Other Than Mother

Choosing Childlessness with Life in Mind

Kamalamani

EARTH

BOOKS

Winchester, UK
Washington, USA

First published by Earth Books, 2016
Earth Books is an imprint of John Hunt Publishing Ltd., Laurel House, Station Approach,
Alresford, Hants, SO24 9JH, UK
office1@jhpbooks.net
www.johnhuntpublishing.com
www.earth-books.net

For distributor details and how to order please visit the 'Ordering' section on our website.

Text copyright: Kamalamani 2015
Poem page 89: Sangharakshita, 1995

ISBN: 978 1 78279 820 0
Library of Congress Control Number: 2015941051

Design: Stuart Davies

Printed and bound by CPI Group (UK) Ltd, Croydon, CR0 4YY, UK

We operate a distinctive and ethical publishing philosophy in all
areas of our business, from our global network of authors to
production and worldwide distribution.

CONTENTS

Foreword   1
Preface   4
Acknowledgments   6
Introduction   9

Part I: The worldly winds   **25**
Chapter 1:   A growing trend of intentional childlessness   26
Chapter 2:   Who are the intentionally childless?   31
Chapter 3:   'Before all else, you are a wife and mother'   34
Chapter 4:   Beyond stereotypes, labeling, right and wrong   41
Chapter 5:   Naturally   47
Chapter 6:   The seven billion mark   53
Chapter 7:   'Mr Fix-It and the Home-Improvement
             Committee'   62
Chapter 8:   Unconditional love   66
Chapter 9:   Meet the parents   71
Chapter 10: Men, women, and children   78
Chapter 11: The miracle of life – and death   84
Chapter 12: The earth from the sky   86

Part II: A private decision with global consequences   **91**
Chapter 13: Decisions, decisions   92
Chapter 14: A soft-voiced prince and a flaming sword   108
Chapter 15: Looking into the 'wheel of life'   114
Chapter 16: Skilful flirting and the art of brewing   118
Chapter 17: A private decision with very public
             consequences   124
Chapter 18: Traditional, transitional and transformative
             women   131
Chapter 19: 'I happen not to have children'   134
Chapter 20: 'By the time I'm 30'   137

Chapter 21:   'You'll live to regret it'   140
Chapter 22:   A bout of the existentials   143
Chapter 23:   Roaming new terrain   147

Part III: New horizons and baby-sized projects   **153**
Chapter 24:   Baby-sized projects and rites of passage   154
Chapter 25:   The bodhisattva ideal   159
Chapter 26:   The bodhisattva/ecosattva at work   167
Chapter 27:   Occupying your body in taking your place
              on earth   171
Chapter 28:   An emerging consciousness   177
Chapter 29:   Giving the gift of confidence   183
Chapter 30:   Family healing and the 'ancestor syndrome'   187
Chapter 31:   Minority report   192
Chapter 32:   Ebbs and flows: never saying never?   197
Chapter 33:   Landscapes of the body and divine women   202
Chapter 34:   Inspiring women   209
Chapter 35:   Going forth   212
Chapter 36:   Big mind and parental mind   218
Chapter 37:   Stillness, simplicity, and contentment   221
Chapter 38:   Red Tara's fascination and boundless love   225
Chapter 39:   Holding to nothing whatever   230
Chapter 40:   The personal is political   236
Chapter 41:   Doing womankind a massive favour?   241
Chapter 42:   Coming of age: pregnant with possibilities   243

Conclusion: 'A child of all life'   245
Endnotes   248
References   251
Bibliography   267

This book is dedicated to my great-grandmother, Lottie Garbutt (née Jones). Apparently she never wanted children, and ended up being a mother of eight.

For the beloved next generation, my nephew and nieces: Thomas, Daisy-Mae, Lolly (Polly) and Boe.

Foreword

Reproduction is a prime imperative in all species. In ours, generations bear culture forward. Children are the emissaries and inheritors of the future and have long been, ideally at least, the focus of familial hope and responsibility. Now, on our planet with more than seven billion human beings haplessly pushing beyond the limits of Earth's natural systems, the decision whether to bear a child or not has a momentous eco-ethical dimension. Nothing could warrant mindfulness more.

For readers weighing the choice of whether or not to try for a baby, or seeking wisdom on decision making *per se*, this clear and gentle, knowing and engaging work will be of excellent counsel. In it the author recalls and refines her own personal experience, brings to bear her professional understanding, and invokes a bodhisattva concern for the other-than-human life on earth. In *Other Than Mother* Kamalamani gives us a timely, compassionate, skilful guide.

I am long past my reproductive years and thrice as many years as that past my highly public declaration that I would remain childless on grounds of ecological concern. Thus I can remember my feminist reveling in the advent of the Pill. At last! A highly effective birth control method whose employment was essentially at the woman's discretion. For biology not to be destiny, and for women to be able to enjoy heterosexual intercourse for its own sake, without the consequence of pregnancy, was an epochal, liberating, and life-complicating development. Now medical and surgical interventions and surrogacy provide technical remedies for infertility, and allow long postponements of childbearing. These developments further untether women's destinies from their fated reproductive biology. They add complexity to our choices, relationships, and possible roles in life.

For significant numbers of women to question childbearing altogether and to realise satisfying lives absent of motherhood is both historically unprecedented and, in these times, urgently necessary.

My life as a conscientious nonparent has been satisfying, but not unmixed. Although it was clearly the correct choice for me, at pivotal times I have revisited the decision, sometimes uneasily. It is a kindness of Kamalamani's book that she understands how this could be, and encourages exploring and accepting such retrospection.

When, in 1969, our numbers stood at 3.5 billion, I was alarmed enough by human overpopulation to vow to bear no children. Considering that it took millennia from our emergence as a species for us to number one billion as of 1890, the exponential growth that has doubled human numbers in less than fifty years is ever more staggering. Human population growth must be curtailed. The children we do invite deserve our true concern. And soon our numbers must decline. Compassion and responsibility must be paramount.

In *Other than Mother* the fundamental precept is choose life. Wisely Kamalamani enlarges upon the meaning of this to include the option of childlessness among the possible life-affirming choices, and illuminates the creative and altruistic possibilities that such chosen – or accepted – lives can offer. Throughout the book she is respectful of, and encouraging to the reader's individuality and responsibility to make the best decision for herself and the wider global community. Kamalamani, who is a psychotherapist, makes no formulaic prescriptions. Rather she presents guidance to assist the reader's self-discovery and discernment. The outcomes can only be beneficial, whether it be a more conscious, settled choice of childlessness, a deliberate and careful decision to try for a baby, or a willingness to pause and reflect further.

Foreword

We can only welcome this worthy book, that encourages the
reader to ponder childlessness – or trying for a baby – with the
totality of Earth in mind.

Stephanie Mills
Author of *Epicurean Simplicity*, and *Whatever Happened to Ecology?*

Preface

A dreaming birth

My friend Vicky and I are walking up a railway tunnel. It is dingy and poorly lit. There is a dull orange and green haze from the bare light bulbs hanging haphazardly from the tunnel's ceiling. The tunnel continues way into the distance, wending its way up a slight incline. I cringe as I walk; I am ill at ease in here, the tunnel is dusty and suffocating.

The one thing that delights and intrigues me in the midst of this strange tunnel is that my friend Vicky is charging up the track, stomping determinedly in her Dr Martens boots as only she can, when she is on a mission. I feel glad to be following her – she clearly knows her way. Sometimes in the past I have tended to be the one taking the adventurous path. This time she is leading. She is determinedly on her path, and it is patently clear to me that it is not the path I shall be following.

I had this dream the day after seeing Vicky, one of my oldest friends, and hearing the exciting news that she was pregnant with her first child, Josh. My own decision not to have children was cemented after this dream, waking with an unprecedented certainty that I would not have children this lifetime. Vicky has gone on to have Sam, her second son, and is a fabulous mother and friend.

In having this dream I realized that my belly had finally caught up with my head and heart in the decision-making process of whether or not to have children. I had spent swathes of the previous three years thinking about not having children on a more rational and logical level – the decision then bubbled up from a deeper, gut level.

The day after this dream I found myself book searching online. I was looking for a book exploring the decision not to

4

have children. At that point I was not looking for an academic work, feminist analysis, statistical explanations as to why approximately one in four women are opting to remain childless in many 'Western' societies, nor a book that bemoaned the existence of children and celebrated the childfree life, although all of the above were, and are, available. Perhaps, with hindsight, I was looking for permission or confirmation that it was okay to be a woman in her early thirties who did not have children, swimming against the tide of prevailing pronatal culture; a culture in which 'family values' were then being re-emphasized in the party political agenda.

I was looking for a book capturing the spirit of how I might 'give birth': giving expression to my nurturing and creative instincts, through living, working, relating, and Buddhist practice. Honoring life, without producing an earthling. Being a woman but not choosing to be a mother. Whilst I found a few interesting books on this subject, they were not quite what I was seeking. In the face of fruitless online searching, I decided I would have to write it. 17 years later and this book has finally been born, along with a wave of many other fine books on the subject.

Acknowledgments

As I reached the final stages of re-drafting this book I had a moment of profound appreciation, thinking of all those who have been instrumental in its birth. A similar thing happened when I was completing *Meditating with Character*, my first book. I felt an overwhelming gratitude to those who researched this area before me, and, in parallel, found myself wishing well those who will continue the tradition – my voice is but one in understanding and living a voluntarily childless life. As I looked back I was glad of the early books and papers I read on this subject, in particular, the work of Mardy Ireland and Rosemary Gillespie, both referenced here.

My sincere thanks also goes to Jennifer Matheson (then known as Sarvabhadri) for the conversations about whether or not to have children we had back in 1997 on a retreat she was leading. I was so grateful for her timely engagement with my decision-making, which was precious and rare. It was particularly helpful because she was a Mom, and I could see a very loving one at that. Our conversations helped me to see that I had a say in my own life, at a time when I was only just starting to realize that having children is a choice.

There are many people with whom I have had interesting and influential conversations about choosing parenthood or childlessness over the past 17 years: in person, and via email in response to articles I have published. As well as talking with childless friends, I am appreciative of the handful of friends who are Moms but have had the courage to be absolutely honest about their struggles with parenthood and how they might not choose that pathway again, although they would not for one minute wish to be without their children. These conversations helped me in de-romanticizing and normalizing parenthood, and highlighted the complexity of the parental bond. My thanks also to the five therapy colleagues who replied to the detailed questionnaire I sent out on a local counseling and psychotherapy network on this theme. In the end I decided not to use interview material, apart from the chapter by 'Miriam' (name changed for confidentiality) entitled 'I happen not to have children', but I very much appreciated learning from your personal experiences.

The latter stages of giving birth to this book have been quite an endurance test, so I am particularly appreciative to readers of the final manuscript for your detailed comments and feedback. Paul Crummay, thanks for helping me find clarity about how to engage others in their process of 'choosing'. To Emily, my sister-in-law, for your encouraging comments about the introduction. Thank you to Maitreyi for your support and urgent encouragement when I was in the grips of the worst self doubt, and for reading and commenting on the final draft with such care and clarity. To Kate O'Halloran for being my doula (birth companion), particularly in encouraging me to 'just say it' and to re-work some of the reflections. Thanks to Sarah Thorne for your detailed feedback and appreciative emails which really helped me to make it to the end of the editing process. To Suhada for raising interesting questions and noticing when I was losing my thread and wandering off piste!

It has been a pleasure to have developed a recent connection with Stephanie Mills, who kindly agreed to write the Foreword. For a long while Stephanie has been an inspiration to me, particularly as an ecological activist and author. Thanks for your immediacy in understanding my purpose in writing *Other than Mother*. Your work has been an inspiring example to me in deciding not to have children with life in mind, I am glad to be continuing that dialogue and hope others continue it in the future.

Finally, thanks again to Paul Crummay, creator of the image on the front cover. Paul is a talented artist and this image was born from a short text message conversation in which I described what I saw in my mind's eye: a woman holding the world as lovingly as a mother holds her new-born baby. Within a few hours Paul had emailed me a first pencil sketch. Thank you, this image and what it symbolizes was an important stage in having the faith to finally publish this book.

Above all, my heartfelt thanks to Suhada, for all the cups of rooibos tea and for your patience during the seemingly endless evenings and weekends when my fingers have been glued to the laptop.

Kamalamani
Bristol, 5th May 2015

Introduction

Life can be messy. We never know how it will turn out. This makes decision-making interesting; another potentially messy process with its own twists and turns, highs and lows. Perhaps the most significant, life or death sort of decision that any of us might make in the course of our lives – although it is often not seen as such – is deciding whether to have children. Now, in the 21st century, having children is still seen as the default thing to do for the majority of the world's population. Remarkably, it is also still seen as a personal decision, despite the fact that as a species we are facing, and have played our part in causing, environmental degradation, climate chaos, the sixth mass extinction, international wars, poverty, and desperate inequality.

For a significant percentage of parents having children is a non-decision, because their babies were unplanned. For many others having children is a non-decision, in the sense that it is just something they always assumed they would do. To some it simply makes sense on the subterranean gut level of what it means to be human and alive. Others have children because that is the preference of their partners. Billions of others on the planet do not have the luxury of access to contraception or live in a place where as many children as possible is still the norm, because of rates of child mortality. Even in countries where contraception is widely and freely available some adopt a 'Russian roulette' approach, knowing that whilst they are fertile, children loom as a pregnant possibility.

Whilst babies arrive with ease and surprise for some, others try for a child for years, to no avail. Many of us will probably recognize ourselves as having been in one or more of these categories. This is the interesting thing about this dimension of life; our beliefs, thoughts, feelings, and behaviors can change as we move through life's cycles – for the majority of us it is far from a one-off decision. In the age of patchwork-like families many people become mothers and fathers in the role of a step-parent, never having conceived a child of their own, but nevertheless having a significant parental role to play.

When we are well beyond our fertile years the issue of child-bearing and rearing can still shape us, perhaps in the form of regret; 'what ifs', or appreciation that we have followed a less conventional path. Some find themselves in later life in the situation where children never quite happened, or they never got round to having children, leaving them with a host of feelings; from deep regret, to a philosophical ambivalence, through to peaceful acceptance.

This book is about choosing life: what that means, and the endless forms life takes. It also takes into account respect for life beyond our immediate loved ones: our wider communities, nations, people living on other continents as well as the effect of our swelling population on other-than-human life and the biosphere. My intention is that this is a book for men and for women (and for those who are more fluid in their gender identi-fication) despite the title. Having said that, the issues for men and women are very different, given the different societal and familial conditioning in which we are submerged. The book is likely to make more sense to women, given that I write having been societally and culturally conditioned as a woman. Also because 'there is much historical and contemporary evidence to suggest that motherhood is a primary status for women in a way that fatherhood is not for men' (Letherby, 1999: 361). Notwithstanding, I hope some men find it of use and I would welcome more men talking and writing on this theme.

Choosing how to live might include choosing to try for children or choosing a life without children. Or perhaps some of you are at a point where you just do not know and do not know how to decide what to do for the best. Or you might be a woman at the end of your most engaging child-rearing years taking stock and reviewing life as a parent, before taking a next step.

My choice has been about deciding not to try for children, a decision-making process that has spanned more than 17 years. This book explores different facets and dimensions of that decision-making process, living with the decision, and life beyond decision-making. Each chapter reflects a different aspect of, or theme about, intentional childlessness. I weave together my personal experience with anecdotes, academic research, and conversations about this subject with friends, strangers, colleagues and acquaintances. Several themes in this book are re-visited throughout its course, particularly questions around non-parenthood and identity, social conformity and finding our place in the world, reflecting how the decision-making process revisits different facets of our lives over time. You will not find in-depth case studies about intentionally childless women and couples in this book, primarily because there are several existing books which already include these (for example: Carroll, 2000; Ireland, 1993; Van Luven, 2006, and Walker, 2010).

When I started to write this book it felt like a journey about a personal decision – whether or not to have children. My perspective has changed radically over the past 17 years. I am now interested in exploring the relevance of the baby-making decision to the current situation we are in as humans living on planet earth. 'A private decision with global consequences', the title of Part II, sums up rather neatly the road I have travelled in my own reflections and understanding.

My research and numerous dialogues have lead me to look at child-bearing and rearing in a way which acknowledges the global consequences of the decision to procreate. The original reason for my provisional decision not to have children was because of my commitment to practicing Buddhism. As I did that, in parallel with mulling over the baby question, the more I realized that an important emphasis in Buddhism is living with a respect for all that lives and our environment. Given the times we are in, I am keen to urge people – Buddhist or not – to think about the baby-making decision with the planet in mind, and in view of the nature of their relationship to their planet and other-than-human life, not to mention the tens of millions of children living on the planet without parents, home, love, shelter, and sustenance.

We know that many children are longed for, nurtured, embraced and brought up with a huge amount of love. We also know of children who are unwanted, abandoned, neglected, abused, with lives sometimes being prematurely ended when that torment of never being wanted becomes too overwhelming and unbearable. In my therapy room I often meet the adult versions of such children. Conversely, some children are *so* wanted, with their parents having such a vision for their lives (even before they take their first step), or living vicariously through their children, that they feel unable to be themselves, to live their own lives, until they have realized the pressure they have been under and that their time is their own.

I am not, of course, the first person to be concerned with the hot potato of child-bearing, planetary considerations, and life on Earth. In graduating from Mill College in Oakland, California, in 1969, Stephanie Mills delivered a college graduation speech entitled 'The Future is a Cruel Hoax', which catapulted her into the national spotlight. The year before, Paul Ehrlich's bestselling book *The Population Bomb* (Ehrlich, 1968) had been published. Mills had been moved deeply by its message that we humans are facing a future of war, strife and famine – victims of our own reproductive success, and exploiting Earth's finite resources. Mills announced to her classmates: "I am terribly saddened by the fact that the most humane thing for me to do is to have no children at all" (Mills quoted in Hymas, 2010). Since that time Stephanie has been an ecological activist, and a lecturer in bioregionalism, ecological restoration, community economics, and voluntary simplicity.

In 1972 the National Organization for Non-Parents was founded in California, later becoming the National Alliance for Optional Parenthood (NAOP). It continued until 1982 as a support group for those deciding to not have children, and as an advocacy group fighting pronatalism: attitudes which over-glorify parenthood at the cost of other life choices. It aimed at educating the public on non-parenthood as a valid lifestyle choice, as well as promoting awareness of the problems associated with overpopulation (Blackstone, 2014). More recently, environmental factors for not having children are less often cited in most of the literature I have come across – although in conversation people I have talked to have occasionally cited this as a reason why they decided not to have children.[1] It is refreshing to come across articles like the ones from Lisa Hymas, published in *The Guardian*: 'I decided not to have children for environmental reasons' (Hymas, 2011a) and 'How green are the childless by choice?' (Hymas, 2011b).

Choosing what to do with the time we have available to us is another hot topic, and an eternal human quest, whether or not we are choosing to try for children. Having the verve to live life – in whatever way we make sense of that – is stretching and challenging. Whilst the great spiritual teachers and inspirers have espoused the importance of living with awareness, authen-ticity and an ethical sensitivity towards ourselves, others and the world, it is, of course, not as easy as it sounds, particularly in a culture which prioritizes individual freedom and pleasure-seeking, often at the cost of community and the health of other-than-human life and the planet. Similar to the arrival of children, life itself does not arrive with a detailed instruction manual, so the art of muddling through seems to apply to many of us, most of the time.

The emphasis upon individual choice, such a key emphasis in our society since the 1980s, can be a myth. Within our society, let alone on a global level, some are free and resourced to choose how they live, serving those doing the choosing; the folk with power, position and wealth, and subsequently, political clout.

Even when we are free to choose how to respond to our life situation and what to do with our time, we do not always *know* that we are, because of our doubt, fear, indecision, restlessness, and the immense pressure to conform. This pressure is experienced acutely in the realm of child-bearing. As Kitzinger reminds us: '...a woman has little value until she becomes a mother' (Kitzinger, 1978: 245). Even though she was writing in 1978, Kitzinger's point is still a valid one. In the last decade or so what is strange is that societal pressure to conform has become more implicit. As Dally says: '...societal pressures provide powerful motives but are seldom voiced' (Dally, 1982: 197), with Pohlman (1969) suggesting that wanting children is primarily due to the need to conform to the pressures imposed by society.

So I also use 'choice' here to throw light on the fact that for many people the decision to have children is still something of a non-choice. Given the strength of pronatal, pro-nuclear family views, certainly in the culture in which I live, we have collective work to do in raising awareness about the public consequences of child-bearing and rearing. The 'natural' option (which we shall explore later) prevailing in mainstream popular culture is to find a significant other of the opposite sex, settle down and have some children. It is still seen as deviant to veer far from that norm – deviant presumably, because of fears of family breakdown and moral decline? I think it takes courage to veer off the path and to take a less well-trodden path. It also takes courage to be a parent, of course. I was glad to be introduced to the work of the philosopher Christine Overall, a mother herself, who poses the question 'Why have children?' (Overall, 2012). She presents a careful investigation of the moral issues surrounding the choice to have a child, rather than – for once – asking 'Why don't you have children?'

Billions of people alive today do not have freedom of choice.

For those of us who do have the privilege of living in a situation of relative political freedom and peace, with the money, food, shelter, care, and access to health and education services to support our lives, the 'choosing' aspect of the title of this book is purposely thought-provoking. The global situation we face in 2015 is hot, and quite literally getting hotter, climate-wise, and having children is a private decision with global consequences. The hot title of Part II is to encourage us to engage with this important subject area, making the decision as to whether or not to have children as conscious as possible. There is also a difference between choice and responsibility. Whilst some have more choices available to them than others, each of us can only live our own lives, no one else can live it for us, or save us, or tell us how to live. So acknowledging a healthy responsibility for choosing how we spend our time is an important starting point.

The matter of 'choice' with regards to child-bearing is likely to be incredibly charged for those of you who would love to have children, but are unable; known in academic literature as 'involuntary childlessness' or 'childless by circumstance'. In this case the notion of choice and choosing life might seem crass – even devastating – in the light of the situation in which you find yourselves. I want to clarify that this book is specifically about intentional childlessness – choosing childlessness. If you are involuntarily childless you might find certain parts of the book relevant – for example, the critiques of the pro-baby-making pronatalism of our society and the stereotyping and prejudices towards non-mothers – but it is aimed primarily at those either still in a decision-making process, or those who have decided not to have children.[2]

The early literature on childlessness had some weaknesses, as McAllister & Clarke (1998: 1) point out, for example, some early studies of childlessness were often not representative, using sampling methods that focused on those who were middle class, married, and female. In some of the early studies of declining fertility there was often no distinction made between intentional and unintentional childlessness. This is a huge and insensitive over-sight, and a reflection of the lack of detailed attention given to these themes and the people whose lives are affected. Having said that, there can be a substantial gray area, if that is the right word, between voluntary and involuntary childlessness. As we shall see, some make a definite decision to not have children from an early age, with some women asking to be sterilized because of their certainty.

Deciding whether or not to have children is often an unfolding decision, changed by: relationships (or lack of), living situations, life priorities, financial situation, to name but a few factors. Those who have been called the 'ambivalent' childless (see McAllister with Clarke, 1998: 3) never make a firm decision about whether or not to have children and do not rule out later parenthood. Some had postponed childbearing, whilst others had experienced fertility problems. In many cases the process is about weighing up possibilities, rather than making a firm and lasting choice either way. There can be an overlap between those of us who do not choose to have children and those of us who are childless by circumstance. From this point of view I rather like Walker's pithy and rather more flexible definitions of: childfree by happenstance, childfree by choice and childfree by circumstance (Walker, 2010: 6).

'Choice' is a problematic word in other ways. For example, I am acutely aware that my partner and I have never tried to conceive. So it is actually not the case that I have chosen not to have children; more accurately, I have tried to not conceive. For all I know, I may have had difficulties in conceiving. Conversely, I may have conceived and never even realized.

This leads me to my other main concern with the notion of 'choice'. In the 21st century those of us in late-stage capitalist societies are obsessed with the illusion of choice. This is most often framed in terms of consumer choice in a world in which we are so often defined and classified as customers and consumers, rather than as human beings living our lives interdependently with other living beings; human and other-than-human. Our anthropocentrism and consumerism can give us the erroneous idea that we are mistresses and masters of our universes. For some humans in our society it seems as though the world exists as a resource-filled playground designed to meet our needs, rather than seeing the world in relation to our place in a complex ecosystem. Hence the title of this book being 'with life in mind'. Not simply because procreation is obviously linked to population, but looking at much wider factors, such as the threat of our runaway consumption, and the way we treat our home – the planet – and *all* the beings that live here.

Trying for children, and indeed, childbearing and rearing are dimensions in which the stark realities of both the robustness and the fragility of life are much in evidence. Experiences from these realms can shatter, in no uncertain terms, that view that we are mistresses and masters of our universes. I only have to cast my mind to friends, family and clients with this in mind: the heartbreak of friends who have undergone repeated IVF treatment, friends whose healthy, happy children have died, the client or family member or friend who miscarries, the friends bringing up children with chronic health problems, the clients who fear that they will never find a partner with whom to start a family, and the friends and clients who abort the children they are carrying. The distress of these varying, yet commonplace scenarios are compounded by living in a society in which so many of us expect to get what we want when we want it – at least in material terms. In facing the fragile, fast-changing, unsatisfactory experiences we are challenged to come to terms with the ongoing reality of the unpredictability of existence. An unpredictability which can be exhilarating and devastating in about equal measure.

Finally, in researching and reviewing the literature about

childlessness over 17 years I have sometimes been saddened by witnessing the hardening of views and polarizations and the throwing around of stereotypes, from 'yummy mummies' to 'selfish, career-driven Bridget Jones types', and worse still, anti-child comments. As Basten points out: '...a number of views expressed on internet forums are often aggressive and acutely self-assertive' (Basten, 2009: 18). In this book I seek to throw light on this particular decision-making process rather than to prescribe whether or not anyone should or shouldn't have children.

Intentional childlessness is still seen by some as rebellious and socially deviant, so this book may be a challenging read for some. A vocal minority of those who have decided not to have children focus their energies on talking about children and other parents in a demeaning way. What I am seeking to create is mutual respect rather than ever more deeply divided camps of people and opinions. There are a thicket of views and opinions about child-bearing, rearing, and parenting - or choosing not to do so. I hope to create a 'pregnant pause' for conscious decision-making with a glimpse of the local and global implications. May we respect one another and respect difference as we take our next breath and form our next word – myself included.

So choice is an interesting, loaded, culturally-conditioned and complex notion. I am fascinated by how we go about choosing. Or whether we tend to do things in auto-pilot. Whether babies just happen along. For some of us life revolves around a well-crafted plan, for others, it all just happens. Do we solely choose how to respond to any big decisions in life? Or do those decisions, to some extent at least, 'choose us'? Perhaps we respond by creating certain conditions to the best of our current ability and see what happens.

Those moments when life 'chooses us' do seem to happen, ranging from times when a particular decision seems somehow 'fated', when the whisperings of a vocational calling will not go away, or when a baby is conceived despite a couple being absolutely determined not to get pregnant. My life is, at best, like a gorgeously emerging work-in-progress sculpture. Some days it is beautiful, flowing, engaging and creative, with others joining in with the odd bit of chiseling. On a more scattered day I stare at the tools and the block of stone, perplexed in trying to recall what I am doing. Perhaps you can relate to that or have your own preferred analogy or metaphor.

This book is about choosing – bearing in mind all my caveats about that tricky word – rather than not-choosing. It is about choosing life and keeping the initiative in how you live. The language around childlessness is generally concerned with lack; the words and names speak of lack: elective childlessness, intentional childlessness, unintentional childlessness. Note the repetitive 'less'. For the sake of shorthand I tend to favor using the term 'childless'. Being 'childfree' seems for some to suggest a greater sense of freedom and choice (Stobert & Kemeny, 2003), whereas 'childless' can sound negative or missing out on something special (Walker, 2010: 3). Personally, the term 'childfree' leaves me cold, implying that freedom from children is automatically a good thing for one's health, a bit like something which is sugar-free or caffeine-free, or is used to refer to childfree environments. Other intentionally childless women identify as being an 'anti-Mom' (Shriver, 2005).

The truth is, I am not all that fond of any of these terms, but they are needed here for ease of discussion. I tend to use the term 'intentional childlessness' or 'choosing childlessness' (or childless for short, meaning intentionally childless in this context) which reflects the fact that this was a positive choice. But please be aware as and when you read other literature on this theme that there is a growing trend for 'childless' to refer to those who are involuntarily or unintentionally so and 'childfree' for those who are voluntarily or intentionally without child.

In writing this book my creative juices only started to flow fully when I realized that its backbone needed to be about choosing life, rather than life being over because of my childlessness. The spirit of 'choosing life' first caught my attention watching a film called *The Shawshank Redemption*. The character Andy says to his friend Red: "You can get busy living or get busy dying". At that time in my life – a time of mourning after my father's death – I was erring on the side of getting busy dying, rather than living, so it was a timely wake up call to re-engage with living. Choosing life is also an invitation to bear in mind all of life on this amazing biosphere and the effect our decisions have upon one another and other-than-human life. For me, the form of choosing life happens to be about choosing not to have children; the main thread of this book. For you, it might be about having children. In my mind if the decision is not set in a broader context of choosing life, explorations of intentional childlessness can end up being perceived as defensive – reinforcing the unfortunate, distorted stereotypes of childless women being weird, deviant, anti-social or at absolute worst, child-hating, by virtue of their childlessness. So this is an invitation into a creative exploration of how to live life, with a particular focus upon the decision of whether or not to have children.

However, I would be mistaken to not capture the sense of 'otherness' that I have experienced in choosing not to be a mother – and I know for sure that I am not alone in that experience. Hence the title 'Other Than Mother' acknowledges that those of us without child are in a minority compared to the majority of women who have children and become mothers, even if their average age may be getting later. That is still the status quo. Most childbearing women have multiple roles, but motherhood remains absolutely central in terms of explicit and implicit social norms. In choosing not to have children I still experience from time to time that 'otherness' from socially accepted norms, and I will explore that otherness throughout the course of this book.

Talking about this sense of otherness and opening more

dialogues about how notions of womanhood are still so inextricably tied up with motherhood are important for everyone – men and women, with or without child – in terms of allowing people to live authentic lives regardless of their gender, sexuality, class, ethnicity, and desire to bear children. Instead of the intentionally childless being seen as deviant or weird, here I invite a celebration of the creativity channeled into other ways of living which do not happen to involve physical child-bearing and rearing.

The content of *Other Than Mother* has been informed by my work in a number of different realms: as a body psychotherapist, as a therapy supervisor, as a friend to women in their twenties, thirties, and forties who are 'umming' and 'ahhing' over this decision, as a friend to men and women who would not choose parenthood if they had their time again, as an ecopsychologist, and as a researcher sifting through the literature on this subject, from statistics about intentional childlessness trends through to mainstream media commentary and academic literature.[3] It has also been hugely influenced by my practice of meditation and Buddhism and a curiosity about how to live. I have noticed how my tone switches in various parts of this book, as I draw on the experience of working in different roles, my own personal experiences and those of folk around me.

A few practical points in navigating this book. Firstly, it is divided into three parts:

Part I – The worldly winds
Part II – A private decision with global consequences
Part III – New horizons and baby-sized projects

These three parts roughly equate to the before, during, and after phases of deciding whether or not to have children. Each part has fairly short chapters with different tones and flavors, and I have structured the book into three parts in the hope that it is a useful way of dividing the material and inviting you into a process of your own reflections, having read some of mine. Do bear in mind that this is not a linear process, it is generally a messy, creative, human process, so although the book is structured in a way which reflects the before, during and after aspects of the decision, life is not quite so tidy... In other words, be as kind to and as patient with yourself as you can as you read. You might also find that you want to read the three different parts in an order that suits you, perhaps delving straight into the decision-making process of Part II.

The title of Part I, 'The worldly winds', is taken from a traditional Buddhist teaching. The eight 'worldly winds', traditionally known as the 'loka dharmas' or 'worldly conditions' are: pleasure and pain, loss and gain, fame and infamy, and praise and blame (see Sangharakshita 1998: 7-8). They blow through our lives to a greater or lesser extent all the time. To give an example, we can feel the loss of not having children. Conversely, if we have children, we are likely, even if only occasionally, to feel the loss of having the time and space for things other than parenthood. The trick of a balancing approach to life is to become so familiar with our patterns in how we respond to pleasure, pain, loss, gain, fame, infamy, praise, and blame that we remain unduly swayed by them. This feels like an appropriate title for Part I of this book, as the worldly winds make themselves very much felt in the area of child-rearing or not, with the myriad of views, assumptions and stereotypes of ourselves and others, particularly around the realities and myths of parenthood and non-parenthood. So Part I looks at the various pulls in different directions as we try to decide whether or not to start a family and how confusing a field this can be; how free are we to choose when we are subjected to the worldly winds?

The focus of Part II is upon the decision-making process itself. How do we approach this process? What might be the factors worth considering in this process? Part II includes many of my own reflections about my decision to remain childless. Despite the fact that it is personal in parts, I hope it extends to more universal themes with wider relevance and resonance. I purposefully wrote this section from a personal point of view as an invitation to encourage you to mull upon your own reflections in this process – and it would be tricky to write in the abstract! The other option is to follow a more 'case study' lead approach, or a more academic, theoretical one. Both are interesting and relevant and are available elsewhere (see the references for some excellent examples). My intention in Part II is to invite you deep into your decision-making process from reading about mine.

Part III focuses upon life beyond deciding not to have children; living with the decision. It is called 'New horizons' because in my experience new horizons open up when you have decided to remain childless. Much energy can be expended in the 'will I, won't I?' or, perhaps more aptly for many: 'will we, won't we?' Not deciding can be draining and, at times, divisive, for ourselves and those closest to us. Deciding, even provisionally, not to have children can be freeing in giving us a flavor of, and taking seriously, other directions in life. Equally, I think it can feel like an odd time when you first decide not to have children, particularly if that has been a real possibility at times, hence the emphasis on the 'baby-sized project' early on in Part III. This part of the book invites a process of absorbing and digesting your decision-making process; maybe initiating a baby-sized project of your own.

Many themes are re-visited during the course of Parts I, II, and III. For example, perceptions of childless women, stereotyping (how we might stereotype ourselves and be stereotyped), how non-parenthood can bring a feeling of otherness because of the prevailing pro-family agendas, and the impact of child-bearing in light of global issues. The reason for re-visiting these themes is because they are themes that I have re-visited in the decision-making process, and, I am sure, will continue to re-visit in the future. The re-visiting of these themes reflects the nature of this decision-making territory and echoes the research in terms of how people decide to have children. For many people who are 'umming and ahhing' it is not an overnight decision. Making an important decision, rather like working as a client in therapy, is about looking at different aspects of the decision for ourselves, rather like looking at the different facets which form the surface of a jewel. As we re-visit different parts of our experience our self-awareness deepens.

As you read this book you will come across suggestions and ideas in the form of 'pregnant pauses' and 'reveries' at the end of some of the chapters. Please feel free to use these in a way which best serves you: reflect on them, brainstorm them, ignore them, or perhaps note them down and share them with a trusted friend. Maybe read them in a more dream-like state, as the name suggests, an important notion in some therapeutic circles, and important as we allow ourselves to be lost in our thoughts and daydreams about this subject matter.[4] This decision-making process draws as much on our awareness of what emerges in a dreaming state as it does our logical, rational minds. Most importantly, please bear in mind that these pregnant pauses and reveries are only pointers and suggestions, and are not exhaustive. I purposely have not included them at the end of every single chapter, as I think that could become a bit overwhelming. Remember, too, there are no 'right' or 'wrong' answers and you do not have to share your reflections with anyone unless you wish to. You may decide to engage with the reflections once you have read and digested the whole book. My hope is that each of the chapters should stand alone and make sense, enabling you to delve into the parts which are of most interest and relevance.

I wish you well as you 'choose' life.

Part I

The worldly winds

Chapter 1

A growing trend of intentional childlessness

When I took my first steps in researching intentional child-lessness I was relieved to find that my perception of fewer women having children in their twenties and thirties was backed by statistics. A significant demographic shift is taking place as a higher percentage of women in the UK and Europe are deciding to have children at a later age, as well as a greater percentage choosing to remain childless:

> More women in England and Wales are reaching the end of their reproductive careers without having had a live birth. The figure rose from one in ten women born in 1945 to around one in five women born in 1960...the 2002-based national population projections assume that the percentage of women remaining childless will increase a little further, to about 22 per cent of those born in 1990 and later. (Berrington, 1990)

In 2011, one in five women in England and Wales reached the age of 45 having never given birth to a child. This data, from the Office of National Statistics (2013), relates to women born in 1966 who were assumed to have reached the end of their childbearing years. Similarly, one in five women born between 1961 and 1965 were childless when they had reached the age of 45. in the preceding years.

A similar picture is emerging in the US and other countries. For example, a 2003 US Census study found that a record 19% of US women between the ages of 40 and 44 did not have children, compared with 10% in 1976 (Cohen, 2010). I recently read that it is estimated that one in four children of my generation (I am 44) will be childless on their 50th birthday.

The USA's CDC (Center for Disease Control and Prevention) reported in their National Health Statistics Report from 2012 that of the 19% of women who remain childless between the ages of 40 and 44, half are childfree by choice. The remainder are unable to have children, due to biological and circumstantial factors (CDC, 2012). The process of researching this area is not without its difficulties. Jeffries and Konnert (2002) found that the researcher's definitions of voluntary and involuntary childlessness were inconsistent with participants self-definitions in one-third of cases. So it is not that easy to get definitive data, again highlighting the gray area between voluntary and involuntary childlessness, depending upon one's perceptions.

In another study, seeking to understand how adults without children define their childless state, Connidis and McMullin (1996) found that 28% of participants said they were childless by choice and 72% by circumstance. However, the researchers found that there was a 60% overlap in the reasons cited for childlessness between the two groups. It is also worth bearing in mind the process of decision-making; from their US-based research, Heaton, Cardell and Holland (1999) noted shifts in childbearing decisions spanning, on average, six years. Similarly, Merlo and Rowland (2000) point out how most women in Australia remain childless after a long series of postponements. These figures show the importance of a longitudinal approach in understanding childless statistics. A longitudinal approach will also be invaluable in understanding how the estimated one in four women who remain childless live with that decision into their middle and elder years.

The origins of a childless/childfree trend started far earlier in the twentieth century, of course. Abbott writes: 'a third of the women born in 1960 went through their twenties without becoming mothers. Those who opted out of motherhood were haunted by the ticking of the 'biological clock' in their thirties' (Abbott, 2003:164). This delaying of having children, or 'fertility postponement' as it is medically called, was most likely a result of the increase in contraception, more women working, and the broader acceptance of alternative ways of living (Daniluk and Herman, 1984).

Preceding these more recent changes was the phenomena of women from different classes being employed on a previously unparalleled scale during the two world wars of the twentieth century. The experience of engaging in non-domestic work, along with the activities of the suffragette movement, meant that women were starting to experience and realize their potential beyond the domestic realm. In the UK women over the age of 30 (who met particular property qualifications) were given the vote in 1918, with suffrage being extended to all women over the age of 21 in 1928 (Crawford, 2000). Prior to this there were calls for 'voluntary motherhood' in the late 19th century; the first name for a feminist birth control demand in the US. This was the response of feminists to their understanding that involuntary motherhood and child raising were important aspects of woman's oppression (Gordon in Walzer Leavitt, 1999).

These figures give a sense of the phenomenon of intentional childlessness, influenced by a wide range of factors: social, cultural, economic, political, ecological, environmental, spiritual, religious, and technological. In the more recent past childlessness is a lifestyle choice for some, for others it can arise out of the pressures of longer working hours and the breakdown of traditional families (Henley Centre, 1999). So choosing childlessness sometimes arises from financial strife and heartbreak, rather than being a positive choice. It is encouraging that childlessness is being more researched, given that in the early days studies failed to even distinguish between voluntarily and involuntarily childless women (McAllister and Clarke, 1998).

The fact that until recently much of the research neglected to distinguish between the intentional and unintentional aspects of childlessness reflects the recent emergence of this field. More recently there seems to be a better understanding of the strength of emotion involved in childlessness, particularly one might argue involuntary childlessness, and the need to be clear about the varying intentions of women of a childbearing age. The strongest similarity between the intentionally and unintentionally childless is likely to be their experiences of living in a pronatal society. The difference is that there is likely to be more sympathy for those who are unintentionally childless, compared to those who choose to not have children, given the continuing pro-family narrative of our society (having said that, it can be shocking to witness the lack of empathy for those who are involuntarily childless in some incidences...).

These demographic shifts raise fascinating and far-reaching questions. What is becoming increasingly clear from the research is that a broad range of men and women are remaining childless. Research to date about childless women challenges the earlier assumption that this figure is mainly composed of successful, well-educated, white, middle-class career women. The phenomena of increasing childlessness challenges conventional conceptions of, and assumptions about, womanhood and how to be a woman. I am focusing on women, rather than men here, given that there remains a widespread societal assumption – implicit and covert – that motherhood remains central to adult female identity and notions of femininity, maturity, and what is considered 'normal' compared to notions of manhood and fatherhood.

The popular media in the UK report that women in their twenties are experiencing something of an early identity crisis as child-bearing and rearing is a far less obvious choice than it once was. Concern is also starting to be more widely expressed about women leaving it too late to have children. Today I read how Kirsty Allsopp, a popular UK television presenter, was urging women to 'ditch university and have a baby by 27' because of her fear that woman wanting children are leaving it too late (Tran,

2014).

I hope this book plays a part in filling out the broader landscape of the decision-making process behind these bare statistics. The reasons why people remain childfree are as complicated, as varied, and as individual as why and when other people choose to become parents. What goes on in terms of our decision-making around procreation? How is it to be a woman who's not a mother? Or a man who's not a father, but who has always dreamed of becoming one? How do we go about 'choosing' – with all the caveats I included earlier about the notion of choice – and how does it vary for different people at varying points in their reproductive life?

Chapter 2

Who are the intentionally childless?

If there is a shared characteristic amongst the interviewees [voluntarily childless women] it is that they are all 'distinctive'. It takes a lot of strength and courage to swim against the tide of convention. (Bartlett, 1994: xi. Author's brackets added)

The last chapter explored the statistical information regarding intentional childlessness. But who are the childless in *real life*, in a more three-dimensional way? Thinking of those I have met, those who chose not to have children are:

- men and women
- lesbian, gay, straight, bisexual, transgender, queer, questioning
- middle class, working class, upper class
- wealthy and broke
- white, people of color, and from different ethnic groups
- atheists, materialists, spiritually-inclined, unsure, undecided
- jobless through to career-focused
- procrastinators
- disillusioned by the free babysitting they provided during their own childhood
- free of obvious 'baby urges' and hormonal surges
- pursuing other things: art, travel, a religious, spiritual, or vocational path
- out of time, having left it too late
- recovering from being born into traumatic family dynamics

- non-committal
- eco-warriors with concerns for the population and the planet (some identifying as a GINK - a synonym for 'Green Inclinations No Kids'. See Hymas, 2010)
- simply not interested in kids or family life

Identity-wise, thinking of those same childless people. Some:

...are happy on the margins

...feel excluded and overlooked

...feel liberated in no longer having to be part of family life

...do not relate to themselves as childless until it is pointed out to them

...see themselves as the black sheep of the family or the 'odd one out'

...are busy getting on with life

...have regrets about not having children: part decision, part circumstance

...are shunned for their decision

...are supported in their decision

In other words, those who choose a childless life have a spectrum of experiences. I include this chapter early in this book for two reasons. Firstly, to ensure that this book stays grounded in the reality that the decision as to whether or not to have children is something that affects real people, rather than those who have been counted and analyzed in quantitative research, with their stories remaining rather faceless and nameless.

Secondly, to challenge the far-reaching stereotype that those who choose childlessness are mainly career-driven, successful, 30-something women (sometimes dubbed the 'Bridget Jones generation', taken from the book and film *Bridget Jones's Diary* (Fielding, 1997)). For some intentionally childless women this career status may be important to their identity in the world and how they are defined. For others, it is less important because their creativity and engagement is expressed in realms of life aside from career or because they barely paused to consider having children. For others still, having children is too far out of reach financially, or in terms of their life circumstances.

Reverie

I long to soften the barriers between how those with children and those without are seen, categorized and judged – and in how we see, categorize and judge ourselves, too. I also seek to break down the stereotypes of those who are voluntarily or intentionally childless. Who are the intentionally childless in your mind's eye? Which friends, family members, of public figures come to mind? Can you notice in yourself whether you see childlessness in terms of lack? Emptiness or wholeness? Or abundance?

Chapter 3

'Before all else, you are a wife and mother'

A woman's capacity to create, bear and nurture a child is the very essence of her womanhood, her unique and special capacity-prized, feared, envied, protected, and celebrated. (Ashurst, 1989: 97)

...Caring and nurturing has historically been seen to be what women do, and mothers have traditionally been seen to be what women are. (Gillespie, 2001: 142)

In this section I start to look at what it means to be 'other than mother' from both a personal point of view and in terms of how our identities are shaped by societal assumptions, rules and norms. The issues around child-bearing, rearing, and identity are loaded, as indicated by the title of this chapter from Ibsen's play *A Doll's House* (Ibsen, 2003: 228).

Until my mid twenties I would have agreed with the quote above from Ibsen's character, Helmer, that before all else, I would be a mother, and that that identity would be central to my sense of myself, my life, and that of my partner. Being a family would have been an important way of belonging to my wider family and local community. I was far less sure about the wife aspect, although I suspect I would have preferred to marry before trying for children, had the situation arisen.

My little mantra was that I would have children 'by the time I'm 30'. From an early age I had a parallel urge to follow a less conventional path. As a teenager I remember recoiling inwardly when a neighbor commented that I would make a 'lovely wife and mother'. He was meaning to pay me a compliment. Outwardly I smiled, but was taken aback by my gut response:

'you must be joking!' I realize, in retrospect, that I was already making other plans.

Throughout my twenties my life was focused upon discovering Buddhist practice, working, and exploring the world. I was frequently travelling to Africa as a development worker, living with a partner with whom I did not want to have children and focusing my attentions on working towards ordination into the Triratna Buddhist Order (then known as the Western Buddhist Order). Childbearing is a spiritual 'calling' for some, but that hasn't been the case for me, mine was taking the shape of meaningful work and Buddhist practice.

Delving deeper into the Dharma (the teachings of the Buddha) had – and continues to have – a transformative effect upon my priorities and what I felt I could offer to the world through my work. My sense of self and my life were not taking the shape I had once planned. Throughout my twenties I became increasingly influenced by the vision of my life: supporting others, serving the world, and adventuring. I was energetic and engaged, and fortunate in doing a job which gave expression to that vision. I was also reflecting on the Buddhist view of self: that there is no such thing as a fixed, unchanging self, that everything is impermanent and in constant flux. These reflections, and the notion that suffering is largely caused when we expect things to run in accordance with our plan, colliding rather dramatically with the five year plan drawn up neatly in my mind. Practicing the Dharma threw light on my less helpful habits and gradually taught me that my little life was/is one life amongst billions of others, human and other-than-human species. It was an eye-opening and expansive time.

I was increasingly drawn to the 'bodhisattva' path, rather than the path of motherhood. In Buddhist teachings, bodhisattvas are beings who vow to save all sentient beings. They are the embodiment of altruism; an altruism which arises from an awareness of suffering. What I loved in particular, and still do, is how the bodhisattva: 'chooses to live within this paradox of knowing deeply the illusory nature of the world he or she inhabits while still being willing to remain within it' (Preece, 2006: 206). I shall return to the subject of the bodhisattva and the bodhisattva ideal later in this book. For some people, of course, the paths of motherhood and apprentice bodhisattva-hood weave together, but that was not to be my way.

I had always assumed that I would have children, and at this point I still anticipated that it would be the case 'one day'. Through my late twenties there was an increasing mismatch between my 'one day' thoughts and the emerging shape of my life. The myths of the 'lifelong learner' or 'eternal student' were much more prominent than impending motherhood. My heart longed for all sorts of things, but procreation was not at the top of the list. By my late twenties I had also experienced more of life; my over-idealism had rubbed up against reality at home and at work and I was a bit more realistic than in my early twenties. Looking around me I was starting to see that the goal of 'having it all' (career, partner, children, leisure time) which was around in society in my late teens was, in fact, a myth, and a myth which was, at worst, disenchanting and harmful for many families and their wider communities.

I appreciated reading recently the words of Lucy Worsley, the Chief Curator at the UK's Historic Royal Palaces and an historian, presenting many popular television history series. She stated publically "I have been educated out of the natural reproductive function" (see Davis, 2012). It resonates with my own experience and the message of prioritizing education over and above all else. Not surprisingly, the tabloid press had a field day with her statement, claiming she was arrogant: 'too busy' to be a mother – perish the thought. In a *Guardian* interview with Angela Wintle, Worsley explained her statement: 'All I had meant was that while growing up in the 80s, the overriding message from teachers and parents was, 'Finish your education', and maybe that early conditioning stuck in a way they had not intended' (Wintle, 2013). Her statement certainly threw more light on the messages of my own upbringing.[5]

Back then I would never have predicted the myriad of responses I have encountered as a woman choosing not to have children. Choosing childlessness provokes interesting reactions – even when one is not being provocative. It was at this point that the pro-couple and pro-family nature of our society started to become blatantly obvious to me for the first time. Having got an education, the 'right thing' – societally, at least – would be to find a nice man with prospects and have some kids. I started to realize in no uncertain terms how identity is formed at the interface, and in the interplay and struggle between our image of ourselves and society's rules and norms; explicitly and implicitly stated.

Societally, and despite the advances made by early feminists, a woman's primary, so-say 'natural' role, is still seen as bearing children. In the wise words of the renowned writer Adrienne Rich:

> Through motherhood, every woman has been defined from outside herself: mother, matriarch, matron, spinster, barren, old maid – listen to the history of emotional timbre that hangs around each of these words. Even by default motherhood has been an enforced identity for women, while the phrases 'childless man' and 'nonfather' sound absurd and irrelevant to us. (Rich, 1978: 261)

Not only are women defined from the outside, but we are also living in times shaped by pronatalism, or, as Elaine Tyler May (1995) calls it: a 'new pronatalism' which began its ascent in the United States and other 'Western' societies in the 1970s, following in the wake of the second wave of feminism which had served to de emphasize the positive importance of motherhood in women's lives. As Gross points out:

37

...pronatalism as an ideology seems to be rampant on the planet; those who mildly suggest that unlimited reproduction is not an individual right and could well be destructive are derided. (Gross, 1997: 293)

There are implications of this for intentionally childless women – myself and all of you reading who have chosen not to have children – given that women are still primarily defined in relation to motherhood (or non-motherhood). It raises questions: how do the growing number of us who choose not to become mothers make sense of our place and identity in the face of a pronatal culture? How do we find a voice and presence as an emerging body of women? Are similar challenges arising as for other minority and marginalized groups? What are the implications for men who consciously decide to remain childless? Whilst men may not be defined so strongly by their fatherhood, for some men this is—or could be—a vital part of their life.

I find questions about identity and decision-making fascinating, straddling the boundary between our public and private realms. An example of this boundary-straddling is the commonplace phenomena of being asked about my childlessness. I do not question a person or couple's decision to have children – unless they are close friends seeking advice or a therapy client, and then I tread carefully – so I am intrigued as to the social rules that apply when a stranger feels free to question my decision not to bear children or to tell me with certainty that I shall live to regret my decision. As a curious person, I am intrigued that few people who question my decision are sufficiently curious to ask what I have chosen in my life as an alternative path, or in fact, whether I wished to have children but was unable to do so, as would be the case for someone who was involuntarily childless and quite possibly in the midst of intense grief.

A host of factors shape the reasons for choosing childlessness, as they can for choosing to have children. In some cultures choosing childlessness is almost beyond belief, often due to economic consequences which affect the survival of the family and the individuals within that family. Having had the good fortune of working with women throughout sub-Saharan Africa in my twenties and early thirties, I am used to being met with disbelief that I had no plans to marry and bear children. The disbelief often dissolved into good humored "well, you are a very sensible woman!" and a surprisingly strong sense of connection. These cultural factors and assumptions and norms have a strong bearing upon this issue and I have found it useful to reflect as deeply as I can on these changing social phenomena more broadly in the light of the cultural, ecological, religious, social, political and economic conditioning of my own life so far.

Ideas around identity and childlessness underpinning the foundations of this book are complex. As Gillespie (2000) points out: 'Cultural discourses on femininity and identity may never have adequately encapsulated what it means to be a woman, in childless women and equally importantly in mothers' (2000: 233). Perhaps, as Gillespie suggests, we are on the nursery slopes in terms of opening up these discourses, and the more they open, the more diversity we are likely to encounter amongst mothers and non-mothers (and fathers and non-fathers). Many women live with an ambivalent attitude towards motherhood. This is not an infrequent theme in my therapy room, and it surfaces in conversation with close women friends who have the courage to acknowledge their ambivalence about motherhood – in parallel with an enduring bond with their children.

The fact that a woman is a mother is, of course, not necessarily an indication that she wanted to become one (Campbell, 1999). Furthermore, as Movius (1976: 58) points out, the desire of some women to terminate pregnancy, and incidences of parental child abuse, reflect the fact that not only do some women (and, in some cases, their partners) not feel ready for motherhood, but also that not everyone has the capacity to offer sound enough conditions to raise a child; another under-discussed, taboo-filled theme. Parenthood is characterized by an irreversibility which is incomparable to any other relationship (Engel, 1998; Rossi, 1969). This raises important questions around identity and how we may conform to and be affirmed by socially ascribed roles, whilst feeling a great deal of inner conflict in that role, with the generation of even more conflict when we feel unable to communicate that conflict to anyone around us.

In these reflections we are moving into the territory of views and assumptions about womanhood, motherhood, and parenthood. Notice which of the points and questions below throw light on your own experience of womanhood, in its heights and depths. If you are a man reading this, perhaps notice the messages you received about manhood and fatherhood as you grew up, and your observations of the conditioning of the women around you.

A pregnant pause

Remember back to your early thoughts of whether or not you'd be a mother or father. Notice whether Ashurst's words ring true: 'A woman's capacity to create, bear and nurture a child is the very essence of her womanhood...' (Ashurst, 1989: 97). How have your views changed over time? Notice whether you agree with Adrienne Rich's point of view that '...motherhood has been an enforced identity for women...' (Rich, 1978: 261). What assumptions about and attitudes towards motherhood have shaped your life, whether you're a man or a woman? And notice associated attitudes about gender, sexuality, and childbearing. If you are without child, what sense do you make of being part of an 'emerging body of women' in terms of your childlessness? Is it exciting or daunting?

Chapter 4

Beyond stereotypes, labeling, right and wrong

As soon as we address the question of childlessness, we are thrust into the realm of cliché and mythology, where no one is protected from the false assumptions: women will not grow up until they're mothers; women who do not have children are selfish, cold; childless women must have been abused when they were growing up. Friends caution that you are missing out on life's most exhilarating pleasure or reason that your partner will not feel any ties to a childless relationship. Some myths are even more disturbing: the persistent notion that lesbians – not to mention poor women, women with prison records, or women with HIV – are categorically unfit to be mothers. (Ratner, 2000:1)

...nothing can prepare you for the indifference of friends who do not have babies. (*About Time,* 2013)

How do we develop new narratives around how we choose to live, whether or not that includes childbearing and child-rearing? How can we bring fresh air, mindfulness, and compassion into a dialogue which respects different ways of living, undermining the destructive energy of taboos? Let us go beyond stereotypes of the childless, particularly childless women and the 'abnormality' of their situation and status. Here we shall explore the popularized stereotypes before thinking about the much-needed new forms and archetypes of voluntary childlessness in Part III.

Women who choose not to have children are seen by some as: '...self-centered, immature, workaholic, unfeminine, materialistic, cold, neurotic, child-hating' reports Terri Casey (Casey, 1998: xiii) with regard to responses towards herself and the childless women she interviewed and wrote about in *Pride and Joy*, a book which beautifully records the lives of 25 childless women (Casey, 1998). Some of these choice adjectives concur with my experience of responses to my choosing childlessness; a sense of misfortune about my life and choices. The fact that I have committed my life to practicing Buddhism adds to this sense of being 'other', even a little alien to some, so personally-speaking, this is familiar territory. I am also fortunate in that I am surrounded by people who have been supportive of my creative endeavors (my 'baby-sized projects' – more of that later). Even my Mom, a proud, hands-on grandma, has come to terms with the fact that my creations are not baby-shaped.

Intentionally childless women have been reported as 'deviant', presumably because they threaten the status quo (see Veevers, 1975). More recent research from Turkey notes how parents are perceived as warmer than non-parents (Copur and Koropeckyj-Cox 2010), and childless men and women see themselves as negatively stereotyped (Somers, 1993). In my twenties I was struck by how often my decision not to have children was questioned. As Dubofsky says:

> While it is somehow become socially acceptable to ask everyone you come across if they have children, and if not, why, that does not make it easier to disclose a complicated answer, which everyone has to a certain degree. (Dubofsky, 2014)

In my experience this questioning can turn into a minor interrogation for those for whom the idea of a world without their offspring is unthinkable. Being a parent sometimes gives a strong voice, identity and a sense of entitlement to have a very vocal – perhaps even 'right' – point of view in addressing the intentionally childless. I imagine how it would be if I started telling parents how to bring up their kids, when I have no experience of parenting? It would obviously be inappropriate and unwise (and rude). That does not mean I might not have a point of view. After all, I was parented, and spend alot of time thinking about parenting and upbringing in the course of my work as a counselor and therapist. But there is having a point of view and knowing when it's wise to share it. As Dubofsky points out, the reasons as to why someone does not have children are often complex. As we are exploring here, each decision to have children and not to have children is unique to the people and circumstances involved.

A further stereotype to which I have already alluded – particularly perpetuated in the mainstream media – is that women who choose not to have children tend to be career-driven super-women in high powered jobs. This is not borne out in the studies that have been undertaken. For example, a 1998 survey undertaken by the Joseph Rowntree foundation in the UK reported that: 'highly qualified women are more likely to remain childless but career identity did not emerge as central to personal identity or personal fulfillment for the majority of intentionally childless people. On the contrary, early retirement proved a popular goal' (McAllister with Clarke, 1998).

Morell (2000: 314) found, unexpectedly, that in her study of childless women in the US 75% of the participants described themselves as coming from poor or working class backgrounds. The participants themselves commonly linked their upward mobility directly to their decision to remain childless.

A further dimension to this stereotype is research undertaken by Sylvia Ann Hewlett into 1,168 of the highest earning US women executives who wished to bear children, but were unable to for a range of reasons. She found that 'the brutal demands of ambitious careers, the asymmetries of male-female relationships, and the difficulties of bearing children late in life conspire to crowd out the possibility of having children' (Hewlett, 2002: 68). So perhaps this is the shadow, unseen, and for the individuals involved, sad aspect of the stereotype of the oft-called 'selfish' career woman.

The selfish question is an interesting, recurring label. Just yesterday, Pope Francis was chiding couples who choose not to have children, saying the decision is a 'selfish' act (Kirchgaessner, 2015). Taking this judgment to its logical conclusion means that those with children are somehow selfless. I have no doubt that bringing up children calls upon parent's selflessness. Yet was their original desire to have children motivated by selflessness? Would more children not be adopted, if there were such selflessness? I found it refreshing when a friend responded to my thoughts about childlessness with great honesty: "Well good for you, I have definitely got the selfish gene and I wish I could have had *even more* kids!" The only aspect of the selfish argument being leveled at those who are childless I understand is when I see folk drifting along, never committing to one thing or another, and being self-obsessed. Most parents simply do not have time for self-obsession, so I can see from this point of view how the selfish label gets plastered across the forehead of the childless, sometimes rather indiscriminately.

More recently I have found myself reclaiming some of the stereotypes applied to the intentionally childless. For example, if 'unfemale' or 'unfeminine' mean that I have found the freedom to explore the myriad of facets of my character and experience, rather than those qualities traditionally associated with what is known as the 'feminine' (which seems to be popularly associated with nurturing, receptive and so on), then I am all for being what is seen as 'unfemale' (even though I personally feel pretty happy being in a female body these days). I have found it useful to get clear about what I mean by 'feminine' and 'masculine' as opposed to 'female' and 'male'. Female and male describe society's rather binary, polarizing way of biologically categorizing men and women, boys and girls – ignoring the preference of those who identify as gender diverse. Feminine and masculine are terms which refer to the qualities or appearances traditionally associated with women or men respectively, which are culturally determined. These distinctions matter, I think, because of language's power in reinforcing the way we make sense of and file away our experiences of the world. Maybe 'feminine' and 'masculine' fall into a similar category to the way we use the term 'nature', more of which in the following chapter. Is there a temptation to assume that we all know what we all mean, rather than getting to the bottom of what we *actually* mean as we talk about these loaded labels?

If deviant means that I have the voice to question things I see going on around me that are unjust, then I am also happy to be deviant and speak out against the status quo. If career-driven is the term applied to having a passion and ambition for the work I do, particularly the work which I think makes a contribution in the world, then I am also happy to embrace being career-driven. Let's be less linear in the way we categorize men and women, raising deep-seated questions, views and assumptions about gender identity, sexuality, and our place, role and function in society:

During the three decades when I asserted my right to remain silent [when asked where my children were], I was constantly struck by the question, "Do you have children, and if not, why not?" This was a question that only women were obliged to answer under pain of being suspected of immorality and selfishness. No doubt cultures exist where the majority of people believe that a man who has not fathered a child is less than a man, but I have never seen a man backed up against the wall and lectured like someone who is suspected of harboring a secret lust to kill puppies. (Mackey, 2000: 30)

Reverie

This chapter reaches the heart of the worldly winds, in particular, the winds of praise and blame, fame and infamy. We can be praised and criticized for being a parent. We can be praised and criticized for not being a parent. We looked earlier at how we might feel stereotyped and stereotype ourselves. Which, if any, of the stereotypes do you identify with in a positive sense and may wish to reclaim in a positive way? Do you think of childlessness as being deviant? Do you enjoy being seen as deviant and 'other', or does it repel you?

Chapter 5

Naturally

'Nature,' as Raymond Williams has remarked, is one of the most complex words in the language. Yet, as with many other problematic terms, its complexity is concealed by the ease and regularity with which we put it to use in a wide variety of contexts. It is at once both familiar and extremely elusive: an idea which we employ with such ease and regularity that it seems as though we ourselves are privileged with some 'natural' access to its intelligibility; but also an idea which most of us know, in some sense, to be so various and comprehensive in its use as to defy our powers of definition. (Soper 1995: 1)

References to 'nature' and 'natural' abound in popular views and opinions about childbearing:

- It is natural to feel broody...
- It is natural for a woman to want a child...
- She had a natural birth...
- Giving birth at home is more natural...
- Naturally, now they're married, they'll have children...
- It is just not natural for two women (or two men) to bring up a child...
- It is unnatural to not have kids...

Childbearing and rearing is, in much common parlance at least, still seen as the 'natural' choice, regardless of research about pregnancy and the maternal instinct. Why is this problematic? Because: 'When motherhood is defined as 'natural', non-motherhood becomes considered 'unnatural' and 'unwomanly''

(Peterson and Engwall, 2013, drawing on Lorber and Moore, 2007; Rich et al., 2011). It seems timely here to roam around the notion of 'nature' and what is 'natural', bearing in mind the underlying societal assumption that it is only natural for a woman to want a child and for a heterosexual couple to start a family.

'Nature' and 'natural' are such over-used phrases, that, as Soper points out in the opening quote, they almost defy our powers of definition. In the realm of childbearing the mention of Mother Earth and Mother Nature crop up time and again. Having children is seen as 'natural' and – another problematic word – the norm. Was there ever or is there consensus on what 'nature' actually means? Perhaps we became more fixated on using the term 'nature' loosely, in a catch-all way, the more we removed ourselves collectively from our earth-touching roots and wilderness (and our inner wild nature), locating ourselves in an urban environment, with its modernity and so-called 'civilization'?

We live in a world which attempts to plan and control life, including our own fertility, with the medicalisation of the birthing of our children. Baby-making is seen and remarked upon as a 'natural' thing. Yet the reality of the medicalisation of labor is a different story, with the degree of intervention, and the emphasis upon hospital births. (Happily this situation seems to be changing, with the suggestion recently that home births should be encouraged for low-risk births. At least more than a half of all expectant mothers in the UK will be offered the chance of being in their 'natural' habitat – their home – as they give birth (NICE, 2014).)

I find myself faintly amused and slightly sobered by my own situation in writing this book about intentional childlessness, particularly in this chapter. I say I have chosen to not have children. The truth is that I have never tried to have children. For all I know I may be unable to have children, with nature deciding my child-bearing status, regardless of what I think and write. This highlights for me the way in which I/we humans act habitually as if we are masters and mistresses of our universes, sometimes making assumptions based on nothing much at all. It can be so easy to fall into the trap of assuming things will work out, and we can be so disappointed when things do not go to plan. Rather than having an awareness of the uncertainty and even the fragility of life, we can tend to erroneously think we have control. This is exacerbated by living in a society which prefers quick fixes to problems rather than deeper, slower transformation, with symptoms being treated rather than causality examined, and in which money, wealth and status are seen as solutions to all ills. I long for the day when we remember that we are each but one being – still unique and significant – part of a vast, interconnected universe within universes.

To say that a woman or a couple should have a child because it is 'natural', or, in the words of Freud, a biological imperative, is fraught with assumptions and complexity. And, yes, it is factually accurate that if a fertile man and woman have sexual intercourse then sometimes the 'natural' consequence is the creation of a baby. It is the blanket use of the term 'natural' – and the judgments and nested assumptions that accompany it – which can cause trouble and lead to confusing worldviews. Equally troubling is the emphasis upon baby-making as 'natural' and a central priority, rather than an emphasis upon other 'natural' human faculties. For example, the immense spiritual faculty of many human beings; perhaps those following in the Buddha's footsteps and practicing the three-fold path of ethics, meditation, and wisdom. I am saddened that the life of someone living simply, without the desire to procreate, perhaps without the desire to have sex – creating a life of stillness, simplicity and contentment – is seen as odd or less 'natural' than those choosing to birth and rear children. The desire to procreate is strong and instinctual, with the understandable human longing to recreate little versions of ourselves and our beloved, but it is certainly not the only valid or 'natural' desire.

I would welcome us into a broader 'church' (or 'meditation hall'!) in thinking through what is 'natural' and how we use the term, witnessing and examining more closely our own assumptions, views, and prejudices, particularly when they are consciously or unconsciously projected upon others. It is simple to fall into judging the life decisions of others against the yardstick of what we see as 'natural' and 'right', often as a way of avoiding looking at and engaging with our own precious lives. Perhaps the day will come when we live with an awareness of the 'natural', as in 'nature' and the 'natural' world as other-than-human life, and by extension, our own inner 'wild' nature, rather than projecting 'wild' onto things and beings which we perceive to be outside of ourselves. We are made of the same elements as the natural world, sharing a high percentage of DNA with all living things. We might live more sustainable lives, cleaning up our act – individually and collectively – and care more for our home, the earth and other species, seeing the interdependent nature of our relationship with our habitat and all that lives?

Right now it is just starting to dawn on us collectively that unless we do that, life on earth will continue to change radically and at an alarming rate, for example, in terms of abrupt climate change, a drastic continuing loss of biodiversity, and environmental degradation. I sometimes imagine a world in which the same amount of time, energy, money, and care, would be channeled into righting our relationship with the earth, as it is into conceiving and bringing up children. It would be an awesome sea change, particularly given the amazing creativity, tenacity, and resourcefulness of human beings. After all, whether or not we are parents to children we have ourselves borne, we are all stewards in handing on the legacy of our time on earth to the next generation of earth dwellers: human and other-than-human.

The importance of stewardship and legacy are easily

overlooked beneath short-termism, and our fixation upon 'me-making' through: educational achievement, job security, career progression, wealth accumulation, finding the perfect romantic partner and creating a nuclear family; all aspects of life which are endorsed by the current zeitgeist. Many of us in the 'developed world' have suffered the loss of our earth-touching, Pagan roots, and with it, our awe for life and our desire for connection. Most have this awe, particularly on returning from a country walk, visiting a paradise island, or meditating, it just gets obscured by other things and the need to keep up with our fast-moving lifestyles. Perhaps the interest in reality TV and the surge in celebrity culture is a degraded form of this longing for something more sacred and divine which we can no longer find within ourselves, maybe we are continually looking to others to fill our hunger? As a species we seem to have lost our full color, our full capacity for life. But all is not lost – the glimpses of life in full color are still there, and there is a waking up process going on.

Radical change is ahead if we decide to adapt to living in a world less reliant upon fossil fuels. In fact, radical change is ahead of us anyway. We need to re-think our relationship with the 'natural world' as we figure out afresh how we grow and transport our food, and distribute other vital resources. In the meantime we can be aware of how we use the words 'nature' and 'natural' and start to unpack the assumptions in those words about ourselves, and views about the 'right' way to live.

As a city dweller I like to bring an awareness of 'nature' into my every day. I watch the phases of the moon, noticing the waxing and waning. I like finding out about the rock strata lying beneath the foundations of our house, and meeting the local flora and fauna with whom I share this neighborhood. As I sit to meditate I sometimes bring to mind the historical Buddha, Siddhartha Gautama. How, after his enlightenment, he wandered, most likely wearing an old, ragged robe, living a simple life; collecting food, finding shelter and sharing his teachings. He would have lived far more closely to the elements, without this artificial split between 'nature' within us and 'nature' outside ourselves.

A pregnant pause

This chapter has roamed the pastures of the views and associations with 'nature' and 'natural'. Do you, or did you, see having a child as a 'natural' choice? What does 'nature' or 'natural' mean to you in this particular context? What do you make of the notion of stewardship? If you take a moment to envision the future, what would you like your life's legacy to be? Not just your legacy in material terms, as captured by having a will, but the legacy of your time on earth, the decisions you made, the work you did, the people you spent time with... In what ways do you feel connected to your family, friends, your community, your locality, and your 'earth-touching' roots?

Chapter 6

The seven billion mark

To admit that human population growth has been bad for the planet is an affront to the collective ego. Suspecting that our species has exploded in numbers beyond right relation to the biosphere is to admit that there might be something to Earth larger and more important than spectacular *Homo sapiens*. (Mills, 1989: 4. Original italics)

Every one of us contributes to the destruction of Earth's environment. We all consume resources and generate waste. (Hoffman, 2012)

According to the media, the seven billionth human being was estimated to have been born on 31st October 2011. This event was accompanied by a flurry of media interest and questions about resource scarcity and the state of the world into which children are being born. Crossing this mark seemed, to some degree at least, to be a wake-up call: 'how did the last billion happen along so suddenly?' World population reached the six billion mark in October 1999, only 12 years earlier (United Nations, 1999). The second quote, above, states an obvious fact about consumption, yet it is a fact which is scarcely mentioned in dialogues around whether or not to have children.

Deciding to choose to have six children remains a non-political decision, even though we collectively face, or in truth, are just turning towards, the challenges we face. There may be sufficient food, water, and shelter for everyone on the planet, but so far we have fallen short in ensuring everyone leads a free, fed life, as well as not only ignoring, but actually compromising the health of the planet.

Extreme suffering – unnecessary suffering – is worsening rather than easing. The suffering extends way beyond human suffering to the suffering of the biosphere and her multitude of species. This isn't, of course, just about population – it is more complex than that. It is about trade policy, foreign policy, how/whether the financial system works (or *for whom* it currently works), the lifestyle choices of the world's wealthiest, educated classes, the loss of biodiversity and extinction of species, and destructive lifestyles of humans living in 'more developed countries', to name just a few, interrelating factors.

Here we enter a fascinating and challenging area. How can we live alongside one another, replacing judgment and blame with mutual understanding and shared stewardship for the earth and all of her species? Can we entertain that possibility, or do we continue being entranced and ensnared by the capitalist dream, and the free choice of the individual, the consequences of which are fast becoming a nightmare of global proportions?

This dilemma is with me most days, reflecting on how we balance the needs of ourselves and other humans, and how we live in a way that supports our species without discounting the lives of other species with which we share the planet. It forces me to look at my own life. What gives me the right to consume almost twice the amount of carbon than is recommended for sustainable life on earth? Because I live in the UK? Because of my color? Class? And I wonder about the effect on each of our psyches, living in the knowledge that billions of the world's inhabitants are today suffering from silent hunger. I raise these questions with the wish for us all to think more carefully about the cost of our capitalist lifestyles, rather than as a guilt trip, which would be fruitless, and unskillful.

The world is hotting up. The world is literally hotting up, in terms of climate change and temperature rises. It is also hotting up in terms of the polarization of lifestyles, views, fundamental religion, and wealth. In the process of writing this book, the

Occupy Movement was born. People who would never before have thought of themselves as politically active have woken up to no longer accepting avoidable injustices and questioning the nature of the mainstream capitalist rat-race in which we live. (I hesitate to include the term 'rat-race' here – would rats treat each other in the way we humans are known to treat each other and our earthly home?)

This is, in part at least, the global backdrop. Many of us are living 'in the red' in our personal lives and in terms of our global bank account, most obviously, in terms of our carbon footprint. And of course, that is a crude and rough and ready way of looking at modern life, because commoditizing ourselves and other beings as something which can be bought and sold – whether through human sex trafficking or animal transportation and slaughter – is one of the conditions that has got us into the mess we are in at present.

How do we, individually and collectively, re-acquaint ourselves with the reality of interconnection and the interlinked nature of our existences? How long can we go on ignoring this? We have timely reminders of this all around us. For example, the fragility of the Eurozone. Even if we notice this interconnect-edness at the level of financial markets and their precarious nature, it might be a useful enough start. Perhaps it can even take us to the point of realizing that the old models are no longer working, with talk of 'growth' as the main objective being far outdated. 'Equity' and 'equilibrium' and true 'sustainability' (for all species) might be more useful.

How we engage with looking at population growth and respect for sustainable life on earth is as important as what we end up actually doing individually and collectively. Those without children could think 'oh I am okay, I did not have any kids' (I do not think that, just to clarify) and those with five kids might think 'I am okay, we have got a good income and it is my right to have as many kids as I want'. The net result: two people locked into their own private worlds, buying hook, line and sinker into an individualistic worldview and not understanding the consequences of their actions. The 'norm' of much of the mainstream 'Western' world is that if we have the money and the time, then what we do is our personal choice. The time has come, whether we welcome or resist it, to open up our worldviews to new perspectives and ways of living, or face pretty certain extinction as a species (and all the while, causing harm or extinction to other species).

We can wait for governments to bring in a one or two child policy which we can rail against and criticize politicians for, or we can start thinking more about the consequences of our own actions as a body of people. It is obviously not solely the government's responsibility to face questions like population growth and resulting resource scarcity square on. It is the responsibility of each of us to know our inbuilt duty of care to the earth and other elements as part of life on earth. It is also incredibly hard to stay with these questions before we resort to our escapist strategy of choice, whether that is self-medication through alcohol, food, drugs, sex, television, or hedonism, or denial or frozen fear. It is so easy and understandable to think we are too insignificant to make a difference in the face of such big challenges, or simply unable to stay with things that are too painful (see Marshall, 2014).

Our connection to and recognition of this duty of care seems to have become seriously compromised. On a practical, everyday level, the more 'civilized' and privileged our lives become, the more tenuous this link. If you live in a village with a well as your only water source, you have a clear idea of how much water you have. You know not to pollute the water in your well, unless you want to cause harm to yourselves and your community. Many of us in 'more developed nations' have become removed from the source of our water and other life-giving elements. We turn taps on and off, adjusting switches and dials as we manage heat, water, and light. We expect there to be an ever-flowing supply of precious resources, a view at odds with the reality of finite resources or holding a tenuous hope for a green-tech solution somewhere in an imagined future.

The loss of knitted-up thinking also seems to apply in the area of childbirth and rearing. We are given the impression, or we buy into the collusion, that it is our birthright to have a child, or as many children as we would like. This is seen as a private decision, rather like deciding to buy a new house or car. Societally there is, sadly, little consideration given to the wider implications of the number of children we produce.

Restricting the number of children is off the political agenda, in fact, the environmental considerations of childbearing are rarely up for discussion. Being aware of cutting personal carbon emissions is only just edging its way onto the agenda in any meaningful sense, with limited interest. In 2007, Tony Blair – then the UK prime minister – had the perfect opportunity to set a 'good' example with regards to carbon emissions, but declared that he had no intention of abandoning long-haul holiday flights to reduce his carbon footprint, stating: "I personally think these things are a bit impractical actually to expect people to do that" (Watt, 2007).

Imagine the furor if politicians added choosing childlessness to their agendas. We've witnessed the criticism of Julia Gillard, former Australian president, by Tony Abbott, head of the opposition. Gillard cited her single, childless and atheistic status as obstacles, as she urged the business community not to write off her or her government (Coorey, 2012). As Day writes:

Perhaps one of the reasons the continuing spats between Abbott and Gillard are getting so much attention is that Abbott says out loud what many think about childless women: that our inexperience as mothers means that we are not really qualified to have an opinion on anything. (Day, 2012)

Bringing childlessness onto the public agenda is perceived as bringing too much bad press and loses the party in power too many votes. It is too hot a potato. And to attempt to raise the issue as a childless woman (or man) you are stuck in the Catch 22 which Day points out above; of not being qualified to have an opinion in the first place. The issue of how many children one has chosen to have is, interestingly, even too hot a potato to enter the public consciousness in terms of being aware of one's carbon footprint. I have been criticized for driving a car by people who have produced three little beings – but at least they cycle to work. I smile and count to ten, given that I am certainly not without my own blind spots... We need to face these questions with great care and respect, realizing how our private and public worlds coincide, and instigate dialogues as we co-create a more sustainable way of living.

In the 1970s and 80s organizations like the National Alliance for Optional Parenthood (mentioned in the introduction) raised discussions about the environmental and population implication of having children. Since then these discussions seem to have become increasingly rare, perhaps given that we are in the latter stages of capitalism, conditioned by the prevailing narrative of economic growth which is more in line with pronatalism and a 'business as normal' agenda coloring all aspects of life (i.e. overlooking the fact that we live in a world with finite resources). For example, a recent article 'Childless by Choice: More people decide against having children, presenting quandaries for governments and the elderly' concludes that:

> ...given the anticipated substantial cutbacks in entitlements – already underway in European nations – it is doubtful that governments can provide sufficient financial and human resources to care for the growing numbers of elderly without children. (Chamie & Mirkin, 2012)

This argument assumes the 'business as normal' point of view with regards to our current capitalist system and our patterns of procreating. It also continues to perpetuate the view of the voluntarily childless as being deviant and a societal burden. Our current financial system assumes that growth is good, despite the harm that our 'Western' lifestyles cause to life, both human and other-than-human. A more open stance on immigration could alleviate fears about population growth, and (sadly) would be in line with the fact that climate change refugees exist and their numbers will increase in the coming decades. Hoffman makes a timely point:

> It would be apparent to a school child that the population cannot keep growing indefinitely. The U.S. has finite land and the world has finite resources. Inevitably population growth must stop. So how will we prevent the economy from imploding when that happens? (Hoffman, 2013)

I am amused and frustrated when people have responded to my chosen childlessness with the response "how would the planet carry on if everyone was like you?" (It reminds me of the response, when I confirm that I am vegetarian, that the world would be over-run with cows if everyone were like me.) I confess, this, along with the 'you are selfish' response to child-lessness, baffles me. I realize I am still in a minority of women and thankfully for the continuation of the species not everyone is like me. If the planet were looking like it was coming to a stand-still due to plummeting population growth I might well think again and I have no doubt others would, too. Although I wonder whether we can even imagine a world in which the earth was given a bit more space from constant human interference and meddling? We should step back and remember that the planet does not need us to run the show (or to be 'Planet Managers' in the words of Evan Eisenberg, 2000: xv).

Looking to the future, I am appreciative of authors like Ellen Walker and her passionate words to potential parents-to-be:

> If you are considering becoming a parent first take some time to consider the environmental impact that a child will have, especially if the child becomes a parent at some time... If you want a child, do so because this life goal is a passion that you believe will be worth the necessary sacrifices. Support organizations that work to protect the environment... Let's all work together to save our world for those future generations. (Walker, 2011)

A pregnant pause

This chapter is full of stirring issues, so take your time in pondering the thoughts and themes which follow. Notice whether environmental, consumption, and resource considerations enter the equation of your thoughts about childbearing. Do you see the baby-making decision as a private decision or a decision with much wider consequences? Notice your own sense of your sphere of influence and sense of agency in the world. What skills, experience, and qualities do you, or could you, offer the world? (Often we avoid taking action or living the life of our wildest dreams because we don't believe we can make a difference.) Are you able to sustain a sense of your own contribution to life and the world without becoming overwhelmed? Or falling into denial? Hedonism? Burying your metaphorical head in the sand? Or are you a climate change skeptic? Give yourself time to notice how you respond to these themes, which can feel insurmountable. Having strategies of choice in working with the insurmountable is inevitable, human, and can be useful. Perhaps

---

the trick is to get to know your strategies intimately, knowing how, when, and whether they serve you and the wider world.

Chapter 7

'Mr. Fix-It and the Home-Improvement Committee'[6]

A lot of the time, people are feeling a loss of connection and love in their marriage, so they kind of hold this fantasy that if they have a child that that will bring everything back to being OK... Part of it is an idealization, and the solution to fixing a problem. (Bensching, 2011)

Babies are sometimes conceived in an attempt to try to fix things. In fact, this seems a fairly commonplace strategy. Perhaps a marriage has gone a bit lifeless. Or a partner is commitment-phobic, or is making it up to his or her spouse for having an affair. Or a woman reaches a point when she is not sure what to do with her life. Or she wants her husband to change through fatherhood. I am not smug about this, knowing very well that I could have easily done many of the above in slightly different circumstances. I think a voluntary childless equivalent is not having children as a result of avoiding things, whether that is relationship, intimacy (not just sexual, but intimacy in friendship and with family), or commitment. We all have our strategies of choice, childless or not...

Babies do not fix things. They do not fix communication in a stagnating marriage or necessarily bring a couple together, even though it is a totally understandable and human and fallible thing to think – or hope and pray – that they might fix these things. Every day in my therapy room I hear peoples' stories of birth and death: those who wish they had not been born, those whose parents wished they had not been born, and who have been told they were unwanted, those who were supposed to have been a girl, those who were born in absolutely dire circumstances, materially and/or in terms of the abuse to which they were subjected, those who regret terminating a pregnancy, those who are in the throes of threatening themselves with death, and those who get pregnant, seeking to get at least one good thing out of a disastrous relationship.

I have empathy with the 'fixing' approach to having children, knowing that I could easily have done that myself. Perhaps I would have unconsciously tried to right things that I did not get when I was young, perhaps to prove to myself that my birth and existence have been and are worthwhile, perhaps to receive praise from others, perhaps to nurture a little being, watching and learning and growing with them, which must be fascinating and rewarding. All of these are understandable human reasons to have a child, or to want to be successful at anything, for that matter, but perhaps not the most useful reasons for having children *per se*, and perhaps not all that great for the life of the new being in question.

This 'fix it' idea is commented upon in everyday life in the form of 'it will be different when a baby comes along'. As humans we are in an age in the 'Western' world when we like problem-solving, and doing so with our whizzy technological solutions. There is a strong 'fix it' culture in many sectors of contemporary life: medical, technological, even increasingly in the professionalizing of the counseling and psychotherapy culture; sometimes being seduced by the false promise of the quick fix rather than deep and lasting healing and change. This fixing obsession is so extreme that Bateson (1972: 498) cites technological progress, along with population increase and errors in our values, as being the three root causes of the threat to human survival.

My concern with an over-focus on the 'fix it' phenomena is that we forget to look at the underlying patterns and to observe – really observe – what is underneath 'the problem' we are trying to fix. I am not suggesting that we should avoid taking action;

rather we should breathe and reflect before acting. There is a real and present danger that we are creating—further colluding with capitalism—a culture of problems and solutions, rather than seeing life in its own wonderful messiness and running at its own pace. This is part and parcel of the way many of us—myself included—relate to ourselves, others, our immediate environment and the earth. We are busy, we are hurrying, and we expect things on time, at the right price. The consumer mindset has taken hold in our hearts and minds, to the extent that we relate to life in a consumerist way even when we are not at the shopping mall. So long as we have the money, it can be easy to fall into the trap of assuming that something or some experience is ours, regardless of the consequences.

When life does not go to plan, we immediately think that there is a problem, rather than pausing to wonder whether what has happened is par for the course and part of life's rich pattern. It is easy to forget, clever egos that we have, that we are not at the centre of the universe. No one is centre of the universe, but our egos trot out a different story in the privacy of our own minds. Consumerist life has tapped into, and found a stronghold and 'natural' home in the nature of ego and its constant craving for things, money, experiences, and certain people.

Having babies is inevitably influenced by these societal trends. Not only can baby-making be a 'fix it' solution; conception has also become big business in terms of the moves towards genetics and baby-making, and the medicalisation of the birthing process. One could even be forgiven for thinking that for some parents (I am sure a tiny minority), having a baby is more about accessorizing and keeping up with their peer group than it is about wanting to nurture and bring life into the world. And as quickly as I have typed that, I feel absolutely sure that that is rarely or never the whole story in childbearing and rearing. We never know what is going on for others – it is hard enough knowing what is going on for ourselves most of the time. Let's

just be as aware as possible of our motivations, whether or not
we find ourselves choosing childlessness.

Chapter 8

Unconditional love

Motherhood continues to be seen as woman's highest achievement: spiritually our society exalts the idea of motherhood based on self-sacrifice and unconditional love. (Bartlett, 1994: x)

...life does not deliver itself to us in a perfect form. Yet all spiritual teachings point out that it is precisely through the ways in which our life is imperfect that we gain the chance to grow in wisdom. (Dowrick, 2010: 311)

In my psychotherapy work I often practice and reflect upon 'unconditional love'. It is most familiar to me as one of the 'core conditions' as outlined by Carl Rogers, the founder of 'Person-centered' or 'Client-centered' counseling. According to Rogers, the three qualities of unconditional positive regard, authenticity and congruence, are the vital ingredients for a healing and effective relationship between the client and the therapist (Rogers, 1994: 61-61). In my practice, even though I do not identify solely as a Person-centered counselor, the core conditions are invaluable and helpful reminders. In practice, unconditional positive regard moves between being a reality and an aspiration. I have the aspiration to have that regard for my clients and, in parallel, I know that my mind is conditioned by things other than unconditional love. When a therapy client – or a friend I am meeting – is 15 minutes late for the third time in a row, as well as feeling concerned, and wondering what the lateness is about, I also start to feel irritated.

I am interested in how the term 'unconditional love' is used by parents with regards to their children. It is often said that a parent's love for their child is unconditional. On one hand I understand this comment, and, on another, I realize that I don't. I remember the feeling when I held my nephew, Thomas, for the first time. A wave of fierce protection, connection, and a huge rush of love – hard to articulate. Those feelings have been there when I have held all my nieces for the first time, too, although I noticed it most strongly with Thomas, as it was a new experience at the time, given he is the first born of the next generation. Perhaps that was unconditional love. I have felt similar feelings for my partner at times, and for friends and clients. But, in truth, I have felt it most strongly for my blood relatives. I would do anything to protect the little life in my arms. I am sure for parents, having *created* this little life, the feeling is much amplified.

What I do not understand about the notion of unconditional parental love is that it is obviously only one part of the picture. Parental love, in its purest (enlightened?) form, I have no doubt, is unconditional. The behavior of most parents towards their children at least some of the time is conditioned by states of mind other than those fuelled by love. I am stating the obvious here. And it feels like the obvious needs to be stated, to throw light on what looks like a frequent over-romanticizing of parental love (the other thing that fascinates me is why unconditional love is so often applied to human relationships, rather than our relationships with other-than-human life, but perhaps that is a subject for another chapter...).

Parental behavior, like other behavior in all other forms of relationship, is conditioned by many things: love, kindness, irritation, patience, frustration, power and control, all sorts of things, and yet, parental love is painted by some as unconditional. Full stop. How about we create more dialogues about love – parental or otherwise, unconditional or otherwise – rather than making sweeping generalizations, and exerting huge pressure on parents, so they feel defensive and protective of their role, especially at times when their love feels far from unconditional (for example, when their children are testing them to the limit)? Perhaps it is time we lightened the pressure of guilt or remorse for the majority of parents who do not feel wall-to-wall unconditional love for their offspring. I long for a world in which we celebrate our imperfections as a way of living more contented, easier lives. I am reminded of a Buddhist teaching about *metta* – translated as universal loving kindness – known as the 'Karaniya Metta Sutta'. It goes like this:

If you know your own good
and know where peace dwells
then this is the task:

Lead a simple and a frugal life
uncorrupted, capable and just;
be mild, speak soft, eradicate conceit,
keep appetites and senses calm.

Be discreet and unassuming;
do not seek rewards.
Do not have to be ashamed
in the presence of the wise.

May everything that lives be well!
Weak or strong, large or small, seen or unseen, here or
elsewhere,
present or to come, in heights or depths,
may all be well.

Have that mind for all the world –
get rid of lies and pride –
a mother's mind for her baby,
her love, but now unbounded.

Secure this mind of love,
no enemies, no obstructions,
wherever or however you may be!

It is sublime, this,
it escapes birth and death,
losing lust and delusion,
and living in the truth!
(Vipassi, date unknown)

This 'sutta', or teaching, provides me with enough material for my Buddhist practice this lifetime. It says all I need to know. I imagine how the world would be if we paid more attention to the lines:

...a mother's mind for her baby,
her love, but now unbounded.
Secure this mind of love...

Imagine if, even for only a fraction of the time, we all acted as though we loved everyone we came across as much as we loved our own children? The Metta Sutta urges us to understand the potential of the unconditional love that a mother has for her child and to cultivate that intention and feeling for all beings everywhere – human and other-than-human. It sounds utopian, and yet, my experience shows me that practicing metta meditation changes me and my point of view, thereby changing my relationships.

20 years ago, during my first visit to the Bristol Buddhist Centre, I was introduced to a meditation practice called the 'metta bhavana' or 'cultivation of loving-kindness'. It is a traditional practice in which you are invited, in five stages, to contact and focus upon the loving-kindness you feel towards yourself, a friend, a 'neutral' person, an enemy, and all living beings.

I was pretty disillusioned at the time. Being taught the metta bhavana meditation opened my eyes to the possibility of how life might be – or will be – when I have the wherewithal to have a response of wisdom and compassion in every moment, rather than at peak moments. I was not a Buddhist then, and was not looking for a path of practice; I did my own thing spiritually. But I was stopped in my tracks by that simple teaching of loving-kindness. In taking up the practice, I soon noticed the effect it had in my everyday life. Most obviously, how hard it was to feel metta for myself, compared to others. How my ill will towards others, particularly those in the 'enemy' stage of the practice, started to soften round the edges, when I made the time to do the practice. What a relief it was to bring to mind all sentient life, even though it felt like a huge leap of faith and challenged my imagination.

If we have not been fortunate enough to have experienced maternal or parental love, a central challenge might be how to learn to love ourselves and others when that was not modeled for us in our earliest weeks, months, and years. The metta bhavana meditation can be invaluable in cultivating that love for ourselves, through to all sentient beings.

Through the process of reflecting and acting upon choosing childlessness, the most important thing I have learned is about love. Love, respect, and care for life and all that lives. Not just love for our lover, children, parents, other family members, and closest friends – love for all beings everywhere, human and other-than-human. Being loving, and communicating across a divide of differing opinions is a tall order, yet contacting the love of my most heartfelt moments is always worth the effort.

Chapter 9

Meet the parents

Share the pleasures of raising children widely, so that all need not directly reproduce in order to enter into this basic human experience. We must hope that no woman would give birth to more than one or two children during this period of crisis. Adopt children. Let reverence for life and reverence for the feminine mean also a reverence for other species and for future human lives... (Snyder, 1995: 33)

In deciding whether or not to have children we are likely, consciously or not, to 'meet' our own parents or significant carers; those who had an important influence upon us in our formative years. This 'meeting the parents' manifests in many ways. The most obvious way is in actually looking at our parent's present-day view of our procreating – or lack thereof – and how those views have conditioned us through the course of our lives. Some of us are likely to have imbibed a strong pronatal message, whilst others may have been lucky enough to have parents and carers who have less investment in our choices. Some of the messages will be delivered directly, others more covertly, perhaps in side-glances and sighs. Some of us might re-meet the parents we were expected to be in our own childhoods, bringing up younger siblings, realizing that deciding not to have children is influenced by the fact that we have already felt responsible for children and are not interested in doing that again:

The role of being a 'little parent' was cited as one of the deciding factors in the choice to remain child-free. For those women the mystique of happy parenting has been blown apart. (Bartlett, 1994: 83)

We are likely to be reminded of our own childhood in mulling over the decision. We might spend time reflecting on how our parents/carers acted towards us and each other, trying to understand our childhoods through our now adult eyes, understanding the complexity of human beings and the world. Our decision not to have children might be a rejection of childhood, or of the notion of motherhood or fatherhood, depending upon our experience of being a child and our subsequent worldviews. For others, having children is likely to be a potentially or actually reparative act, healing wounds, and perhaps 'putting things right', which did not feel right in their childhoods. For those who experienced relatively happy and contented childhoods the decision as to whether or not to have children can appear to be a non-decision; why wouldn't one re-create something that was positive? For some, going anywhere near a conscious decision-making process is too painful to contemplate, because of the pain or neglect of childhood and the wish to avoid ever risking that for another little life. Or perhaps we feel ill-equipped to become a parent.

It is also possible that we'll meet the inner, internalized version of our parents or early carers in thinking about child-bearing. This internalized version may or may not resemble our present-day parents, if they are still living, or our parents as they were, if they have died. Reflecting on our sense of our parents within can be a valuable exercise in understanding the norms, rules and assumptions that govern us and our everyday decisions. And, of course, in parenthood, those internalized parental voices are often expressed when we find ourselves saying things that were said to us.

If we are in a relationship the chances are that we will also meet our partner's parents – both within and in real life – and their familial expectations and norms, which may be similar or incredibly different to our own, with a clash of cultures. It might be useful not only to dialogue as much as possible with partners with this in mind, but also to sift through our own conditioning, hopes, fears, and expectations as embodied in our worldviews, inherited family views, family stories, rules and myths. Perhaps give time for unconscious hopes and fears to bubble to the surface. Meeting our partners in this way can be helpful in whichever decision we end up making, as well as improving our relationships and communication.

It can, of course, be useful to meet our parents in the present-day, updating our historical and/or internalized parental views. Bartlett (1994: 115) cites how an American professor of psychology runs a course that encourages women to write their mother's biography, having interviewed them about their lives as children, adolescents and young women before they became mothers. Bartlett notes how if we did this it would be like 'meeting our mothers for the very first time, getting to know them as women in their own right and not just in the role which relates to us'.

If you have tended to avoid the subject of procreation as a way of avoiding the pain of looking at your personal history it can be useful to ponder, perhaps with help, how to approach this in yourself. I find it particularly poignant witnessing friends and colleagues with avoidant strategies reaching their mid forties, realizing they have run out of time to have a baby – a process which may have been hard but extremely reparative. Women and men in this heart-breaking situation can take considerable time to feel peace and reconciliation with their circumstances, without turning to further self-punishment and failure. And often they suffer alone and in silence, with the danger that they'll pull away from social contact and the thought of the pain of being surrounded by friend's children. If you know you tend towards avoiding this topic, perhaps take time to reflect on the pregnant pause suggestions at the end of this chapter and bear in mind Bartlett's words:

The constant postponement of making a decision can also be seen as emotional paralysis; the woman constantly living in a state of division with a resulting lack of direction and an enormous drain on her energy: sitting on the fence is hard work. (Bartlett, 1994: 101)

In thinking around this theme of meeting the parents I find myself wanting to fly the flag for the courage of most birth parents and adoptive parents everywhere. I see friends and family as parents and applaud their love, energy, commitment, hard work, tenacity and care. Given that we are imperfect beings there is no such thing as perfect parents, even though it is held up so strongly as a cultural aspiration in our child and nuclear-family-centric culture. Perhaps an awareness of the fact that parents can only ever be good enough, rather than perfect, is worth bearing in mind in whatever course of action we choose.

We reach a point in adulthood where meeting our inner parents or carers – regardless of whether or not we can actually meet our flesh and blood parents in the way we wish to – is vital for our own sense of who we are, where we are and what is true now. In suggesting this I am not for one minute suggesting quick-fix forgiveness, overlooking the fact that some people survive hellish childhoods, or suggesting that the process is easy and quick. I just think it is useful to 'meet' our parents somehow or another before we die, and, ideally at least, before they die.

No parent can shield us from sickness, old age, death and all the ordinary ups and downs of life. No one can shield us from life's challenging circumstances. Just as a therapist cannot magic away our difficulties. Hopefully parents are around to share some of the joy and happiness. Life is as it is, even though our parents' or carer's response to life obviously has a huge historical bearing on our feelings of safety, security and nourishment. Our parents might have had the best intentions and things might still have been incredibly difficult in our childhood. Or they might have been largely negligent. It is our job to figure out our relationship and responses to what happens and has happened to us, knowing what we are responsible for and what we are not, what we need to carry and what we need to find a way to heal or let rest.

Having children certainly offers an opportunity to grow and mature. That is not solely a good reason to have children and it is obviously not a guaranteed outcome. There are plenty of other ways to grow and mature. As with many paths in life, it is not necessarily what we do, but the degree of awareness and authenticity which we bring to the task. But for the moment I am thinking of how I have witnessed some friends blossoming as parents, relishing their relationship with their child, despite the sleep deprivation and money pressures. They have 'grown up' in the best possible sense of those words – still playing and retaining their child-likeness rather than childlessness.

I can also think of friends and acquaintances without children who exude a sense of being eternally young, rather than youthful, in a perhaps not so helpful way. They seem a bit lost, confused, rootless, unsettled, ill at ease and searching. Some of these friends have consciously chosen not to have children; others have remained ambivalent or not consciously approached the subject. Of course, it may well be the case that these friends might have been prone to rootlessness had they had children. I guess if that were the case at least they would have had a considerable objective task to fill their time. I think a strong downside of our current cultural climate in the 'West' is that in a certain way there is also too much choice and an illusion of freedom in that choice, which, in fact, can be experienced as more like being trapped in a prison of indecision.

In becoming parents, through having our own children or adopting, we meet our parents and revisit our own childhoods, perhaps more vividly than ever. If our parents are still around our family relationships change and shift as the next generation arrives and a new set of dynamics are co-created. In witnessing parenting I am reminded of those 'oh my God, I am becoming my mother' laughs I have shared with friends as we catch ourselves echoing the words or actions of one or both of our parents: 'do not come crying to me when...' Some friends who are parents develop a lot more empathy for their own parents – many with a good dose of acceptance and understanding – as they undertake the Herculean task of parenting. Others seem to expect even more of their parents, for example, in the form of full-time baby-sitting and financial support.

As the next generation takes shape there is the re-telling of old family stories, repeating of patterns and well-worn family grooves. In choosing to not become parents we also continue to 'meet our parents'. At different stages in our own lifecycles our experience changes. We have the opportunity to continue to see and re-see our parents; who they were, how they were, warts and all. Both of my grandmother's and my father's deaths were a precious lesson in seeing that you tend to die as you live. The older I get the more I see the fallibility and the immense life energy of my mum and the new lease of life she has experienced since my father's death. That is the great, and perhaps unexpected, thing about parents – about all of us, in fact – we keep on changing. It can be tempting to typecast our parents as the people they were when we were growing up. Perhaps this is truer in some families and for some individuals, but for most people it is not the case.

So meet your parents – inner and outer, living or dead, birth and/or adoptive parents, now and then – whether or not you decide to have children. And meet the parent in yourself, whether or not you physically plan to create children. We all have a part to play in having and creating visions for new, more life-honoring ways of life. In this vein, I love the opening quote from Gary Snyder and his exhortation to 'share the pleasures of raising children widely'!

Reveries

Meeting our parents is a life-long task, as is meeting ourselves, so these reveries are just a starting point. In meeting our parents we become more aware of how our own views, beliefs, and assumptions have been formed and shaped by our interactions with experiences of the world. Cast your mind back to the stories you were told about your parent's childhoods, and their experience of childbirth, childbearing and their views on family. Notice how free you've felt to follow your own pathway through life. Have you tended to follow the path of least resistance and most social acceptability in conforming and fitting in? Or have you tended to do your own thing? Have important life decisions been respected by your closest family? If you are adopted, how has that brought particular challenges to the decision as to whether or not to have children? How do you feel different and similar to other friends who are not adopted? Notice whether you lose yourself in anxiety, indecision, or distraction, putting off looking at the 'baby question'. Maybe spend time reflecting and dreaming on the reasons for this, particularly if you do not have as many childbearing years left as you would like.

Chapter 10

Men, women, and children

Not everyone wants to parent, which is a choice that should be respected for both men and women. But if we only choose to interpret compassion for children as parenthood, we seek to dismiss the interest and efforts of many who are invested in the well-being of our kids. (Beck, 2011)

I find it virtually impossible to write about intentional childlessness in a way that encompasses what is relevant, current, and interesting for an audience of both women *and* men. I realize that in one sense it is a misnomer to split the potential reading population into two along gender lines, and in another sense, given the very different gender conditioning of men and women, it is a vitally important to do so (and I'm aware that I am oversimplifying things in not talking more about gender diversity).

Different things are still expected of men and women, not to mention men and women of various cultures, ethnicities, ages, sexuality, and those who choose not identify as either a man or a woman. Woman bear children and can decide, in the UK and some other countries, whether or not to carry their child to full term. Once the baby is born, in the majority of households, but obviously not all, it is still the mother who takes the primary role in caring for the child or children.

I am aware of my own prejudices and shortcomings here and invite that awareness in you as you read. I am a human being with a woman's body and a particular set of familial and cultural conditions of relative privilege, which I share, in part at least, with other 40 something, mainly white, middle-class, educated, voluntarily childless women living in the UK. I was born and raised in these conditions and have chosen others since, for example: being a Buddhist, vegetarian, urban-dweller.

It is important to raise this point about gender and audience, because it is a struggle that is indicative of societal struggles and misunderstandings in the arena of gender, identity, childbearing and rearing. In grappling with the struggles, creative dialogues will hopefully arise about difference, as we navigate through the minefields of blame and polarization within and between men and women. I hope this book is as useful for a man figuring out whether it is time for him to be a Dad as much as a woman in a same-sex relationship working out whether parenthood is for her, or a woman alone without a partner wondering whether she will ever have children.

Reflections about these themes need to be accessible to all, because childbearing and rearing include all of us, not just parents – although they clearly have the life-giving role to play. Each of us play a role in being aware of the worldly conditions and web of relationships into which babies are being born, whether or not we are, or ever will be parents. As Sabonfu Somé says: '…it takes a whole village to raise a child' (Somé, 2013). In my mind it is the 'splitting off' that occurs in this arena which causes problems. For example, the most obvious split that we have been exploring, of women as mothers having more status than women who are childless. Or the split-off view that parents have sole responsibility for their children. They obviously have responsibility in terms of the everyday raising and care, but they do not in terms of the societal conditions we offer our children; which are created and maintained collectively.

For example, being an auntie is an important part of my life, as well as personally having been a significant rite of passage. My nephew and nieces matter to me very much and I love being in their company. Their births marked many things: the passing of time, the joy of life and new beginnings, moving into early middle age and growing eldership, witnessing my brother as a father, as well as knowing him as a brother and work colleague, and, in turn, him witnessing me as an auntie, as well as a sister and work colleague. Perhaps as voluntary childlessness becomes more acknowledged and accepted, we will reconceive family structures. I am struck by the words of Blackstone and Dyer Stewart in this regard:

> The consequences of deciding to remain childfree specifically for the lives of children have not yet been considered. What role do childfree people play in the lives of children and how do those relationships differ from parent-child relationships? What does it mean for our cultural understanding of "family" if increasing numbers of families do not include children? (Blackstone and Dyer Stewart, 2012)

I also want to include the words of Dally here, who brings an important and related point about gender and 'motherly' qualities:

> ...motherliness is a human quality and by no means confined to women. The use of the phrase 'maternal instinct' is often used by those who wish to assert that only women should care for children or that the details of childrearing are beneath the dignity of men. In fact, many men have motherly qualities and many more could develop them if society and circumstance would permit it. (Dally, 1982)

Dally's point is relevant and timely, given the widespread assumption that I have encountered in researching this book, that men are much more ambivalent about childbearing and rearing and that it is women who want children. Is this really the case? What about the men who long to be dads, and long to talk about potential fatherhood, but have no context in which to do so? Or those men who strongly identify with having motherly qualities, to which Dally refers? What about dads who go along with having another baby to keep the peace? Or have a child to keep their relationship? Perhaps dads or dads-to-be do not get the air time they need, because of the emphasis upon parenthood being so inextricably linked to women's rather than men's ascribed identity.

I am increasingly and acutely aware of my own ignorance and lack of knowledge on a personal level about men and the baby question. Despite researching this area for more than 17 years, I have had very few conversations with men about babies – apart from those with whom I have been intimately involved. What a shame and a loss. I do not think that that is through a lack of interest in my male friends. Perhaps it is another sign of the way our society still ascribes and gives permissions for women to do the emotional work and men to be the rational ones, being more encouraged to make their mark in the world. We know that there are still remnants of the stereotype of women being at home with an inward orientation, and men being at work, running the world, with a more outward orientation.

Having the experience of being in a woman's body means that I am continually reminded of my potential for procreation. My body's most prominent processes: hormonal swings, ovulation pain, PMS, and period pain, make for a physical, sometimes vivid experience of my body's potential ability to create babies. I say potential, because I have never tried to create a baby, so do not know for sure that it would work. But the potential is all there in theory. I find it tricky to imagine what it would be like to have a man's body and the different physicality of that experience, which limits my confidence to comment. And sadly, the physical experience of being a man, perhaps bar jokes about sexual prowess, is a subject which is not talked about all that much in the mainstream, even amongst close friends.

Earlier in life, particularly through puberty, being a body is often exciting and sometimes bewildering for children on the cusp of adulthood. All those swirling questions: 'what the hell's going on?' 'Does he/she/they fancy me? How do I know?' 'Why have I got hair *there*?' 'Is it going to be this painful every month for the next 40 years?' Thankfully, for most people the vividness of puberty calms down as we mature. Although questions about attractiveness and body image, sexuality and gender, often prevail. The other big question for women as they become sexually active is the risk of unwanted pregnancy and sexually transmitted diseases. Perhaps this was more acute for my generation, growing up in an era of a heightened awareness of the actual and potential impact of HIV-Aids.

My fear of getting pregnant when I was younger was huge. Not because I played Russian Roulette, conception-wise, but for lots of other reasons. I had the remnants of 'no sex before marriage' rattling around in my mind from a church-going upbringing. I knew from a young age that I would not be able to go through with having an abortion, in parallel with supporting and witnessing a few close friends having them. Perhaps because I knew there were many things I wanted to do in my life which were not to do with bearing children (perhaps even back then part of me knew, without rationally 'knowing', that I would remain without child).

Knowing the potency of my body and, I then assumed, its baby-making powers, felt like a responsibility. It is a potential responsibility, and one which seems to be felt more keenly by women than men, given that women carry babies. Getting pregnant and carrying a baby to full-term must be immense in terms of the hopes, fears, communication and a forming bond between mother and child.

I would love to know how this process is for men in their impending fatherhood, and at the births of their children. I have a sense of this, and I have seen friends go through this, but I am sad to realize that they nowhere near parallel the blow-by-blow birth stories of women friends. Our storytelling creates our shared histories and it feels a loss that I do not have the same sense of how male friends have found this event. I am appreciative to John and Tom, both therapy friends and colleagues, with whom I talked about this book. John and I had a long and fascinating conversation about the birth of his son. I was glad to hear him tell me the story of his son's birth in detail – how it was and how it is now – and his hopes and fears in deciding whether or not to try for a second baby. In reflecting on this conversation I realize, sadly, what a rare species of a conversation that was.

Am I – are we – enquiring and inclusive in looking at the baby-making decision? I remember a response to an article about intentional childlessness I wrote in *Therapy Today*, the journal of the British Association for Counseling and Psychotherapy. The month after my article was published a man wrote a letter to *Therapy Today* saying he found it disappointing that the article was aimed at women. So, to the man who wrote that letter I would like to say: write something! Let your voice be heard on this subject. Because I am not sure I can write a very meaningful piece aimed at men, given my style of writing. I can raise useful points of reflection, I can point out how pronatal our society still seems to be, I can empathize, I can write of my sadness about the prejudice and disempowerment that goes on, creating trouble for men, women and children, but I cannot write that article from the experience of having a man's body and a man's conditioning.

I am also reminded of the response of a dear female friend to the research questions I sent out on this theme to a forum of counselors and psychotherapists. Her assumption, reading the email, was that they were only aimed at women, when, in fact they were purposely gender neutral in their content. The assumptions, rules, norms and prejudices of our societal conditioning seep into every corner of our being.

Chapter 11

The miracle of life – and death

Birth is a miracle. It is amazing and awesome. Each child born matters. Each life matters whether it is planned, a surprise, wanted, or rejected. What happens at conception, during gestation, and at birth, shape how we become a body, how embodied we are in our relationships with others, and whether we embrace or reject life and the incarnation of consciousness. Each child and life is unique: constellating around a particular time, place, web of friends, family, carers, influenced by the backdrop of world events. Something happens at birth which is akin to times of death and passing. It is as though time stops, fleetingly. Maybe it is because of that prevailing sense that things will never be the same again – although things, of course, are never the same again in any of life's moments... Maybe it is because the only universal certainties are birth and death and what happens in the middle is unknown and unknowable. Our parents and carers provide the conditions for our lives, and throughout our adult lives we make of it what we will.

Every sentient being born matters. Every species that is now extinct mattered. Every new day matters. Every new season matters – in fact, our lives depend on them. Many folk tend to focus less on the miracle of other-than-human life and death, in our anthropocentric world, although when we remember to remember we still marvel at the new blossom, the bird taking its first wobbly flight, the crashing of stormy sea, the soft unfurling of a bracken leaf, and feel familiar sorrow when our animal friend dies. This book's cover picture says it all for me: I urge us to be as in love with the world, and all of life, as we are with our individual, baby-shaped creations. Maybe that is idealistic and impossible, but that is my hope and challenge. It echoes the words of the metta sutta included earlier in Part I.

Tragically, life often is not respected, whether that is the life of a child or the life of an animal. The preciousness of life is overlooked, even trampled, as we can get caught up in the worldly winds, forgetting to pay attention to what matters. As much as being about whether or not to bear children, this book is about life – the constant flow of life and death. It is not about a lack of something, which the word 'childless' can so often denote, particularly in the context of childlessness being judged harshly. It is not about negating or disapproving of life and those who wish to procreate. Essentially, it is about consciousness and honoring the children who are already on the planet and those who are yet to arrive, welcoming them as fully as we are able. In the words of Kahlil Gibran, it is about knowing that:

Your children are not your children.
They are the sons and daughters of Life's longing for itself.
They come through you but not from you,
And though they are with you yet they belong not to you.
You may give them your love but not your thoughts,
For they have their own thoughts.
You may house their bodies but not their souls,
For their souls dwell in the house of tomorrow,
Which you cannot visit, not even in your dreams. (Gibran, 1991: 22)

Chapter 12

The earth from the sky

> Among do-gooders, it is bad form to be a pessimist, but I cannot seem to get that extinction crisis out of my mind. Or that population explosion. Or global climate change. Or the consequences of an era of trade agreements. Can't get those billionaires; those landless, homeless, jobless billions; those new diseases; that global casino of finance capitalism; the corporate capture of the media; those aging nuclear reactors; those surveillance satellites; those crowded prisons out of my mind. (Mills, 2002: 28)

Much of this book's content feels weighty so far. I guess that is not surprising, given that the decision to have children, or having children whether or not you decide to, or not having children whether or not you decide to, all touch the nature of existence: 'Why are we here?' 'What are we doing?' or 'What have I done with my life?' These are the sort of questions we ask ourselves at different ages. Childbearing is itself a weighty decision, given that it leads to the creation of a new life, and is ever more weighty in the current climate. It can be easy to feel a bit doom and gloom looking at societal conditioning around having children and childlessness: the stereotyping of the childless and the public consequences of what, superficially, looks to be a private decision.

This chapter is a pause to reconnect with our inspiration, creativity and our human nature – there, I used the dreaded 'nature' word! – before we move to Part II of this book. As I thought of the title of this chapter the image that immediately came to mind was the picture of the earth from the moon. I still find it spine-tingling after more than 40 years. In the days when

I still flew in 'planes I used to savor the view of the earth from the sky. It never ceased to amaze me: the changing light, the textures of the weather, and of different landscapes beneath us.

I also find myself wondering at the phenomenal nature of human beings: their achievement, fascination, inventiveness, creativity, and compassion. So far I have brought in themes that perhaps do not show humans in their best light. I wonder whether this is because we are living through rather cynical times and forget, on a collective level, to appreciate our species. We can often be pre-occupied with scandals, the latest 'natural' disaster, war, or our inhumanity to one another. Even when kindness is reported in the mainstream media it tends to be the grand acts of kindness, rather than the many acts of kindness that you and I witness in our every day lives.

In this spirit of celebrating humanity and the qualities of our species I can see exactly why people have children. Because 'life is king' – the line from a poem I quote at the end of this chapter. New life is awesome. I only have to recollect holding one of my nieces or my nephew for the first time to feel that sense of the miracle, beauty and wonder of new life and the newborn's little breathing body and fragile dependence. Creating new life must be even more awesome, particularly if it is with one's beloved. (And in my non-baby making life moments of creative endeavor fuel my fascination and engagement.)

I dream sometimes how life would be – how the planet would be – if we could sustain that sense of the miracle, beauty and wonder of not just human life, but of all life. Not in a gushing way, but more in the way we feel that deep appreciation and connection when holding a newborn baby, or gazing at our lover, or being deeply and deliciously alert in meditation, or saying goodbye to someone close to us, or watching the snow gently fall; whatever the occasion happens to be which stops us in our tracks.

I imagine that we would feel more acutely the loss and pain

of trashing other species on the planet. Perhaps we might trash less, the more we stop ourselves in our tracks. What if we were to connect with the horror of how it would feel for the starving child on the news to be our own child? If we had to give our own children water from a river polluted with chemicals perhaps we would clean up our act and be prepared to live a simpler life? If we let more of the beauty of life in more of the time, *we* would be more beautiful and act more beautifully to ourselves and one another.

Most people are decent, honest, kind beings. In fact, I think most people I know are walking miracles when I think about the richness of their lives to date: the ups and downs, the sorrow, and the happiness. Yet at the same time, and particularly at the moment, collectively we cannot seem to face the fact that a 'business as normal' approach to life is not working globally and is literally costing billions of people and animals their lives. Perhaps our imaginations have shrunk as we have become more addled by the busyness of having to be wealthy and successful. Perhaps we have stopped dreaming on a social and communal level as we are so focused upon the survival of our family or simply ourselves, and our vision has narrowed. I have to be honest here, I am glad at this point in time to not have any children. I feel deeply concerned about my nephew and nieces and the how the world will be by the time they are my age.

Societally I think we place a terrible collective burden on children in so-called 'more developed' countries. On the one hand children represent hope for the future. On a personal level perhaps one good reason to have children is to continue one's family line, leaving a legacy. Yet as well as creating children, shouldn't we be thinking ahead to ensure that they have air which is clean enough to breathe, a stable enough climate to produce food and shelters or homes?

I dream of a planet upon which we all, even only occasionally, connect with a sense of the miracle, beauty and wonder of life in the midst of our everyday lives.

Life is King

Hour after hour, day
After day we try
To grasp the Ungraspable, pinpoint
The Unpredictable. Flowers
Wither when touched, ice
Suddenly cracks beneath our feet. Vainly
We try to track bird flight through the sky, trace
Dumb fish through deep water, try
To anticipate the earned smile, the soft
Reward, even
Try to grasp our own lives. But Life
Slips through our fingers
Like snow. Life
Cannot belong to us. We
Belong to Life. Life
Is King.
(Sangharakshita, 1995: 285)

Reverie

In the Preface I recounted the 'dreaming birth' of this book; how my decision not to have children emerged, in part, from a dream. Having finished Part I pause and notice what occupies your sleeping and waking dream. Scan the reflections below, noticing which attract your attention...

Is raising a family part of your dream? If yes, what does it look like in your mind's eye and what will move you closer to realizing this dream? If no, what are your dreams for your life? Draw a circle or 'mandala' of your life – a mandala is a circular symbol representing the universe in Buddhist and Hindu symbolism. Near the centre of the circle write down what is central to your dreams, surrounded by things around the edges which are less important, but still significant supports to, or aspects of your life. Experiment using post-it notes in creating your circle, so that you can move things around, trying out different options.

What are the habitual stories of your life? Maybe you think of yourself as a roamer, never settling in a conventional sense? Or perhaps you feel rather stuck in a rut and fear change? Note which patterns recur in your life. To what extent are these shaped by the stories you tell yourself about your experience, rather than being present with your current experience? When you think of your life and how it is, what do you want to change? What are you able to change? What can't you change? What's fine as it is?

If you are intrigued by dreaming but find it hard to remember your dreams, maybe before you go to sleep invite your dreaming state to tell you what you need to know. Setting an intention like this can be helpful in finding out the dreaming mind's wishes for you.

Part II

A private decision with global consequences

Chapter 13

Decisions, decisions

> Making a decision is scary, whether it is to have children, or not. There are tremendous losses and gains on both sides and it is a mammoth task to weigh all these up. Some women sit on the fence, effectively not making a decision until the menopause arrives and nature makes the final resolution. This could be seen as a positive stance; being always open to change. (Bartlett, 1994: 99)

The flavor of Part II is more personal; I shall say how I came to the decision not to have children and you will have the chance to explore the factors influencing your own decision-making. Having looked at the broad, global, themes of Part I we move to a personal focus here, and Part III then extends outwards from this personal focus to look at the horizons beyond the decision to not try for children. For now we are looking at the actual decision-making process, so a change of focus and a change of gear.

It is a slightly strange thing to devote a whole chunk of this book to discussing why not to have children, given that one rarely hears people discuss in detail why they have children. Until recent decades both scenarios would have been hypothetical, given the lack of access to reliable contraception. It is amazing how society has been changed by contraception and, in parallel, how slow cultural discourses associated with femininity and motherhood are to change (Gillespie, 2001: 147).

There have been particularly influential life events that stand out in my decision not to have children, which I shall explore in more detail later. Once it dawned on me, aged 27, that there is a choice involved in trying for children, I gave myself time to experiment, firstly by living with a provisional decision to remain childless. That provisional decision gradually evolved into a firmer, more lasting one. It did not happen overnight, but was marked by a series of small events and then the gradual acknowledgement that my life was not heading in the direction of baby-making.

This opening chapter is based largely on my own brainstorming process as to whether or not to plan for children. This sounds quite mechanical for such a significant decision, but it made sense to me in my twenties, the time of my brainstorming, when my approach to decision-making and processing information was to: write lists, draw mind maps, do SWOT analyses etcetera.[7] In more recent years I have become more curious about different facets of myself: the logical bit, the creative bit, the liminal bits, and the dreaming body...

I made this list in the early stages of researching this book as a way of tracking my process and seeing what changed in response to the prospect of not trying for children. It can be useful, and sometimes surprising, to commit to paper the thoughts and feelings skulking around in our awareness. So I thought I would include these here. This is obviously not a definitive list and it would change if I wrote it afresh today. It is a starting point and potentially useful prompt for you to consider your own pros and cons in approaching the question of having children. If you've had children, now might be a useful point to stop and reflect on the reasons why you had them. It is a question that is less often asked, but, I think, just as important as reasons for *not* having children.

Why I would have tried for children:

1. Because I would love to carry a child and experience giving birth
2. Because I met the potential father of my children

3. Because the biological clock is ticking loudly
4. To be a 'proper' woman
5. To do something with my life
6. To do something completely different from my paid work so far
7. Because I would love to see what I would be like as a mum
8. To make my family happy (picturing my mum's face as I break the news...)
9. To live a fantasy-like 'Mother Earth' dream
10. Because I have a womb
11. Because others tell me I would be a good mum
12. To create descendants

1. Because I would love to carry a child and experience giving birth

This is the strongest pull towards motherhood, hence its first place on this list. I love the thought of giving birth. Rationally, this makes no sense, particularly after hearing scary birth stories: "It was just too quick and shocking" through to "It went on for 72 hours and I was absolutely exhausted". I am fascinated by the miracle of life. Interestingly, in recalling those birth tales, what immediately comes to mind is death tales, too. So perhaps the appeal of giving birth is the attraction of the intimacy in the ordinary yet extraordinary cycle of life and death. I continue to deepen my interest in birth – my own, and that of my psychotherapy clients – through having trained in pre and peri-natal psychology, and focusing upon birth issues in my therapy practice, which is a fascinating area and a critical time of life.

2. Because I met the potential father of my children

This has been a tough one. 15 years ago I finally met and started a relationship with a man who I could tell would be a great dad, and shortly afterwards, decided definitely not to have children.

On reflection, I realized that the two factors were related; I felt freer to choose whether or not to have children, given that I knew it was a possible option, rather than an imagined, projected-into-the-future 'one day, when I meet Mr Right' sort of fantasy (although I have to confess that the 'Mr Right' and 'Mrs Right' thing has always brought a frown to my face – surely there must be more than one Mr Right? Or Mrs Right?).

Sometimes it feels difficult to have met the man with whom I could happily have children and know we are not doing that. Fortunately, we feel similarly about this decision. We could both have imagined having children together, but equally, it has not turned out to be our main priority this lifetime. We both love being around children, and children seem to like being around us. And we occasionally experience pangs of 'what if?'

3. Because the biological clock is ticking loudly

Tick tock, tick tock. Hurry, hurry. The white rabbit in *Alice in Wonderland* springs to mind (Carroll, 2015). The biological clock is an important, big factor and a prominent one in the present climate. Leaving it too late to have children is causing heartache for some of my generation, as the childbearing age increases and some women encounter problems they imagined would be solved easily by medical fertility interventions.

I had not realized myself how strong an underlying thing the ticking biological clock can be. In my mid thirties I sat in the dentist's waiting room, flicking through the pages of a women's magazine, and waiting my turn. A statistic stating that female fertility declines steadily from the age of 30 leapt at me from the page. I suddenly felt sick. Intellectually I knew this to be the case, but emotionally, I realized that this meant me, this body, and my fertility.

It was a useful wake up call. It prompted me to take a fresh look at what was beneath this physically sick feeling. It seemed to be a more embodied acknowledgment that there is an end date after which I will not bear children, and that that end date was approaching faster than I cared to realize. I also noticed a feeling of slight panic that as we get older, our choices in life wane, and we either live with, or resist – the choice is ours – the consequences of the choices we have made so far.

4. The 'proper woman' scenario

A recurring theme in this book and in my own process is the feeling that I, and others, are not 'proper' women without children. This fear is hardly surprising, given the myriad of views and behaviors towards choosing childlessness, which we have already touched upon. Researching and writing this book has confirmed that the view of voluntarily childless women as selfish and career-driven prevails for some. I have also realized that thinking about not having children is still a significant threat – potential and actual – to many women's identities and their view of themselves and their affirmed place within their families and communities. I can understand this from my own experience, and given the pronatal forces we have been exploring.

Despite all the recent changes in family structure and family life, with fewer people getting married and having children – and given the global challenges we face – we are still conditioned that having children is the norm, giving a positive, socially-affirmed identity. Being seen as the quirky, unusual one can be entertaining for a little while, except when you become pigeon-holed as the quirky unusual one or the butt of other people's jokes... I am gladdened to say, at the age of 44, that I cannot remember the last time I personally felt that I was not a 'proper' woman as a result of not having had children.

5. To do something with my life

I am grateful that I have done interesting things, met great people, travelled to fascinating places, practiced Buddhism, and had a rich life so far. At this point in my life I find it harder to contact a sense of why I would have had children in order to do something with my life, though it was an important thought in my twenties. I am blessed to be fulfilled in my life, work and relationships, so no longer feel a sense that having children would be the making of my life, as I know is the sentiment of many of my good friends.

6. To do something completely different from my paid work so far

Again, this point feels rather out-dated in my current life, but I can remember it being an important factor. Back then I remember thinking that I would like to take time out from my current jobs, doing something completely different, with having children fitting that bill. At the time I think I would have struggled to have made that space for myself without the good reason of becoming pregnant. If I had, having a child would have been 24-7 work rather than nine to five work. (Although running two businesses means that I rarely work from nine to five, so perhaps the adjustment might not have been such a shock to the system, at least practically.)

7. Because I would love seeing what I would be like as a mum

I am still curious about this one. Would I be a good enough mum or would my impatience, over-protectiveness and perfectionism take over? A mixture, most likely. I would probably be good at playing and encouraging, and supportive of learning and creativity. But in reality, I have no idea what I would be like, so all of this is speculation!

8. To make my family happy (picturing my mum's face as I break the pregnancy news...)

This factor is on the wane, but I would still have love to have given my mum the pleasure of being a grandma again. I remember watching my late dad, then ill with leukemia, playing with my little nephew Thomas. My body shouted out with a pang: 'Give him another grandchild before it is too late!'. It was a poignant, urgent moment. This response was partly because my dad was such a great granddad, his health was declining, and deep down, I am sure that I thought in a childlike way that if I produced offspring for the next generation, I might be able to magically prolong his life.

I am happy to report that my mum has got used to the idea of me not having children. I appreciate her love and support and genuine interest in the 'baby-sized projects' which have filled my post-decision horizon to date, as well as her enthusiasm as a grandma to my nephew and nieces. I am proud that she has felt able to understand my reasons for not having children and respects me and my life as it is, a reflection of her generosity of spirit and grace.

9. To live a fantasy-like 'Mother Earth' dream
Now we enter the realm of fantasy. I occasionally used to harbor a secret dream that if we had children I would be at home all day, growing vegetables, baking cakes, painting pictures, making things, and not giving two hoots about the mess. We would live in happy, shabby house with a rambling wild garden. If I picture having a family, the Spanish film and book *Like Water for Chocolate* comes to mind, one of my favorite books (Esquival, 1993) and films. This story, with its passion and dramas, is probably a more realistic depiction of family love, duty, jealousy, and tension, and a useful corrective to my Mother Earth fantasy.

10. Because I have a womb
I used to have the thought, almost on a monthly basis, of 'Why am I going through all this if I don't end up having children?' The mood swings, the short-temper, bursting into tears at three days to go, then the pain and a lead-like lower body. Then it all

happens again three weeks later. I am sure I should appreciate being 'in touch' with my body, and its cycles – especially given that I work as a Body Psychotherapist – but I have to confess, it sometimes gets a bit repetitive. These days I am more in sync with my month, sometimes even enjoying the different emotional tones of my cycle.

11. Because others tell me I would be a good mum

"But you'd be a great mum!" I have heard this many times in my life, which is sweet, and thanks to those of you who said it and meant it. Who knows whether it would have been true, but it is a response with which I am familiar, particularly when I say I/we are not planning to have children. Most people assumed I would become a mother, including myself, until my late twenties.

I have been around children a lot in my life, as a babysitter and aunt. I like childrens' company. I like most other people's children, too. They matter to me as much as the thought of having my own, which is a funny thing to say, but it is true. I love being an auntie by blood and an auntie through friendship, roles I take seriously, and playfully, especially when we are trampolining. I have little doubt that, had I had children, I would have loved them like I have never loved anyone else on the planet (as well as experiencing the accompanying and inevitable heartache and worry).

12. To create descendants

Since brainstorming this list of reasons why I would have had children more than a decade ago, I have become interested in ancestry, genealogy and family healing. For this reason I found that I needed to add this last point. A while back I had a spell of researching intensively our family tree. It was fascinating finding out about the different ancestral lines. I recall a sobering moment when I realized that I am and would be someone's auntie, great auntie, sister, daughter, but that I would never be someone's direct ancestor. That was a weighty moment. In my experience of researching, aunties and uncles, however many times removed, are useful in determining whether I have found the 'right' relative, but they are no way as important as the people you know are a part of your direct lineage. I am reminded of a poignant moment in an interview with Tracy Emin, the UK-based artist, in a web clip advertising her appearance on the BBC television programme 'Who Do You Think You Are':

The fact that I am never going to have any children means that I am the end of my line. After me, I stop. I am the last of my kind, there is no more. (Emin, 2011)

For the first time I could understand why people have children to keep the family name going. It strikes a chord with the feeling I had when I held my nephew for the first time, a strong and embodied sense of duty towards him, to be as good an auntie as possible. Interestingly, in holding him, I also felt relieved that my brother and his partner had begun to have children, diverting the familial pressure from me to have them.

Why I did not end up trying for children:

1. Having children was not a priority
2. Because the planet does not need me to add to the population
3. I want to explore nurturing self, other, world, rather than create mortal children
4. Because having children would not fix suffering
5. The myth of 'having it all' is simply that: a myth (and a capitalist one, at that)
6. To minimize the dusty household life
7. Truth be told, I just do not want children enough

1. Having children was not a priority

It became clear to me at some point in my mid thirties that there were things more important in my life than having children, in particular, my practice of meditation and Buddhism. In practicing Buddhism I can see that my work has started to make a difference – most likely only a small difference, but a difference, nevertheless – in terms of the time I have to commit to teaching, mentoring, writing, friendship, and supporting women in their process of treading a Buddhist path and being ordained. I would have struggled to have done this to the same degree, had I become a mother. It would not have been impossible, of course, but I sense I would have felt conflicted and probably that I was falling short of fulfilling my work either as a mum or as a Dharma-farer.

My work is also an important aspect of my life, including my work as a psychotherapist, supervisor, writer, and running my family's business with my brother, and aiming to be a fair and supportive employer. Work is an important channel for my practice of the Dharma. My practice is at the heart of how I work, my relationships with others, figuring out ethical dilemmas, prioritizing how I spend my time and feeling my way into new areas of work and ways of working.

2. Because the planet does not need me to add to the population

The drive to consume, consume, consume in the 'Western' world is out of control. I have probably already said that, so my apologies for being repetitive. Yesterday I re-calculated my carbon footprint. To live my current lifestyle, we apparently need getting on for one and a half planets, rather than the one planet that we actually have. That is sobering. It could be worse, my carbon footprint's lower than average, apparently, but it is still sobering. And we still only have one planet. I need to look afresh at how I am living with this in mind.

A frustration with these online calculators is that they do not factor in whether or not you have had children, which is a significant decision in terms of one's carbon footprint, particularly if your children go on to procreate. This is obviously a complex calculation, given that at some point, perhaps on becoming an adult, a person becomes responsible for his/her own carbon footprint. However, it is surely worth being aware of this as we reflect on our carbon usage, direct and indirect. Gies (2012) points out how a statistical survey from Oregan State University, published in Global Environmental Change in 2009, highlights the environmental impact of childbearing. In addition to the resources a child will use in his or her lifetime, there is the exponential power of population growth. 'Under current conditions in the United States, for example, each child ultimately adds about 9,441 metric tons of carbon dioxide to the carbon legacy of an average female – which is 5.7 times her lifetime emissions' (Gies, 2012).

I sometimes hear an argument for having children which goes something like this: "I'm going to have children. Even though I'm concerned about the environment, you never know, our child might help solve global problems, or be the next Einstein". I am curious about this. Maybe I lack self-confidence and aplomb but why would my partner and I produce a super-genius? And would I want to put that much pressure on my offspring? How could I presume they would be interested in the same issues as I am? I think, and hope, that I would mainly wish them health, peace of mind, and a good dose of kindness and ethical sensitivity towards themselves, others, and the planet. I guess this sort of argument illustrates the hopes and expectations which become invested in the creation of a new life and the pressure children face, and which we might have faced as children.

3. I want to explore nurturing self, other, world, rather than create mortal children

When I made the provisional decision to not have children in my late twenties, it gradually dawned on me that what I wanted was to be a mum without being a mortal, flesh and blood mother. I wanted, and still want, to explore what is possible in terms of nurturing myself, others, and the world, without giving birth physically, explored in Part III.

An important aspect of this for me draws upon the inspiration of what is known as the 'bodhisattva ideal' in Buddhism, which I introduced earlier. This is the vow taken by bodhisattvas to save all sentient beings. Bodhisattva literally means 'body of awakening', with bodhisattvas representing the altruistic dimension of Buddhist practice, which has been an important motivating factor in my practice. In Part III I shall explore in greater detail how different dimensions of apprentice-bodhisattva activity have been important in my life.

4. Because having children would not fix suffering

I was not far into my own reflections on thinking through whether or not to have children when I un-earthed my 'super mum' myth. If I had been a mother I would have tried to juggle everything perfectly. And most likely, failed miserably. Part of me certainly wanted to have children to put right the things that did not go so well in my own childhood, to heal my own past through creating new life, not an uncommon unconscious motivation. I soon realized that this 'super Mum' myth would be an unfair persona to inflict upon any little living being with its own identity, will, hopes, and fears.

Going deeper in my practice of the Dharma was helpful in illuminating this area of my experience. I learned early on in my Buddhist training – with some relief – that it is not possible to fix some basic facts about life. We/I cannot stop people hurting, getting ill or dying. We/I cannot fix samsara; the term used for an existence which is conditioned by the three so-called 'poisons' in Buddhism – greed, hatred and delusion – on its own terms. So trying to fix my own life through creating new life suddenly looked like a limited and limiting strategy. I realized I had to live my own life, healing the bit that needed attention, rather than 'putting right' through bringing about the life of another – a high risk strategy.

5. The myth of 'having it all' is simply that: a myth (and a capitalist one, at that)

I realized this was a myth in my early twenties. It was patently obvious that those around me attempting to follow the myth of having it all (partner, children, career, friendships, leisure time) were struggling. Exhausted, pulled in too many different directions, and perhaps resentful that they had been sold a myth. When did this myth begin? Perhaps in Thatcher's Britain, perhaps before that, I am unsure. Worst still was the element of competitiveness and presenting-well in public; proving you had succeeded in having it all, trying to hide the obvious exhaustion and ill-effects.

On one hand it was a myth that part of me could have found rather alluring. I like a challenge, I have a lot of energy and I am quite focused. But even I realized that having it all and enjoying at least some of whatever 'it' was, looked like a stretch beyond reality. A small voice inside warned me not to try to rise to this, much as I relish a challenge. Trying to raise children well enough, whilst already being committed to my working life and Dharma life looked complicated, and I knew ahead of time that something would have to give. Seeing friends around me, my fear is that the things that tend to give are a woman's sanity and sense of perspective and worst still, the wellbeing of her children. I was not prepared to take that gamble, particularly if I ran the risk of letting my resentment about not having enough time to work or teach pour out over the heads of my children-to-be.

6. To minimize the dusty household life

Although I have moments of loving being a domestic goddess, my natural talents are not in the realm of house tidying and chores. However feminist my views, in theory, I fear that in being a mum I would end up running the risk of being mother to a child, to my partner, and the whole family, knowing how good I am at taking too much responsibility and doing the emotional work. I did not want this for my life. I felt so relieved when early in practicing the Dharma I came across a quote in a Buddhist teaching about the limitations of the 'dusty household life':

Household life is confining, a dusty path. The life gone forth is like the open air. It is not easy living at home to practice the holy life totally perfect, totally pure, like a polished shell. (Thanissaro Bhikkhu, 1997)

7. Truth be told, I just do not want children enough

It is only in the latter stages of writing this that I have realized that I simply didn't want children enough. I have certainly longed to have children for spells in my life and have felt the full-throttle strength of that instinctual hardwiring. But that longing was not prolonged, for reasons I will go on to explore. I am surprised that even after all these years it feels taboo to say this out loud – let alone commit the words to paper and have them published. There is something terribly counter-cultural to admit you do not want children enough to have them. As I type I notice flickers of failure and disapproval – and a sense of relief, too.

I remember talking to one of my early Buddhist teachers, Achalavajra, about having children. I would often talk with teachers and friends about whether or not to have children in my twenties – I hope, looking back, I was not too boring and repetitive! His comment was simple and illuminating: "Well, if you were going to have kids, you probably would've had them by now!" Recalling that now, 18 years later, I realize that he was spot on. I was 26 at the time and was engaged with doing things that mattered to me, which did not include procreation.

Having explored all of the above, I realize that somewhere along the line, the decision not to have children 'made me' as much as I made the decision. I do not mean this as a cop out, but as a reflection of what actually happened. Maybe I am a dewy-eyed optimist, but I think that if we approach the baby question in a conscious and curious way, the right thing happens. Looking back I can see that there were times when my decision could so easily have gone the other way, notably, had I not had the experience of meeting my ailing dad and my new nephew in the course of the same afternoon, more of which later. With child-bearing there is something over and above – or under and beneath – rationality, logic, and reasoning which leads to the happening along of children, which is perhaps why such a high proportion are not planned. It is difficult to not go along with our procreative hardwiring, but it is worth having a good look at our views, assumptions, and conditioning in this arena.

If anything, the child-free raise the status of parenting as they do not view it lightly; seeing it as a precious vocation that demands special qualities and skills, rather than something that anyone can do. (Bartlett, 1994: xiv)

A pregnant pause

There's a lot of material to mull over here, so take your time. If it's useful, brainstorm your own list of pros and cons in deciding whether or not to have children. If that feels too linear, maybe try speed-writing, starting with 'I want children because...' and/or 'I do not want children because...' and see what emerges (write for five minutes non-stop, without lifting your hand from the page, and avoiding the temptation to edit yourself as you write).

I mentioned making a provisional decision not to have children at the age of 27, to see how that felt. Check out with yourself whether it would make sense to you in your current life circumstances to do the same. Notice your responses as you ponder your own pushes and pulls in this decision-making. Which parts of you are interested in this exercise? Which parts have switched off? Listen as carefully as you can to your resistances, and perhaps your ambivalence in engaging with the process. Stay with them, rather than judge or diminish them, bearing in mind that our resistances are often resisting something for a good reason – or at least have been, historically.

Chapter 14

A soft-voiced prince and a flaming sword

Learning meditation and being taught the Dharma (the teachings of the Buddha) were to shape my life in a way that would have been unimaginable to me when I first stepped through the Buddhist Centre door. In this chapter I am rewinding to look at the events in my life leading up to making the provisional decision not to have children, with meditation and Dharma practice becoming an important part of that process.

I went to my first meditation class in my early twenties and loved the metta bhavana (loving-kindness) meditation practice we were taught that night, which I wrote about at the beginning of Part I. The metta bhavana was one of three foundation practices which were taught to beginners. I was fascinated by the dancing eyes of Dharmbandhu, the man who invited us to contact metta for: ourselves, a friend, a neutral person, an enemy, and finally, for all sentient beings. As I recall that first session of being taught the metta bhavana practice, I am put in mind of one of Sharon Salzberg's book titles, *Loving Kindness: The Revolutionary Art of Happiness* (see Salzberg, 2002).

The metta bhavana seemed – and still seems – to me to be a radical practice. Contacting and cultivating loving kindness for myself and others, through to all sentient life, made a lot of sense to me. My own wellbeing was and is interconnected with the wellbeing of all other beings; human and other than human. It was a relief to hear and to practice this, particularly in 1995, which was a challenging year. Having started to learn to meditate, I relished reading about 'the noble eight fold path', a traditional Buddhist teaching (see Sangharakshita, 1990). This teaching invites the practitioner, once they have had a first glimpse (right vision), or felt the first longing to live in a different way, how to practice right emotion, right speech, right action, right livelihood, right effort, right awareness, and right concentration in everyday life. This book was an invaluable and practical map at the time.

Falling in love with the Dharma, and, strange to say, it was a falling in love, was like no other experience. The emotions and strength of feelings were the same, but without focusing those feelings upon another mortal, fallible, beautiful human being. In that moment of wanting to follow in the footsteps of the Buddha I felt my own potential and potency. I recognized how millions of others before me had reached the same point, stretching back through the mists of time, committing themselves to a Buddhist path, quest, journey or unveiling of how things are – words fall short in describing the experience.

Falling in love has the potential to be a small awakening. In falling in love, whether with a person, a new idea, or something sacred, we have the potential to see beyond ourselves, to see new vistas. Falling in love is part of the universal search for love, purpose and connectedness. Yet its expansiveness can shrink and our hopes can be dashed when we pin all our energies, hopes, fears onto another being, losing sight of the potential of love for all beings and what the process itself can teach us.

At this point I deepened my commitment to the Triratna Buddhist movement, asking formally to become a mitra (or 'friend') and, shortly afterwards I asked for ordination into the Triratna Buddhist Order. This was the beginning of a new phase of my life. Being a Dharma-farer has been the most fulfilling and challenging thing I have done. At the time it fully met my late teen and early adult longing for the ultimate challenge – something which would stretch me beyond my imaginings emotionally and intellectually. It also allowed me to give expression to the faith I have felt since I was a small child. I experience this faith as an ordinary feeling which is not attached to or belonging to any particular religion, doctrine, or way of life.

For me that faith has been in the many amazing qualities of human beings, in the everyday miracles of nature and life – human and other-than-human – and faith in my own potential experienced through my interconnection and interactions with other beings. Practicing the Dharma has given me a sense of the vastness of life and its potential as well as a set of tools to use and reflect upon, particularly Buddhist ethics, on days when I lack perspective. The only thing that I knew for sure in my twenties was that I would continue to practice the Dharma this lifetime.

Preparing and training for ordination into the Triratna Buddhist Order, then called the Western Buddhist Order, became an important aspect of my life from my mid twenties to my early thirties. This was something of a Buddhist 'apprenticeship': deepening meditation practice, understanding and engaging with Buddhist ethics, studying and practicing the Dharma and befriending others treading the Buddhist path. It was a profound and multi-faceted process. It was inspiring at times, frustrating at others, but always worth the effort. As well as being a sound training for ordination, the public and private ordination ceremonies were significant rites of passage.

To my surprise, it was on a study retreat in 1998 at Tiratanaloka (a women's Buddhist retreat centre in the Brecon Beacons) that I provisionally decided not to have children. I had not gone on retreat with that on my mind, and it was not relevant to the study material, but that was the time it arose. Perhaps it is not so surprising, looking back. For the year or two prior to that it had started to dawn on me that if I wanted to have children, I had better not put it off for too long, especially as I had always said I would have children by the time I was 30.

I talked a lot to friends and teachers at the time, mainly mothers and non-mothers, which was invaluable, and, of course, provided no straightforward yes or no answers as to whether I should have children. What I suddenly realized on that particular retreat in 1999 was that it was not compulsory to have children –

I had a choice. I am embarrassed to say that this was a revelation to me at the time, because I think it was the first time that I actually saw it as a choice, and the realization presented itself in an unusual way.

As I moved between restlessness and dozing off to sleep one night I found the baby question surfacing in my mind. The conditions of my own childhood had also been on my mind that day, particularly the burdening sense of responsibility I habitually felt, which I was starting to reflect on in the course of my ordination process. I was gazing up at the beautiful picture of Manjushri, the bodhisattva of wisdom in the Tibetan Buddhist tradition. In this picture he was depicted in golden form, wielding a sword in his right hand. In his left hand he holds a book, resting on a blue lotus: the Prajnaparamita sutra, an important Buddhist teaching.

As I gazed at his lovely form I became aware of words forming: 'You are a strong woman Emma (as I was then known) take up the sword!' As I listened quietly I realized that although I was gazing at the form of Manjushri, it was actually the voice of Prajnaparamita I was hearing, the golden Buddha depicted in female form. She is said, mythically, to be the mother of all the Buddhas; an archetypal mother figure with whom I felt a strong connection at the time.

I was no stranger to messages like this, being curious about information from all channels, rather than just more obvious ones. So my semi-awake, semi-sleeping 'encounter' or whatever it was with Manjushri and Prajnaparamita was not disturbing, but aroused my curiosity. It felt like an invitation to free myself, cutting away attachments to the world. In traditional Buddhist symbolism the sword can be seen as a weapon which, used skillfully, cuts through our greed, hatred and delusion, freeing ourselves to move towards deeper contentment, compassion and wisdom for ourselves, others and the world: connection with all that lives. In his book *Meeting the Buddhas* my teacher,

Vessantara, entitles the chapter about Manjushri: 'The soft-voiced prince with the flaming sword' which is a rather lovely and apt depiction of this bodhisattva (see Vessantara, 1993: 149).

It was on this retreat, the day after this 'meeting' with Manjushri and Prajnaparamita, that it dawned on me for the first time that I could choose whether or not I wanted to try for children. It was the first time in my life that I had given myself the opportunity to consciously dwell in a sense on what it would be like to decide not to have children, and to live with the possibility of this decision for a while. It felt both incredibly liberating, and yet blindingly obvious (but is it blindingly obvious? Perhaps we are so conditioned to pro-create that it is not all that obvious at all for some of us).

Until this point I had continued with my rather vague, 'one day' approach to whether or not to try for children. I was taken aback by the feeling of freedom and lightness, simply in realizing I was in a position to make a choice and to make a provisional decision to not have children and see what that felt like. Another part of me sensed that this would be the first step in a long and, at times, challenging process of coming to a final decision not to have children.

The few years that followed were full and busy. I was content in my relationship with my live-in partner. I didn't think we would have children, and I feared that our relationship would end before long, due to my growing interest in Buddhism, and his strengthening feeling of being threatened by that growing interest. I was travelling to sub-Saharan Africa for my work as an international development worker, and teaching as a university lecturer, and loved being stretched by my work. I was engaged with Buddhist practice, the ordination process, and was active around the Bristol Buddhist Centre with study, supporting classes, and meeting friends. The end of this particular phase of my life came rather abruptly at the end of the twentieth century, literally the end of 1999 and the beginning of 2000.

A pregnant pause

I have talked here about my practice of Buddhism and how it changed the course of my life more than I would ever have imagined. This exploration may feel alien to you, or it might be familiar, in that you have spent quite alot of your life exploring your spiritual path. In your reflections notice what has occupied most of your time so far – Work? Education? Family? The point of this chapter is not just about me exploring Buddhism, but about the things that have mattered to me which have ended up taking priority over childbearing and rearing.

Think about the priorities in your life and whether they have meant you have moved towards or away from child-bearing. Building on your reflections from Part I, perhaps recollect whether there have been key moments in your decision-making process so far? What were the circumstances and conditions of your life in those moments? Who was with you, what were you doing, how were you? Has there been a spiritual or transpersonal element in deciding whether or not to have children, or experiences emerging from times of prayer or quiet or inspiration? Has meditation, prayer, or contemplation been an important part of your life? How has it changed you?

Chapter 15

Looking into the 'wheel of life'

Impermanence means the essence of life is fleeting. (Chodron, 2001: 166)

The period around the beginning of the new millennium was incredibly influential in shaping my final decision not to have children. My life was in flux: my long-term relationship was ending, my employer had recently and rather surprisingly gone into voluntary liquidation, and tectonic shifts were afoot in my family. The worldly winds, to which I referred in the title of Part I, were blowing a gale. I was on a work trip to Kenya during the first week of March 2000 when my nephew was born and my Dad was diagnosed with leukemia. Flying home overnight, I could barely contain my excitement at the thought of meeting my new nephew for the first time. Sleep eluded me as I imagined holding his tiny hand and hearing the story of his arrival four days earlier.

My mum met me at a gray and overcast Bristol airport. From a distance she looked as striking as ever – head to toe in a bright red ensemble. But the red of her outfit couldn't disguise her crumpled, defeated posture. She cried as we hugged, saying that dad was in hospital, and did I mind fetching him from the airport. I was fine with that, of course, and momentarily relieved that the doctors were finally taking his chest infection seriously by sending him for tests. As I shared my relief she crumpled further, telling me that the previous day they had been told that dad had pneumonia, not a chest infection, and that in testing him for pneumonia, they had discovered that he had a chronic form of leukemia. Then it was my turn to crumple.

I shall never forget that journey from the airport to the hospital. The sky was extra gray and harsh with low, heavy cloud. My world fell into disarray; it felt like great cracks might actually appear in the sky or in the earth. My mind began to reassemble – temporarily, at least – around a new reality, accompanied by the mantra 'my dad has leukemia, my dad has leukemia'. The words felt foreign, other, and most of all, very unwelcome. I would have to let go of my dad so painfully soon after only recently having got to know him, as a colleague working alongside each other in our family business.

My dad was hardly around when my brother and I were children, which haunted him in his later years. In my early years he travelled on business. When I was four he set up our family business, investing most of his energy in its building and running. It was in my adulthood that we properly got to know each other. There was no way I felt ready to let go of him, but knew instantly that day that that process had begun.

When we reached the hospital I was surprised to find my dad happier and energetically lighter than I had seen him for months. He had been diagnosed with depression in the previous autumn, and had been given anti-depressants. His happiness, or at least, relief, was a result of his being diagnosed with leukemia. He finally understood why he had felt like he had been, in his words, 'pushing a double decker bus single-handedly up Park Street' (Park Street is a long, steep, hill in central Bristol).

I went back to my mum and dad's house. I sat next to him on the sofa eating marmite toast, one of our few, shared, past-times. I leaned against his chest, child-like, listening to his heartbeat. The time came to leave to go to visit my new nephew. To my surprise, leaving my dad's side that day was one of the hardest moments. It was the first step in letting him go. It put me in mind of locking the door of my Nana's house when I had cleared away her things after her death two years previously. She was gone, and I felt the physical blow that we would never meet again, at least, not in person.

An hour later I was at the home of my brother and his girlfriend, holding my nephew for the first time. I was overwhelmed with a feeling of duty and protection towards this gorgeous bundle, feeling the ties of blood more tangibly then ever. His newness was awesome and amazing. He looked, smelt and felt so soft and perfect. He was so little. His soft skin, bright eyes and new smell were in such a stark contrast to the aging, wrinkled, tired dad I had just left behind sitting on the sofa.

I drove home that evening along a particularly beautiful stretch of road which runs along the side of Chew Valley lake in North Somerset. It was a dusky evening in late winter, with not long until the arrival of early spring. The light was pink, with a dark flash of gunmetal gray cloud extending across the sky, very different to the heavy cloud of the morning. It was an evening of promise. That was my felt sense – a surprising sense – an evening of promise. I was not to know then what it meant.

The vividness of the colors, the emotions and the day's changing skies stay with me. The world-weariness of my dad contrasted starkly with the seemingly perfect new life of my new nephew, all taking place in a cocktail of joy and grief. Things are born, grow, blossom, mature, age, grow sick and die. The natural cycle of life for all beings who live an average life span. Perhaps it was a fuller recognition of life rolling on come what may. Maybe it was seeing that life rolls on regardless of whether I would decide to have children or not. Perhaps I did not need to contribute another new life, given that life simply rolls on? Maybe I saw the uniqueness and the smallness of my life as part of the mingling of all that lives and dies on the planet.

That day was an important turning point in my decision to not have children. My experience of that day reminded me of a traditional Buddhist image: the Tibetan wheel of life (see Khema, 1991: 37; Sangharakshita 2002: 13 - 29). This image depicts a circle divided into segments, with each segment relating to a different realm of existence. These realms can be seen as mirror-like reflections of our internal states of mind at different times, for example: the human realm, the animal realm, and the God realm.

The wheel keeps turning, keeps turning, keeps turning. Life keeps on moving. My experience that day was a deeper, or perhaps more direct encounter with the wheel of life and the experiential knowledge that life and death keep happening; keeping the wheel turning as sure as night follows day. I also felt the worldly winds of pleasure and pain, loss and gain, in equal measure; the most bittersweet day of my life so far.

These events took place three years before my dream of Vicky and I walking up the railway tunnel, which I included in the Preface to this book. It is said that the death or serious illness of a close family member or loved one can lead to a stronger urge to procreate. I certainly felt this following the death of my grandmother. I felt that the family was incomplete and I was drawn to make it complete again. I did not feel like that when I heard my dad was ill and when he later died. Something urged me to reflect deeply on my experience of that day, which was to change the shape of my life and have a significant impact in my decision to remain childless.

A pregnant pause

My life and the lives of my immediate family were in upheaval at this moment of looking into the wheel of life. Turning to the circumstances of your own life, and that of close friends and family: Does the symbol of the wheel of life have any resonance for you? Does it help you to make sense of your own circumstances? Have there been times when changes in work, illness, loss, influenced your decision as to whether or not to become a parent? (Longing for a child can often happen after the death of a close loved one, for example.) Do you know anything about the circumstances of your own birth? How has this had any bearing on your own decision to try for children?

Chapter 16

Skilful flirting and the art of brewing

Chronos is clocks, deadlines, watches, calendars, agendas, planners, schedules, beepers. Chronos is time at her worst. Chronos keeps track... Chronos is the world's time. Kairos is transcendence, infinity, reverence, joy, passion, love, the Sacred. Kairos is intimacy with the Real. Kairos is time at her best... Kairos is Spirit's time. We exist in chronos. We long for kairos. That is our duality. Chronos requires speed so that it will not be wasted. Kairos requires space so that it might be savored. We do in chronos. In kairos we are allowed to be... It takes only a moment to cross over from chronos into kairos, but it does take a *moment*. All that kairos asks is our willingness to stop running long enough to hear the music of the spheres. (Breathnach, 1997: 12)

The best decisions I have made have been borne from a fine balance of weighing up pros and cons in a reasoned way, surrounded by a much messier process of listening to my hopes, fears, doubts, fantasies and dreams. The tonnes of self-help and management books about effective decision-making – and I mean 'effective' in the sense of including all of yourself, the effect on others, and your environment, rather than effective in the sense of purely being about profit or efficiency – is testament to the fact that decision-making is an art rather than a technique. Decision-making involves all parts of us: logic, intuition, reason, past experience, future hopes, magic, a bit of luck, our ingrained habits, as well as the influence of those around us. That is a heady mix. It also requires us to be mindful, in the sense of knowing our body-mind well enough to make a good enough decision and giving the process due time and space.

The way we approach the decision-making process is important information with regards the baby question. It is a significant decision because it: tends to span more than two decades, is emotionally charged – with the result that it can be harder to think and act clearly, depends upon mutual decisions and circumstances coming together which can add a sense of urgency – and depending upon your perception of how much time you've got, is about the rest of your life, given that it is an irreversible decision which changes you in ways you could or would never have predicted. If you are a woman there is the added pressure of a limited window of opportunity, and you may already be towards the end of that window feeling pressure to make the 'right' decision. Even then, you potentially face further uncertainty in knowing whether or not you are able to conceive.

In my twenties I used to start an important decision-making process by listing the pros and cons or working my way through a 'SWOT' diagram (exploring Strengths, Weaknesses, Opportunities and Threats), brainstorms and mind maps. I would then get a bit tired of logic and strategizing and put those to one side, not looking at them for a while. The swirl of life would intervene for a few weeks, or months—depending upon how pressing the decision was – until the next time I was reminded, often thanks to some synchronicity or uncanny event.

I might then listen carefully to the thoughts and advice of trusted friends. Then I would leave the decision to 'brew'. This brewing might mean that I would completely forget, consciously at least, that I had a decision to make. Thoughts, feelings or sensations would emerge in dreams, meditation, daydreaming, or showering. Or it might mean me grappling with deeper fears on a subterranean level, particularly if it was a big decision, which drew heavily on my time and resources.

This largely describes my process of deciding not to have children. The 'brewing' time is absolutely vital. It is mysterious.

It operates more along the lines of 'kairos' time as referred to in the opening quote. The ancient Greeks had two (or perhaps more?) definitions of time. 'Chronos', which referred to what we think of as chronological time, and 'kairos', which signifies time 'in between'; a moment of indeterminate time in which something special can happen or arise. Some decisions are too important to rush, and, in parallel, too important to leave for too long, as that biological clock ticks. Kairos time is worth thinking about – or better still, entering into.

The other vital ingredient in decision-making, is noticing life's 'flirts'. I feel indebted to Arny Mindell (2002: 5) for his naming of these, a phenomena which has been made sense to me all of my life. These are those relational signs and indicators and synchronicities which nudge and point me in the direction of uncovering information that is timely and relevant. For example, bumping into a friend from the past at a moment which is opportune for both of us. Or being offered an opportunity at just the right moment, perhaps at a time when I've been shedding projects that seem a bit out-dated or no longer a priority, intuitively clearing a space for the new. Mindell calls them 'mutual dream-like interactions' (2002: 5) and I thoroughly recommend reading more about them, and, better still, being receptive enough to let them attract your attention.

These days decisions seem to come more easily to me. When I have a big decision to make I am more likely to write or dream about the subject and see what emerges. Synchronicitous events and interactions with people often throw light on the way ahead. I am much more likely to pay curious attention to the everyday 'flirts' than to spend much time listing pros and cons, and I cannot remember the last time I drew up a four boxed page with 'strengths', 'weaknesses', 'opportunities', and 'threats' heading up the four columns. Not to say that the SWOT analysis is not useful, just not my method of choice any longer.

'Flirts' are easily missed when your receptive antennae are

turned off or when you are hell-bent on using only one of your faculties to make a decision; perhaps too much logic and not enough intuition, or too much emotion and not enough reason, or too much self-absorption and not seeing wide horizons. Flirts can also seem to mysteriously disappear when you want to make something happen in a willful way. In this way they are a useful reminder that, in the words of the poem of my teacher, quoted at the end of Part I: 'Life is King' (Sangharakshita, 1995: 285). When we forget that life is king we tend to try and push the river, rather than being curious about conducive conditions.

'Flirts' are those often intangible-seeming signals which provide us with enough information to keep moving in a particular direction. Like the time when you start following a particular course of action and doors start opening in the nick of time. At other times doors can slam shut in our faces and we start wondering whether we are missing something really obvious (maybe because we are caught up in a blind spot) or slightly heading up the proverbial garden path and needing to go back to the drawing board. Or needing to relax and let life go on for a while.

The broad phases in my own decision-making process around baby-making went something like this:

Teenage years – I imagine children will happen to me 'by the time I'm 30'.

Aged 26/27 – I discuss whether or not to have children with friends and Buddhist teachers. I buy my first flat and ask for ordination into the Triratna Buddhist order – one foot in Buddhist practice, one in work and life, surrounded by good friends and family. My practice of Buddhism has yet to infuse my everyday life.

Aged 28 – I realize for the first time that I have a choice about whether or not to have children.

Aged 29 – A long-term relationship ends and, later in the year, a new one begins with a man I can imagine being the father of my children.

Aged 31 – I dream about Vicky and I walking up the railway tunnel, included in the Preface. The fact that I will not be having children starts to sink in on a more embodied, visceral level.

Aged 32 – The birth of my nephew, the first born of the next generation, and the diagnosis of my father with leukemia. The beginning of a decade of reflection about life, the wheel of life, death, children, not children. My understanding of the Dharma and my experience of life collide and coincide more fully and influence how I live my life.

Aged 34 – I am ordained into the Triratna Buddhist Order. On the morning of my public ordination I find myself walking in the early morning mist and spontaneously reciting under my breath a passage from the *Bodhicharyavatara: A Guide to the Bodhisattva's Way of Life*: 'Today my birth is fruitful. My human life is justified. Today I am born into the family of the Buddhas. Now I am the Buddha's son' (or daughter, even?) (2008, Shantideva, Williams, Crosby and Skilton).

I am not so much leaving my existing family, as joining a different lineage alongside my ancestral lineage. It is an expansion rather than a rejection. I have a strong sense that my ordination is not just for me, but for everyone alive.

Aged 34-41 – The brewing phase. Children are not happening to me this lifetime. I love meeting my nieces as they are born, getting to know them as they grow and change. I build up my private practice as a counselor and Body Psychotherapist, loving the process of giving time and space to others in the therapeutic process. I write my first book; my first 'baby-sized project'.

Early 40s – I rarely think about the baby question. I have the occasional twinge of 'what if'. I sometimes feel sad I will not be a mum or grandma. I love being an auntie more than ever. My practice of Buddhism and my practice of work and life are now much more integrated. My feet are no longer in different camps, as they were.

Right now I am spending a considerable amount of my time and energy thinking about choosing childlessness in the final preparation of this book. It can be hard to stay focused, because this is not a hot topic for me anymore. I want to finish this book in case it is useful to others grappling with the decision. I surrender more fully than before to the creative, Zen-mistress-like nature of writing, as the final stages of book writing feel like a birth process. The time coincides with undertaking further training in birth psychology and practice. After 17 years, this book is ready to find its feet and leave home...

A pregnant pause

Given what you know about yourself now, how would you say you go about making significant decisions? Think about what I said about 'kairos' time. Are you drawn to the notion that things happen 'in between', in moment of indeterminate time? Notice whether it is easy or tricky to allow lulls during a decision-making process and the light that that sheds on your particular patterns and strategies. Have you been aware of 'flirts' or synchronicities in your process of deciding whether or not to have children? Consider drawing a timeline of your decision-making process so far, which includes key events, themes, and important synchronicities.

Chapter 17

A private decision with very public consequences

There is no point bleating about the future of pandas, polar bears and tigers when we're not addressing the one single factor that is putting more pressure on the ecosystem than any other – namely the ever-increasing size of the world's population. (Packham, 2011)

The child you have contributes to the planet's level of greenhouse gases. By choosing not to have a child, you can reduce your contribution to global climate change. Your decision alone cannot reverse the current situation, but, with enough people making similar choices, change can be effected. Suddenly the argument becomes much more controversial. Logic goes awry, rationality retreats, and emotions take over. (Webb, 2009)

Global issues have fascinated and concerned me, in about equal measure, for as long as I can remember. I decided when I was five that I would be a teacher, at seven that I would write, and at 13 that I would work in Africa. I was a serious little girl and young woman and am happy to report that I am far less serious as I age, although I have not yet lost my hope or care for social and ecological justice, and continue to engage with the 'big picture' in and through everyday life.

I have already mentioned how my secondary school geography classes about population growth, urbanization, and inequality caught my attention. I remember vividly the lesson when we learned about exponential population growth, Malthus' work and the consequences of population growth. These lessons urged me to begin to think seriously about my time on earth and the lives of those around me. I loved studying geography, but was pained by the realities of the world: billions of the world's inhabitants lacking access to food, water, shelter; our damaging environmental habits, and yet, we keep producing babies! In my over-simplistic young mind I couldn't understand why we carried on having babies when there were all these orphans in the world. Shortly after this, the scale of the plight of Romanian orphans emerged, baffling and saddening me further. Of course, I know now that we need change at all levels: individual, community, at the governmental, policy level, as well as at an intergovernmental level, but I didn't then.

Sustainable living involves complex and challenging questions, ranging from finding appropriate technical solutions through to a seismic shift in our individual and collective behavior and consciousness as a human species, calling for huge changes in the distribution of power, wealth, and voice. Until we notice that we share the planet with other beings, that resources are finite, and that our actions are having dire consequences, those shifts are unlikely to happen. Our attitudes, behavior and interpersonal dynamics are complex. They are made more complex by the system in which we live; very often there is not the political will at a policy or corporate level or an individual willingness to engage with the difficult questions we face as individuals and societies around climate change, ongoing threats to biodiversity, population growth and demographic imbalances, the 'silent hunger crisis' (Farming First, 2009) of malnourishment and poverty, and environmental degradation.

What dawned on me through young adulthood was that deciding to have children is a private decision with global consequences. I cannot claim that I was a 14 year old eco-warrior who decided on the spot to not have children in order to save the planet, but a seed had been sown, it was on my mind, and I got involved in the work of the charities Amnesty International,

Friends of the Earth, and Greenpeace. Conditioned as I was, I still assumed I would have children one day, even though I was increasingly engaging with the global picture. If I had wanted them enough, I would still have had children. I am not claiming I did not have children solely to save the planet, it is more complex than that, and my actions are fuelled by many things other than altruism.

What I have found dismaying over the years is the reluctance of others to engage in debate leading to fruitful action. I am not at all surprised, I hasten to add, because these debates are challenging, calling for a view beyond our individual lives, and often involving soul-searching and acknowledging the grief of the loss of human and other-than-human life, which we humans have caused. But I have been disappointed when I open up these conversations with those I thought might engage. I am also very appreciative to those of you who have been prepared to engage fully and creatively with these themes, whether we agree or disagree. I was familiar in my youth with being dismissed as 'too idealistic' or 'too sensitive' or told "You'll change your mind one day, just you wait and see" (with a knowing look and nod of the head).

The reluctance to engage with hot themes reminds me of the time when I became a vegetarian in my early teens. I kept quiet about it, as I realized I was deviating from mid 1980s behavior. In fact, I felt a bit freaky and embarrassed. Fortunately, my geography teacher did not see me as a freak, although, to my adolescent horror, he did hold me up as some sort of right-on paragon of animal-rights (nightmare-ish at that teenage stage when absolutely *everything* is already totally embarrassing). I was criticized left right and centre, taunted by "But what about your leather shoes?" and bombarded with "You'll grow out of it, wait and see", although I am waiting for that day, three decades on.

I am also reminded of a theme from my current situation. 12 years ago I decided to stop flying. I did this as a way of engaging with the reality of the global situation we are in, in a way that I knew would sufficiently challenge my emotional status quo to wake me up to look more closely at my views and habits, particularly, but not only around carbon consumption. I did not want my carbon footprint to be a right-on idea, rather something I considered in day-to-day life. I did not find it difficult not flying at first, but it was harder over time. I love travelling. Travelling alone has given me some of my most exhilarating and growthful experiences of people, other places, and other beings, and has catalyzed me to go deeper in my awareness practice. Not flying has brought to the fore different, lesser-known parts of me. It has also surprised me. I was shocked at the indignant inner voice which emerged: "Of course I should be flying, after all, I can afford it, and therefore I can fly". My consumer conditioning was way more deeply embedded than I cared to openly admit. Despite railing against Mrs. Thatcher and her numerous destructive and, to my mind, narrowly-focused policies, the 'free' market indoctrination of my formative years had obviously seeped in while I was not looking.

I have since found a bit more equanimity about not flying. I have had to engage my imagination more fully in mind travel, rather than actual travel. I have also practiced in greater depth the third Buddhist precept (or training principle) of 'stillness, simplicity and contentment'. I have grown increasingly appreciative of the beautiful places of England and of other nearby countries within non-flying reach. I am also acutely aware of my privileged position, and that for a large percentage of the people on the planet flying is an abstract idea, as they are more concerned with their daily survival. What seems like a hardship for me is beyond the reach of billions of people. What I also find difficult, yet strangely familiar, is just how big a conversation-stopper it is when I mention that I do not fly. Yet again, similar to when I was younger and decided to turn vegetarian, I have tended to be rather quiet about not flying, to the point of hiding myself, a situation I am addressing.

Choosing not to have children seems to fall into similar territory. Now in my mid forties, it is much less common for those around me to ask whether my partner and I intend to have children. But that is not really the point, the point is whether, and how, we can collectively create a climate in which the decision as to whether or not to try for children is recognized for what it is: a private decision with global consequences. Taboos surround this area, and being part of a minority who have decided not to try for children, it can be difficult to give voice to one's experience and point of view without being written off as 'other' (compared to the majority voice of the status quo), odd, and holding overly unconventional and so-called 'way out' opinions (as the voices of minorities have been throughout history, in the eyes of the majority). I talk more about this later in the chapter entitled 'Minority Report'.

The point here for me is not about preaching that you or anyone else shouldn't have children – that would be a pointless and narrow-minded exercise. It is not about whether having children is right and not having children is wrong, or vice-versa. That is also missing the point. It is about understanding the consequences of our actions and the sphere of our influence. There is much confusion and lack of clear thinking around having children being seen as a personal decision and the public impact of that decision. Gross puts it:

...pronatalists regard reproduction as a private right not subject to public policy, even though they usually insist that the results of their reproduction are a public, even a global, responsibility. (Gross, 1997: 294)

We need clearer, more open thinking about childbearing and more awareness of the fact (and traditional Buddhist teaching) that actions have consequences. We need to be more conversant in the strong emotions which this subject elicits. Whether or not to have children could be brought into wider and more public awareness, with discussions in sex education from primary school onwards. With approximately one in four women deciding not to have children, it seems a bit misguided and outdated to not take more seriously this growing social trend, and its positive consequence, in terms of lowering carbon footprints and, of equal importance, creating an environment of more conscious parenting.

It is taking time and energy in bringing about a change in this decision-making culture. As with talking about issues such as carbon usage, we need individual and collective courage to open up an area that is still often considered to be a personal rather than public matter. We'll need courage to express our viewpoint as well as to face our hopes and fears for the future in looking at such themes. After all, an important factor in having children – consciously or unconsciously – is that it gives us a present and a future, and, of course, is largely still seen as our default way of being.

Or perhaps, it has been until now. Whether or not this is our default, or 'natural' way of being, or seen as 'normal', is it realistic to think we can continue to treat procreation as an automatic individual right, in the face of potential and actual planetary disaster? Because we might not personally be faced with issues of food security, soil degradation, and water scarcity it can be easy to believe that this is still a personal choice. The reality increasingly looks as through these issues will be more prevalent in the experiences of our children and their future lives.

The other reason there will need to be sea change to bring about a stronger and more open culture of dialogue about this subject area is because not having children is still seen, curiously, as being a selfish choice. For some folk having children is somehow seen as selfless. To have children is to contribute to the common good. Hand in hand with this, when I have said that I have decided not to have children, I have often been confronted immediately with the 'But what would happen if everyone stopped having children?' argument (which parallels my experience of the 'But what would happen to all the animals if we all became vegetarian?' debate, so it is familiar territory).

The 'choosing' aspect of this book's subtitle includes a plea for us to open up a space in which more dialogue can take place, where we can face our hopes and fears for our own futures and for the future of the planet and our species regardless of the differences in how we choose to live.

A pregnant pause

Maybe re-read your reflections from the chapter 'The seven billion mark', which touches on similar material. You might also reflect on the following: What has been your experience of changing your behavior or making a decision (in my case, becoming vegetarian and not flying) which has attracted attention from others? Was the attention supportive or critical? How has that felt, and what impact did it have upon you? If you are without child, have you been referred to as being selfish for not having children? Notice the effect that's had on your subsequent decision-making. I mention the precept of 'stillness, simplicity, and contentment'. Are there life changes you have made with simplifying and quietening your life in mind?

Chapter 18

Traditional, transitional and transformative women[8]

> Few people had made an early irrevocable decision not to have children. Deciding not to have children was a process that took place in the context of other life events, particularly partnerships. (McAllister with Clark, 1998)

There has always been a minority of women who have chosen a life without children, most visibly those drawn to religious, educational, and vocational work. Yet even amongst those folk it is important not to overlook the fact that some may well have turned to a vocationally-lead life in response to discovering that they were unable to bear children. Given this, the historical scale of intentional and unintentional childlessness can be hard to know.

This chapter is biased towards exploring a woman's decision to not have children, compared to a man's, primarily as there is more information about this phenomena and it is made more culturally prominent, compared to men's decision-making. It is not automatically assumed that a man should be a father, compared to the strength of the assumption made about women, motherhood, and identity. This chapter looks at how this decision takes place over time, from our teens until the menopause. There are a wide range of motivations as to why women decide to remain childless, not least the factor of partnerships, as pointed out by McAllister and Clark in the opening quote of this chapter (and it is worth bearing in mind that those who decide in theory not to have a child can, and often do, end up pregnant 'accidentally').

Over the years writers and researchers have started to categorize those who remain childless depending upon their circumstances and/or motivation. I have found these useful in understanding my approach to decision-making. UK research from 1983 divides childless couples into four groups, based upon their temperament and circumstances: altruistic idealists, easygoing hedonists, partisans of a particular lifestyle, and ill or older people (Baum, 1985: 153 cited in Lisle 1999: 5). Cannold refers to 'waiters and watchers': women who are ambivalent and undecided about parenting, with neither maternity nor childlessness being a fixed part of their imagined future and identity (2004: 7).

I have found Mardy Ireland's categorizations most helpful (Ireland, 1993). She draws distinctions between three categories of women who choose not to have children: those who are traditional, transitional, and transformative, as quoted in the title of this chapter. Women in Ireland's 'Traditional' category are not childless by choice, but, in her words and emphasis child*less* (Ireland, 1993: 17-40). These women have been unable to have children for biological reasons. 'Transitional' women are in Ireland's words: '...living in the stream of social change. They want to pursue the social and career possibilities that are now open to women, but they also want, or think they might want, to have a family' (Ireland, 1993: 41). For a whole variety of reasons, 'Transitional' woman delay childbearing until it is too late to conceive. Ireland refers to this category of women as 'Child-free and Child*less*'.

'Transformative' women are those women who positively chose a childless life (or, in her choice of words, a 'child-free' life) and can be defined as active decision makers, often deciding in childhood to remain childless. Ireland's work reflects how women arrive at their decision in different ways, from ambivalence, through to a definite decision and a rejection of motherhood; in the case of 'Transformative' women:

> When the transformative woman decides to remain child-free, she is saying to the world that she is on a personal quest in which motherhood plays no part. (Ireland, 1995: 71)

There is still a strong cultural bias which prioritizes the decision to try for children over and above other life decisions, with procreation being a woman's main job and role. This cultural bias is easing, but it still has a strong gravitational pull, particularly for women in their late twenties and early thirties. The beauty of the work of authors like Ireland, who have looked at the different sorts of women who may remain childless, is that it questions the social norm of womanhood equaling motherhood. Perhaps the categories above throw light on your own situation? It can be illuminating – even liberating – to understand how we arrive at the decision as to whether or not we will try for children, helping us to better understand ourselves, each other, and our life purpose. Let's hope we reach the point where parenthood is but one amongst several different life choices which are open to us – when following a vocation is encouraged and celebrated as much as bearing a child.

Reverie

The decision as to whether or not to start a family can take many twists and turns, is a snap decision for some, and a non-decision for others. Personally I wandered between being a transitional and transformative woman. How's it been in your life? Maybe revisit the timeline from earlier, this time looking at the people who have been influential in shaping your decision-making process over the months or years so far. Of Ireland's categories: traditional, transitional, and transformative, which draw you and which repel you? What light do these different categories throw on your own circumstances? Or do you see yourself a 'waiter and watcher', in Cannold's words? (Cannold, 2004: 7)

Chapter 19

'I happen not to have children'

With all this talk of choosing, decisions, and freedom to choose, it is timely to mention the men and women for whom the child-bearing question is something of a non-question. Being identified as childless – whether voluntarily or not – is a misnomer to some. It feels important to have a chapter in Part II giving expression to those who see themselves as simply not happening to have children, borrowing the quote above from a therapy work colleague I interviewed in the course of this research. Her life, and the lives of a few others I have talked to, has not just been shaped around the baby question or the overriding desire to find a partner and procreate.

It is important here to represent the views and lives of the women and men who have simply never had a yearning for a child, or, at least not a strong or sustained enough yearning to pursue parenthood. A minority seem to have come to an early decision not to have children. I am reminded of a friend who grew up surrounded by nephews and nieces and simply did not see the need to create any more babies in her mushrooming family – she spent the best part of her teenage years babysitting.

Another colleague reported that she would say to friends and family that she had not ruled out having children and it might still happen, knowing in her heart of hearts that she did not actually want children. She pointed out how:

> ...nobody supported it, as nobody understood it. Literally all my women friends had or wanted children. As this was 30 years ago it was a strange thing to say then. Possibly it is even now. It was always questioned and sometimes challenged. I think I was regarded a bit strange...women just are not

supposed to say this kind of thing. It was seen as a bit unnatural.

This colleague, in her mid fifties, has built a successful career, is financially secure, and has been on a lifelong journey of personal development. Whilst she occasionally wonders what her life would have been like with a child, she does not regret her decision. She eagerly awaits the next generation in the family as she enjoys children and likes being involved with them and their lives. She is sometimes saddened:

> ...when people know you have never wanted kids they expect you not to be interested in their children. This is far from the truth. When newborns get passed round I notice how I get left out, and the babies are passed to the women who have had kids. I feel this as a judgment – albeit unconscious. I think women who do not have children for whatever reason do get seen as lesser in some way.

My colleague's identity and the fact that she 'happens not to have children' is a situation which is very different to my own. The baby question, as I call it, for the sake of shorthand, was a pre-occupation in my late twenties and early thirties. The 'will I, won't I?' questioning took up a fair amount of my energy. So I find it refreshing (and I have to admit, am slightly envious) when I come across friends and colleagues, men and women, for whom this is a non-decision and for whom the categories of 'childfree' or 'childless' are meaningless to a great extent.

In my mind, hearing from women and men like my colleagues is invaluable as a counterbalance to a culture in which pronatalism is still seen as the norm and women are still primarily identified as mothers, with all the accompanying sets of rules, norms, assumptions, associations and behaviors. Hearing my colleague's story was a useful reminder that for some men and women whether or not to raise children has been something of a non-issue, as they have focused upon other things and had other priorities. I hope this chapter helps to normalize those who happen to be without child, opening up our acceptance to the variety of people in the world and their lives.

Chapter 20

'By the time I'm 30'

One of my favorite television series of the 1990s was 'Northern Exposure', which originally ran on CBS in the USA, and was screened here in the UK on Channel 4. It is a drama series based upon the lives and events of the inhabitants of a small, remote Alaskan community, including the surrounding flora, fauna, and wildlife. It is a touching mix of everyday community events, pathos, culture clashes, shamanism, philosophy and all-round quirky characters and story lines.

In an episode entitled 'The Letter' (series six, episode four), Maggie O'Connell, one of the main characters, re-reads a letter on her 30th birthday which she wrote to herself as a 15-year-old. In reading the letter she realizes just how different her life is to how she envisioned it, encouraging her to re-examine her life against the ideals of her 15-year-old self. At that point she, too, is without child. At the risk of being a plot spoiler, towards the end of the programme 15-year-old Maggie shows up, and the 15 and 30-year-old versions of Maggie reconcile their respective hopes and dreams.

Perhaps this episode of Northern Exposure had more of an impact upon my choosing childlessness than I have realized until now. I was in my late teens when I first watched it, and full of plans. I was extremely fond of Maggie's character, who I guess was a significant role model; her quirky life and the nature of her relationship with Joel, the town's doctor. Struck by my own inner mantra of having children 'by the time I'm 30' and remembering this particular episode of Northern Exposure, I felt compelled to try writing my own letter.

So I wrote a letter to myself in my late teens from now, my mid forties. It was a useful and poignant exercise. I could feel the gulf of the intervening years; parts of me are more life-weary, parts of me are much more confident, and I am far more comfortable in my own skin. I could feel the loss of youth – poignant and heart panging – and the loss of some friends and family who are no longer here on earth. I re-contacted the burning idealism of my late teens, and how that has been tempered by life, death, loss and gain; those worldly winds making themselves felt yet again. But most of all I could feel continuity between the values of my late teens and the values I hold dear now. That was surprising and reassuring.

We never know what life will bring and the best laid plans can easily be de-railed and need re-imagining. My idea that I would have children 'by the time I'm 30' was made in my mid-teenage years. Life rolls on. What I have found invaluable is living life with the help of understanding the Dharma, the teachings of the Buddha: seeing and experiencing the inevitability of joy and loss and, as far as possible, keeping my feet on the ground through both of those states. Experiencing the ever-changing, fluid nature of life, and learning to witness that flux and flow in myself, rather than keeping on grooving the more fixed, less fluid stories and habits, which can be horribly constricting.

The best laid plans can go pear-shaped, or exceedingly well, or a whole new life can emerge. Even with the clearest decision-making in the world, the realm of childbearing and raising is as uncertain as any other area of life, and we are not in control of anything much, beyond our responses to life. So reflecting and clear decision-making is great, and life continues to twist and turn, in Shaw's words:

Life is far from simple; paths cross unexpectedly, relationships break down, careers move in unanticipated directions, illness disrupts familial networks, all of which may overturn rational decisions made previously. (Shaw, 2010: 159-160)

Perhaps reflect on those twists and turns in your own experience. What can be most satisfying is holding lightly to life. Deciding something and then seeing where the decision takes you. Paying attention to the fluidity of life. Knowing that there is only ever this moment – the past has gone and the future's a fantasy. Appreciating that nothing is fixed, solid, permanent, or there forever can be extremely liberating, as well as scary.

Reverie

Recall role models who are, or have been, important to you. This might include people you know, as well as those from films, music, literature, the arts, and the sciences (there'll be more reflections on this in Part III 'Inspiring Women', so this is a warm-up). If you are also in your middle years, how is it to get older without a child? How has it changed from when you were in your teens or twenties? Can you relate to the intention to have kids 'by the time I'm x?' If so, has that early intention helped or hindered you? Maybe take the time to write a letter to yourself at a point in time when you were full of plans of how things would be (whether or not about childbearing), and see whether it is helpful in reconciling different aspects of yourself, and different ages of yourself, freeing the parts of yourself which might be frozen or stuck in the past.

Chapter 21

'You'll live to regret it'

To many mothers, Rebecca de Saintonge says, she is a Woman Deeply Flawed, perverted and selfish. Why? Because she has chosen not to have children. But if the reasons for that decision may be complex, one thing is clear: hand on heart, she has never regretted it. (Bauer, 2004: 20)

I admire the clarity of Rebecca de Saintonge in never regretting choosing childlessness. I also admire her for having the courage to be open and public about that clarity. It is not an experience I share, given that I have had moments of regret in being without child. They have not lasted long, but they have been strong when they have happened, and I would not rule out their re-occurrence.

Fear of regret and fear of the unknown are pivotal drivers in the arena of deciding whether or not to have children. They are not the only ones: fear of not fitting in, fear of conforming, fear of missing out, fear of being left behind, and fear of being left 'sitting on the fence' are prominent others. But fear of regret and fear of the unknown are big ones and ones which seem to motivate people to have children, even when they have a history of being ambivalent or even disinterested in child-rearing and childbearing. I guess fear of regret feels particularly pressing because there is a limited time window for childbearing. The good news is that: '...research on older childfree adults finds few if any negative consequences for these individuals' (Blackstone & Dyer Stewart, 2012: 5). And Bartlett finds:

This fear that a woman might suddenly be consumed with baby longings seemed to fade with age. By the age of 40 most women felt that it was now extremely unlikely that they would find themselves chasing after prams. (Bartlett, 1994: 60)

We can, of course, live to regret any of our major actions. I understand the fear of regret for not having children, given that this remains such a culturally affirming, biologically gratifying and for many, very fulfilling role. It is not so clear to me why some people have children to look after them in their old age, as is often stated, given the social and geographical mobility of many of us in this generation. Still, I am often taken aback by the seemingly fragile playing-card-like tower of views and assumptions upon which we base life-changing decisions.

I guess many of us have children because as humans with bodies there can be an alluring, instinctual draw to procreate little beings in our own, and our loved one's, image. Or perhaps you just get pregnant. Life begets life. "Babies happen along" as I was once told by a woman supporting women through pre-abortion counseling. We are hard-wired to plug in, live life, and having sex is one of the most obvious, pleasurable, sometimes confusing, of life-affirming activities. For some sex is their peak experience in terms of intimacy and pleasure experienced in and through the body in contact with the body of another. That, combined with love, lust and perhaps the longing to bear and bring up a child is a heady mixture.

I sometimes think any other reason given for having children might just be window dressing. Our strongest instincts are most at work in this realm. I have empathy for those who have children out of a fear of regret or fear of not knowing what the future holds; with childlessness looking like a potentially bleak future to some. I also empathize with women who end up having children because of the pressure put upon them, given that being questioned can become tiresome and undermining.

Regret can be an embittering thing to live with. I have known people who have come through that sense of fear of future regret, and have done amazingly creative, altruistic and generous things with their childfree lives. In a culture in which there is much fear and concern with what others think of us, perhaps we sometimes need to become more intimate with our fear of regret. What is our experience of regret? How do we know what we regret? Does it change over time, as new life events occur and people happen along? Or is it as solid as concrete, as some would have us believe? Is it regret we fear, or is that the nearest label we reach out for in describing other emotions? What do we do to our body-minds when we feel and live with this level of fear?

A pregnant pause

Having read this chapter notice your responses to regret, both past and present. Perhaps 'living to regret it' is a very real fear as you mull over the baby question; perhaps you are a parent who regrets the decision to have had children; or perhaps you are unable to bear children and live with the regret of never having had the chance to be a mother or father.

Perhaps spend time reflecting on a decision you have made which you regret, or an action that you regret. What would it take to make peace with it in the present day? Did you have the chance to do anything different at the time, or were you doing the best with the knowledge available to you, in the circumstance you were in? What emotions other than regret do you notice? What have you learned about yourself from the entire experience?

Chapter 22

A bout of the existentials

I used to find myself wondering whether I had my mid life crisis early as a result of not having had children – let's hope so. What has become clear in the 17 years since provisionally deciding not to have children is the uncomfortable realization that my life is dispensable compared to many around me. I know on one level that this is a daft view, because every life is unique, important and yet ordinary. On another, it is true. At least on a practical level; when I die, the implications will have far less impact than if – heaven forbid – my sister-in-law, a mother of four, were to lose her life. I have no dependents. When I die some people might be sad for a while, but life will roll on and soon I will take my place in friend and family history. Occasionally I might come to mind, perhaps on my birthday or the anniversary of my death or when someone picks up one of my books to browse.

It is absolutely true that I will never, in this lifetime at least, know the joys and sorrows of being a parent. It is also true that parents will never know how it is to age with the feeling of that dispensability and freedom. As I said earlier, I felt my heart sink on the day that I realized I would be nobody's direct ancestor on our family tree. It was a sobering moment. In fact, not to put too fine a point on it, my ego – alive and kicking – screamed inwardly in horror. So creating descendents and lineage could have been a strong motivator for me in procreating.

My own response to this feeling of indispensability has been to go deeper in my practice of meditation and Buddhism. In going deeper in my spiritual practice I have touched on new energy in 'giving birth' to a number of creative projects, particularly as I have gained confidence throughout my thirties and early forties, re-gathering myself after my father's death and other significant life events. My mind and focus have been sharpened in terms of what I want to do with my time and being more aware of my experience.

What became increasingly clear to me throughout my thirties was wanting to be of service in the way I live. As well as appreciating the altruistic dimension of Buddhist practice expressed most fully through the bodhisattva ideal, I am appreciative of the Buddhist precepts or 'training principles' in living with loving kindness, generosity, stillness and simplicity, truthful communication, and clarity of mind.

In the Buddhist tradition bodhisattvas are beings who wish to attain enlightenment for the sake of all beings. Translated from Sanskrit, the name literally means 'awakened or enlightened being'. Studying and reflecting upon this ideal has been influential in shaping my life and work in my late twenties and early thirties. Not just what I do, but how I do it. When I see my life as a life of service, in the best sense of the word, rather than wanting something or achieving something because I think it will make me happy, I tend to live in a more satisfying and wholesome way.

I can see how, being childless, I could have become a bit self-obsessed, particularly without a path of meditation and spiritual practice, and, in particular, ethical practice. On one hand I can see how some of those who identify strongly with being childfree feel the need to defend and uphold their position as a way of life and, perhaps, part of their identity, given those without children still come under frequent criticism. Personally I am not interested in building a strong childfree identity in and of itself, even though I can see why others do. I think it is useful and important for people to share their experience of being childfree, to the same extent as others talk about their experiences of parenthood. Equally, I can see how those dedicating their lives to parenting are agitated by the outspokenness of some of the childless and how the whole thing can easily become polarized.

'Baby-sized projects' – more of which in Part III – became

important in channeling both my sense of purpose and the desire to nurture, which might otherwise have gone into being a parent. I have also become increasingly interested in the nature of existential questions which arise in parents and non-parents. Given the work I do as a counselor and Body Psychotherapist witnessing fear is commonplace in my working week. In Buddhism there are said to be three forms of suffering: physical suffering (we get ill and suffer), psychological suffering, and existential suffering (the big questions: why am I here? what am I doing with my life?). I witness all three forms of suffering in my therapy room. Existential suffering seems to be the most pervading and deep-seated. Clients who are parents fear their child dying, or perhaps fear leaving their child behind. Those who remain childless sometimes fear their lack of status, and a life without meaning.

In the words of the title of this book, I notice that being 'other than mother' is becoming less and less important to me as the years roll on, and causing me far far less existential suffering. As I have explored, in my thirties whether or not to have children was a pressing issue, drawing my attention and having its own intensity. That has changed. In my forties I think infrequently about motherhood and what I have missed. I am more focused on many other fruitful things: my work as an auntie, therapist, writer, lover, and gardener. Not being a mother is no longer a huge part of my self-identity, although, of course it is a factual reality.

What is increasingly clear to me is that the life work of each of us is to find out what to do with the time and health we have available to us. I do not think that we are all on the planet to have children, in fact, I am starting to wonder whether in our generation, a growing minority of us are here to start to redress the attention we pay to our relationship with the earth and other elements, and our effect on them as a human species, rather than creating more new lives. I don't think family is the most important thing. It is an important thing, certainly to me in my life, but relationships in whatever form are important—human and other-than-human. In fact, looking around me, it seems to be the case that relying on lover bonds and/or family blood ties alone breeds imbalance and difficulty.

A pregnant pause

Take care as you reflect on the themes from this chapter. If you are feeling even slightly below par then reflecting on your own mortality can feel sobering. On the other hand, on a day when you are brimming with purpose it can feel liberating to reflect on the existential questions around choosing childlessness. Ponder the questions below and see which are useful:

Whether you are a mother or father or not, do you have a sense of what your life's for? This mightn't be in a high falutin way, but in terms of perhaps serving a cause you care about, or creating things, or being there for those you love – notice how that sense of purpose (or lack of it) has ebbed and flowed over time. What is it that currently gives your life the most shape and purpose? What do you enjoy? Who do you like spending time with? Include the smaller details of life as well as the bigger considerations.

Chapter 23

Roaming new terrain

..the voluntarily child-free path has not been well mapped and so each woman seems to be travelling alone, cutting through the underbush, unaware that others are on the same road ahead and behind her. (Morell, 2000: 321)

Leave the door open for the unknown, the door into the dark. That is where the most important things come from, where you yourself came from, and where you will go. (Solnit, 2006: 4)

Even contemplating entering the terrain of childlessness can be exciting and liberating. Many women experience great freedom in being childfree. At first it might also elicit feelings of aloneness, invisibility, social non-conformity and disconnection, especially when we find ourselves swimming against a pronatal tide. It might even feel taboo to let yourself enter this terrain, even provisionally sitting with the possibility that it is not compulsory to have children. I am aware that whenever I have written and published an article about choosing childlessness I have been contacted by women who are pleased and relieved to see voluntary childlessness being acknowledged. So even though Carolyn Morell in the above quote was writing 15 years ago, we still have mapping work to do.

We are reaching the end of Part II of this book and I hope that you have found the exploration of the different aspects of decision-making useful in understanding more deeply your own priorities, values, motivations, and experiences. The purpose of this chapter is to support you in the process of entering and thriving in the terrain of childlessness and to see what you learn about yourself and your environment. In the longer-term, this new terrain is about those of us contentedly living without children creating new traditions which recognize and honor our contribution to life. Perhaps this process is also about uncovering, dusting down and re-imagining and remembering childless archetypes and role models who might have been lost in the mists of time.

When we are feeling lost in new terrain we hopefully recognize our need for a map, compass, protective clothing, sustenance, shelter, and, from time to time, the support and company of others; a wilderness guide perhaps, or at least someone who has trodden the path we are starting on, and who may be able to light our way from time to time. My intention is that Part III of this book offers you some material that can help in beginning a process of map-making in a way which makes sense to you and those around you.

Embodying our childlessness, particularly in a society in which having children is the prevailing norm, is initially likely to feel like being lost in unknown terrain. Being lost and losing ourselves means we are more likely to discover a fuller, more up-to-date version of ourselves. Entering 'the door into the dark' in Solnit's words in the opening quote, can be fruitful, as can a map of how to get around. The map of a childless life does not have, of course, the recognizable mountain range or landmark of becoming a parent. We may or may not respond to the more traditional and established maps of the childless following the stereotypical paths of career, vocation, religion, or art and creativity. We need to fill in our own landmarks on this path, creating new traditions, communities, initiations and rites of passage. Of course, path-making is true for everyone living life, it is just that there are, as yet, fewer voluntarily childless role models lighting the way.

What will be our metaphorical compass? Who or what will be our 'magnetic north'? What will be our signpost? Who will help show us the way? Perhaps other friends with similar thoughts and feelings, perhaps books and blogs? Perhaps through the creation of new networks and the gathering of like-minded people.

We will also need protective clothing, to continue this new terrain analogy. Unfortunately, developing a thick enough skin to deal with the criticism and derision of those who are not supportive of our choices and decisions is not as straightforward as putting on our anorak. If only. But the protective clothing analogy is timely and significant. We may well, at times, need protection in this decision-making process. Ideally we cultivate enough emotional robustness to be able to allow the comments and criticisms to wash over us, like water off a duck's back. Of course this might not be the case at first; we might – understandably – feel saddened that others do not give the time of day to a childless viewpoint, particularly if it challenges or upsets their own worldview and status quo.

What seems valuable is that in the long-run we can remain in dialogue – to the extent that that is possible – with those who see our life situation as strange or eccentric. A sadder outcome might be an entrenched polarization where we become so convinced of the 'rightness' of our point of view that we stop listening.

I recognize this tendency in myself in my late teenage years; a determination to demonstrate my own rightness about certain things that were close to my heart, and finding my feet in expressing confidence. I suppose a sort of misplaced idealism. It is probably an inevitable developmental stage, but it is a meager substitute for the grounded, yet fluid, sense of presence when we are able to embody the decisions of our own life without having to make anyone else's life 'wrong' as a result (and it is certainly not a good way to make or keep friends). Deeply respecting difference and being able to hold a space, a genuinely open space, between different standpoints, is different from having to constantly point out difference, often causing further divide and unnecessary hostility. So protective clothing is useful and it is something we put on and take off, depending upon the clemency of the weather and our surroundings.

On embarking upon this terrain we shall also need to know what and who helps to sustain us. What will be the equivalent of our fruit and vegetable 'five a day' as well as the equivalent of the odd bar of chocolate in spiritual emergencies or wild blowing of the worldly winds? Knowing and fostering the conditions which support us to live effectively and make good decisions can be more challenging than it sounds. It is also made up of smaller questions we ask ourselves and answer in the course of living each day. These everyday decisions create the habits that inform the shape of our day and the backbone of our current lives. Hopefully our backbone will be fluid and adaptable. Sometimes we can seize up a bit; our habits seem to fossilize and change seems less possible.

Knowing what sustains us consists of a lifetime quest of twists and turns as well as the immediate decisions: what shall I eat for lunch today? Conditions and relationships are changing all the time, nothing is fixed. Buddhism refers to this in the teachings of the three marks of existence (or 'lakshanas'). This teaching points out how everyday life is marked by impermanence, insubstantiality and unsatisfactoriness. Impermanence refers to how life is fleeting and ever changing. Insubstantiality refers to how all beings and phenomena are devoid of a fixed, unchanging essence. It can be easy to think of ourselves as a fixed entity, rather than as an interconnected being, subject to the process of change. Unsatisfactoriness is created when we expect fleeting life to be fixed and unchanging, in the hope of everlasting happiness and pleasure.

People and community can be an important support in our post-decision terrain. We can be supported and support others in life beyond choosing childlessness. It can sometimes be easy to forget this and forget our own sense of ordinary potency, particularly if we are feeling alone and invisible in the process of choosing childlessness, perhaps standing alone in our particular friendship group.

Hence the importance of meeting – in future, perhaps becoming – a wilderness guide in your exploration of this terrain. We need friends; living, dead, and mythical, on this journey. My best and most valued wilderness guides in the process of choosing childlessness have been Buddhist teachers, the great grandmother whom I never met who never wanted children but gave birth to and raised eight, Tara, the bodhisattva of compassion in Tibetan mythology, and all the women (and a couple of men) who, on hearing about this research and writing, have said words to this effect: "That is such an important theme, you must write it!" Thank you all.

Reverie

As you roam this new terrain, donning your raincoat and pulling on your walking boots, turn over these reflections:

Does the analogy of entering new terrain work for you, in thinking about choosing childlessness? Does it appeal visually? Kinesthetically? Mythically? What has thrown you 'off course' as you have reflected on whether or not to have children? Who have been or might be your 'wilderness guides' in this decision-making process?

Try mapping how this terrain has been for you so far; the post-decision-making landscape. Perhaps use a large bit of paper (the back of wall-lining paper, for example) or use stones as markers and work outside in physically mapping your experience (key turning points, watersheds, and people) so you can see it emerge before you. Consider enlisting the help of a trusted friend – perhaps your wilderness guide – as you do this.

Part III
New horizons and baby-sized projects

Chapter 24

Baby-sized projects and rites of passage

Margaret Mead suggested that the generative impulse could be expressed in other ways, such as passing ideas onto the younger generation through teaching, writing, or an inspiring example. (Mantel, 2013: xiii)

Part III explores the territory – the new horizons – stretching beyond making the provisional or lasting decision to live a life without children. Like Parts I and II this phase has its own distinctive flavor. Engaging fully with decision-making is important, as is knowing when the decision-making process is complete enough, when to follow your life into the next phase of living with the decision. Endlessly keeping one's options open can result in never committing to anything, feeling frustrated, restless, and dissatisfied. Sometimes it is important to make a decision, then give yourself time to re-visit that decision, if necessary, re-deciding with fresh information about yourself and the circumstances shaping events.

My way of understanding this post-decision phase has been through seeing the organic arising of 'baby-sized projects'. I found that once I had provisionally decided not to become a mother, new projects and horizons started to present themselves. Perhaps this was because I was starting to clarify what I wanted to do with my time and energy and widening my choice of pathways. On an energetic level, far less of my energy was pre-occupied with the intensity of thinking about whether or not to become a mother. Of course, your new horizons and my new horizons are likely to be different. So Part III presents the new horizons of my life since deciding not to have children, touching on diverse areas. My hope is that there will be enough coincidence of interest that your process of reflection continues in this post-decision phase, so you build supportive conditions in your life without children.

'Baby-sized' projects seem an apt name to give to creative, useful, projects emerging in the process of deciding not to have children. In my case, these projects marked the transition between wanting and deciding not to have children. In using the language of birthing and babies I am aware that I appear to be staying in a pronatal vein. Or am I? I was curious to read an article in which Jennifer Aniston is criticized for saying she has 'birthed' and 'mothered' many projects, in response to being criticized for not having children. In fact, Ellen (2014), writing in the UK's *Guardian* is enraged: 'The fact that any childless women would feel driven to legitimizing their achievements by appropriating maternal terminology enrages me on their behalf' (Ellen, 2014).

I see where Ellen is coming from here, in terms of women – me – feeling that we are more socially acceptable if we use the language of motherhood. And yet, there is something about birthing and mothering which is a hugely important act or process, the language of which I wish to reclaim. I am not using maternal terminology as a way of seeking the legitimization of my achievements, but because there is something about the creativity of the post-decision-making phase in being childfree which feels like a new life, a birth, a relief, mixed with threads of other emotions. With those caveats in mind, and a dose of poetic license, I reckon that the notion of a 'baby-sized' project is useful, valid, and honors my womanhood.

In choosing not to have children we are likely to have more time and energy to pour into other creative endeavors which may become 'baby-sized projects'. These can be invaluable, particularly during the transition phase of holding in mind the tender possibility that there might be richness to life having decided not to have children. In my experience 'baby-sized' projects spring into life of their own accord, once a decision has been made; they are not something to be manufactured or relentlessly sought after. They appear in their own time and at their own pace and they have the capacity to be a form of rite of passage in our lives without children.

Societally we need to do more to honor creativity in all its manifestations, rather than focus primarily on procreation, so let's start here. When someone has a child it potentially marks a transition or rite of passage. Having a child might mark the transition from young adulthood to parenthood, perhaps leading to a phase of intensity in terms of the new demands on our time, emotions and resources as we learn to parent and grow into the new identity of being a mum or dad. This transition has the potential to be a rite of passage. I say 'potential' as this depends upon the extent to which the mother and father accept this rite of passage, consciously or unconsciously. Some parents accept it wholeheartedly, others may veer away from the responsibility or cannot handle the change of identity. Or perhaps the rite of passage takes longer in circumstances where there are early bonding difficulties for whatever reasons, which is a fairly commonplace occurrence, with only about a half of all women feeling an immediate sense of love for their babies (Bartlett, 1994: 155).

Those of us who choose not to become parents might also benefit from rites of passage as markers or metaphorical gateways we pass through at different points in our lives. Let's hope that over time those of us who choose not to procreate evolve new rites of passage in honoring our creative processes. A 'baby-sized' project might be a way of honoring the focus, creativity, and energy that is so often reserved for procreation. And, of course, the two are not mutually exclusive. I know a handful of friends and colleagues who combine the creativity of a baby-sized project with bringing up a baby.

I have had several 'baby-sized' projects, although in the recent past I have moved from a 'baby-sized project' phase into an opening out into a new phase of life, now that I know for sure I do not want to have children. Perhaps the most important 'baby-sized project' was writing my first book *Meditating with Character* and having it published in 2012. For me this marked a transition from being someone who always just wrote and longed to write a book to someone who was published as an author. It was a 'coming out' in terms of my creativity, with that creativity being witnessed by others. It acknowledged my work role and practice of Buddhism, as well as drawing upon my experience as a counselor and Body Psychotherapist, meditating Buddhist and ecologically-minded human being.

The other characteristic which, in my mind, meant that *Meditating with Character* was a baby-sized project, was that it meant I faced many unknowns. I had no question about the content of the book: encouraging meditators to go deeper in their practice of meditation through engaging with their body awareness. There were, however, far fewer certainties in the process of writing, editing, being edited, being published, and then promoting the book. I met new terrors as well as uncovering more courageous, creative facets of myself.

The process of having a book published is a good one for facing the unknown: rejection, criticism, and praise all feature, both inwardly and outwardly. Whether or not a publisher says 'yes' to your book is out of your control. I was fortunate that my book was only rejected twice, but even then, I pretty much re-wrote it for the first publisher before they decided to turn me down. Whilst this was humbling and disappointing, it was good for my tenacity and certainly tested my patience and editing skills. The heart-stopping bliss of eventually reading the words 'we would like to publish your book' will stay with me until my last breath; one of those moments when I felt more ready to die, knowing that I had done what I could.

Each baby-sized project has its own beginning, middle and

end. It includes moments of uncertainty and long nights of the soul. It culminates in the celebration of something or someone. Other things I have done in my life which have been akin to a baby-sized project were being ordained as a Buddhist and completing my training to become a counselor and Body Psychotherapist in my thirties.

Many of you are likely to have your own baby-sized projects gestating, well under way, or complete. For those of you who are childless and who have perhaps felt a bit rootless or meandering for the past few years, particularly if this meandering has been due to not knowing whether to try for children, do bear in mind opportunities arising for the emergence of a baby-sized project. This might be re-training in the line of work you have always longed to do, following a vocational calling, going travelling, moving house, or creating a home. In the current climate it feels pressing to share the reality that there is plenty to life beyond having children. Whilst that is stating the obvious for some people, for others it is not such a commonplace realization. There are many ways to create without creating babies.

A pregnant pause

Notice whether a 'baby-sized project' might be useful and relevant for you right now. Although I call this a 'project' it could, as I've said, include a new job or vocation, a new start in a different place, and any number of other new ventures. Do you have 'baby-sized projects' on your horizon? What do they/might they look like? In what ways can you imagine such projects being a sort of rite of passage in marking the end of a decision-making phase and the beginning of the rest of your life?

Chapter 25

The bodhisattva ideal

When you look at what is happening to our world – and it is hard to look at what is happening to our water, our air, our trees, our fellow species – it becomes clear that, unless you have some roots in spiritual practice that holds life sacred and encourages joyful communion with all your fellow beings, facing the enormous challenges ahead is nearly impossible. (Macy, 2009: 240)

A central foundation of Dharma practice for me is what is known as the 'altruistic dimension of going for refuge'. In the Buddhist tradition the term 'going for refuge' refers to the repeated act of taking refuge: meditating and practicing with a deepening engagement and strengthening orientation towards the 'three jewels': the Buddha, the Dharma (the teachings of the Buddha and the path way) and the Sangha (the spiritual community of practitioners) in one's heart, and at the heart of one's practice.

Going for refuge to the three jewels, a central commitment for Buddhists worldwide, is concerned with becoming increasingly aware, skilful, and empathic. The 'altruistic dimension of going for refuge' can sound rather grand. In fact, 'alteri' simply means 'other', so altruism means being or becoming more other-regarding, taking other people into account as much as or even more than oneself – hence overcoming the clinging and fixing activity of our egos.

Altruism is an everyday thing. It is certainly not reserved for Buddhists. It is as simple as an ordinary, kind, gesture in which you are engaged with the well being of others as well as yourself. It is interesting that selflessness and altruism are qualities which are often attributed to parents. Altruism is, of course, something we all can practice, and many most likely do without even thinking about it, parents or not, Buddhist or not.

I have already mentioned bodhisattvas a few times through the course of this book; those beings who vow to practice to save all sentient beings. Some energetic and focused folk practice the bodhisattva ideal in the midst of raising children. I take my hat off to you, because I realized in my late twenties that I would not be amongst you. Partly I do not have the energy and partly because I did not want my children to be the primary focus for the practice of altruism when there are already so many other beings in the world. Raising children is, for some, an intense, lifelong, fulfilling and important spiritual practice. Many things we choose to do with our lives can be a creative part of the expression of our spirituality. Having children is not in and of itself a spiritual practice, although some seem to discover the sacred through childbearing and rearing.

Reflecting on the ethics of intention is useful here – what motivates us to do what we do? Anything can be a 'spiritual practice' if our intention is to become more aware, perhaps more compassionate, perhaps more mindful, or whatever is our skilful spiritual aspiration. Meditation is not even necessarily in and of itself a spiritual practice. It most likely is for some of us some of the time, but actually these days meditation and mind-training are used for any number of aims, from excelling at work, to being more powerful and persuasive in relating to, and managing others. Our intentions vary hugely in our daily activities. I meditate because I want to be more consistently kinder and wiser, transcending my everday state of mind which can be unkind and is sometimes foolish. Having said that, I do not always remember to connect with that purpose, sometimes I am just bored and restless! But that is my over-arching aim. Reflecting on ethics and my intentions feel like a gift in that they inform what I do and how I do it.

My choice to not have children was due to my attraction to the altruistic dimension of practice. I did not have children because I knew that I did not want parenting to be the main focus of my practice, with other things fitting round the edges. If I had had children, parenting would have been the main focus of my life, given the size of the task in hand.

In the early days of practice I wanted to know, and I still want to know, how to deepen my engagement with the altruistic aspect of my practice, through everyday work and life. Not just individual acts, but embodying altruism as a way of being. How do I keep the balance of paying attention to myself and to others? How can I practice generosity, in parallel with acknowledging my own needs? How can I be an apprentice bodhisattva, with one leg in meditation, and one leg stepping down into the world to save all sentient beings? (Reflected in the posture of Green Tara, another well-loved bodhisattva.)

I love to burrow beneath the surface of the sometimes seemingly lofty vision of the bodhisattva ideal to figure out how it works 'on the ground' as it were; in the ups and downs of daily life. I am reminded of a quote about spirituality, which I love, from my colleague, the Jungian analyst and public intellectual, Andrew Samuels:

> I seek to advance a vision of spirituality that is regular, ubiquitous and permeates every aspect of existence. It is not intended to be a lofty, exhortative, sermonizing approach. Quite the opposite. My take on spirituality discerns its worm-like nature, not its eagle-like nature. Spirituality as an underneath as well as an over the top thing. And because approaches to spirituality so easily go over the top, it is often better to stay underneath. (Samuels, 2002)

So how do I 'stay underneath', in Andrew's words, still practicing this lofty idea of the bodhisattva? Well, easily, really, when I remember to remember. In my teens I bought a colorful postcard. I cannot remember the picture, apart from its vivid colors, but I do remember the words: 'Practice random acts of kindness and senseless acts of beauty'. I have no idea who wrote the words, but I loved them. This pithy saying points at kindness which is not pious and not about being seen to be a good Buddhist. It is just about being kind because, hell, you are alive, I am alive and here we are. Random acts of kindness and senseless acts of beauty bring the poetry of devotion to everyday life. Superficially, or wrongly interpreted, Buddhism and meditation can be conceived of as being a bit detached and intellectual. Perhaps some practitioners are a bit detached and over-rely on the intellectual. Random acts of kindness cut through the over-thinking, over-analyzing mind into the immediacy of relating to ourselves and others as we are.

Having been inspired by that colorful postcard, I was glad to discover that Buddhism has a name and a myth for giving expression to random acts of kindness in the form of the bodhisattva ideal. Yet, even now, writing about the bodhisattva ideal feels challenging. Well, it *is* challenging. I guess that is the point; the ideal, and the practice of the ideal goes beyond 'me' and 'mine' to the point of ultimately loosening any ego distinction between self and other and dualistic ways of relating to the world. We become who we truly are without that 'who' being perceived of as a fixed, unchanging entity.

Seeing and going beyond the narrow confines of the world of 'me' and 'mine' is a lifelong project. Writing about practicing the bodhisattva ideal feels risky with regards to my decision to not having children partly arising from altruism. I can fear that I am being too 'big for my boots' or putting my head too high above the metaphorical parapet, when, in fact, I am just trying to live in a way that makes sense.

With these caveats safely in place(!) the bodhisattva has never-theless been a guiding principle in my Dharma life over the past 20 years. Perhaps the most obvious inward and outward expression of the bodhisattva ideal took the shape of the vows I took at ordination into the Triratna Buddhist Order. Being ordained was about making a lifetime commitment to orienting my life around the Buddha, Dharma, and Sangha. In the ordination ceremony itself there are four lines of acceptance which we recite, as we accept our ordination. One of those is: 'for the benefit of all beings, I accept this ordination'. Gulp. That was a weighty commitment to make, witnessed by friends, family, and teachers in a crowded village hall in the Brecon Beacons on a sultry midsummer a decade ago. Ever since my ordination I notice my slightly quickening heart beat as I chant the refuges and precepts (the ten training principles which are an important part of the ordination ceremony) or witness others expressing the four lines of acceptance, reminding me of the commitment I made at ordination.

An important reason why I asked for ordination was because I knew I would not be able to sustain practicing as a Buddhist on my own. Having a strong drive towards self-sufficiency, that was hard for my bruised ego to admit. Harder still was mediating between the part of me that likes to 'go it alone' and the part of me that longed to be part of a collective of people practicing together – a longing part which I had kept well hidden for decades. This tussle has softened over time, particularly as I have seen the importance of being part of a community of practitioners.

But what has Dharma practice and ordination into a Buddhist order got to do with altruism? In my mind this works in different ways. One of the most important ways I can express altruism is through embodying the spiritual qualities of wisdom and compassion. To the extent that we aspire to embody wisdom and compassion, or mirror-like clarity, or fearlessness or any number of other enlightening qualities – we are living a more skilful existence, rather than a more tangled, confused existence, which can create and leave a wake of confusion, fear and ill will.

Embodying wisdom and compassion to whatever extent we are able, starting with small random acts of kindness, offers up new space and ways of being in relationship. For example, when I am more in touch with these qualities in a real, tangible sense, I am freer to give my energy and attention to another, or the task in hand, whilst still being aware of what is going on in me. When I am feeling spacious and relaxed in this way, I move more loosely, freely, and more easily through life, like a horse being ridden with a loose, rather than a jerking, constricting rein.

In this state I feel less conflicted by worrying about what I should do with my life, instead responding to events, opportunities, and people, in an intuitive, yielding and trusting way. Years ago my 'save the world' driver was alive and kicking. It is still thriving, although a few things have changed. I have realized that some of the energy I was channeling into saving the world was actually about seeking to solve my own problems, projected outwards. I am learning that there are many ways to save the world. We need to start at home with our own thoughts, words, and deeds, in parallel with staying engaged with action in the world. That is an interesting and lifelong dance, and an essential thread of my Dharma practice, balancing self and other, now and then, being and doing, inner and outer. Playing with the polarities which can give birth to transformation.

If we launch headlong into saving the world when we have not started sifting through our own hopes and fears, we run the risk of becoming part of the problem, rather than being part of a more fruitful and wise future. I still hope we figure out how to solve world poverty and live more peaceably, and I am more aware of the work I need to do in sustaining inner abundance and harmony and in relating to others. I have also got older, and whilst I remain an idealist at heart, I suppose the process of loss and gain and seeing the rich mix of one's own motivations and actions is a great, and important, leveler.

The Buddha, Dharma, and Sangha offer a powerful method of

understanding the joys and sorrows of the world, best exemplified by the bodhisattva ideal. It is not the only useful vision, of course, but it is the one that makes most working sense to me. The three jewels give us the wherewithal to understand our own role in suffering, giving us tools and insights to understand the nature of mind. They offer us tried and tested meditation practices for exploring different states of consciousness which profoundly influence the way we operate in the world, going beyond ourselves without denigrating ourselves, until the moment when we realize that there is no such thing as 'ourself'.

Practicing the bodhisattva ideal keeps my heart ajar, it reminds me that Buddhist practice is not confined to personal development or relaxation and it connects me with all other living beings on the planet; human and other-than-human. In practicing the bodhisattva ideal we are repeatedly giving birth to new versions of ourselves, going beyond our sometimes fixed notions of selfhood in connecting – potentially at least – with all that lives. It is a practice that is accessible to Buddhist and non-Buddhist practitioners alike:

> We cannot think of a Bodhisattva as simply an extraordinary being. The Bodhisattva is not literally a person at all... But however lofty the spiritual attainment of the Bodhisattva might be, Mahāyāna Buddhism encourages absolutely everybody to make that their aim. That is to say, it encourages every single person to co-operate in what it describes as the great work of universal transformation. The Bodhisattva ideal is therefore universal in its aim, which is nothing less than supreme Buddhahood; it is universal in its scope, which encompasses all sentient beings; and it is universal in its frame of reference, which is infinite time and space. (Sangharakshita, 1995: 15)

A pregnant pause

The bodhisattva ideal is likely to be unknown to you, having said that, I am surprised and pleased these days that the bodhisattva ideal is discussed far beyond Buddhist circles. Mull over the following questions, as you think about how altruism and random acts of kindness are, or might become, a more important part of your post-decision-making landscape. What guiding archetypes and ideals or principles have been instrumental in shaping your landscape? Do you think of yourself as having a spiritual life or spiritual path? If so, does that encourage the practice of altruism? How does altruism express itself in your life? How do others express altruism towards you? How do you balance care for yourself with care for others? Notice whether it's easier to receive or give love. Which aspects or phases of your own life have called forth a deepening in your spiritual practice, or in going beyond yourself?

Chapter 26

The bodhisattva/ecosattva ideal at work

As the Buddha's enlightenment reminds us, our awakening too is linked to the Earth. The Earth bore witness to the Buddha, and now the Earth needs us to bear witness — to its dhyana, its steadfastness, the matrix of support it continually provides for living beings. New types of bodhisattvas – 'ecosattvas' – are needed, who combine the practice of self-transformation with devotion to social and ecological transformation. (Stanley and Loy, 2011)

The work I do has been an important crucible for change and growth. It has been a vital aspect of Buddhist practice to do the work that matters to me, and which I hope is of service to others and the world. I love work: writing, teaching, doing business, communicating with work colleagues and Sangha friends. I appreciate entering the crucible of the therapeutic relationship with clients, and the supervisory relationship with supervisees. I love working with training groups, particularly working and living outdoors. It is at work that I face and work with my most challenging, humbling, confusing edges. It is becoming increasingly clear to me that my work is about service; serving myself, others and the world in the best sense of the word. When I approach work (and life) with a sense of service I am less caught up in a more ego-bound, solely self-serving view and approach to life, getting out of my own way. In short, things flow.

I am the daughter of a late workaholic father, so I have seen first hand the slowly eroding damage that an out of balance relationship with work causes, in relationships and in family life. My dad gave me a huge parting gift on the last afternoon of his life. "Don't be a workaholic like I've been"; a powerful and painful acknowledgement which I hope freed him in wherever his journey took him next. His words have certainly freed me from following the less helpful aspects of this, for which I am sincerely grateful.

Even though I love, cherish, and am challenged by work I do not especially connect with the notion of being a career woman. I imagine I outwardly look like her, in part, but I don't feel like her. I feel like someone who works hard, and the more I follow my nose and intuition, the more I end up doing the right work with the right people. It's taken me years to learn to do that. I used to make five-year plans and brainstorm endlessly. That was, until the time of both of my grandmother's and father's illnesses and subsequent deaths. It took most of my thirties to get the wind back in my sails after those bereavements in quick succession, so that I could trust life enough again to follow my nose. I study hard, work hard and have been fortunate to work with some gifted individuals – my father included – who, shortly after his death, was described as a 'legend in his industry'.

In terms of not having had children, I have been called selfish, driven and plainly a bit sad. Those judgments are made less and less these days, and the emotional impact of them is less; I am getting older and people are more familiar with my childless status and my interest in intentional childlessness.

It is easier to not take those judgments too personally now, because I know the riches of my working life, and many other facets of my life. I feel increasingly less obliged to justify my existence – a most welcome aspect of being over 40. I do, however, feel sad that those who remain childless and are in the midst of that decision-making process are subject to these views and opinions in an often invasive and sometimes less than helpful way.

In the intentional childless literature I am saddened that women are so often automatically pigeon-holed as driven career women when they decide not to have children because they value the role of work in their lives, perhaps valuing how they are of service in what they do and how they do it. Even if a woman is driven, or motivated, by her career, whether or not she decides to have children, it is a shame that this is presented extremely negatively or seen as something which is either out of order or out of the ordinary.

This negativity is rarely, if ever, applied with the same vehemence and judgment to her male counterparts. We still have a long way to go as a society in loosening the views, expectations, rules and norms around gender, roles and child-raising and allowing women to excel outside their traditionally assigned roles. The world will not fall apart the more we accept diversity. The reverse will happen, and the growthful aspects of living and respecting difference will increase our understanding of and engagement with one another.

An important underlying aspect of my work as an apprentice bodhisattva, therapist, and childless woman, is supporting others to look afresh at the roles and expectations which are ascribed to them at birth. These can be deeply limiting in a world which needs creativity and big, blue-sky thinking and living, or, in the words of my teacher, Sangharakshita, drawing on the closing quote of the previous chapter, the perspective of universal transformation arising from the bodhisattva ideal. Increasingly my interest in the bodhisattva ideal at work is about working at the interface between the Dharma and the social, ecological, political, economic and cultural aspects of life in the 21st century. Bringing an age-old system of practice and guiding ethical principles into relationship with our extraordinary world calls forth the qualities and developing vision of the apprentice bodhisattva – or, in the words of Stanley and Loy, the ecosattva.

Reverie

By now I hope you are getting an idea of what the bodhisattva ideal is all about!

What are your emerging bodhisattva or ecosattva qualities in your work? How do you embody those qualities? For example, in your engagement with your work community, as well as what you are actually doing for work. In what ways has your work been an expression of your values and/or creativity? Do you relate to being an apprentice, or perhaps a master/mistress in your trade/sector? Or perhaps you are the master/mistress – passing your knowledge, skill, and experience on to apprentices. If you relate to being a career woman, how is it to positively reclaim that label, compared to having it applied to you as a criticism in your childless state? If you are at a stage of looking back at your life, what has been your life work – your *magnum opus*?!

Chapter 27

Occupying your body in taking your place on earth

> For it is the body, the feeling, the instincts, which connect us with the soil. If you give up the past you naturally detach from the past; you lose your roots in the soil, your connection with the totem ancestors that dwell in the soil. You turn outward and drift away, and try to conquer other lands because you are exiled from your own soil. (Jung in Sabini, 2002: 73)

Until my thirties my experience of being a body was, at times, like being in a battleground, sadly rather commonplace for many girls, women, and a growing number of men. Tugs of war around attractiveness, body image, food, and nurturing have all taken their toll. And yet I have learnt the most from these tugs of war. This learning has stood me in good stead in knowing how to live, how to be present and how to relate to and empathize with others. Not being born a perfectly proportioned, petite, neat-boned size ten has also played its part. Being broad-shouldered, crazy of hair, and being described as anything from curvy and curvaceous to a 'fat bitch' has been character-building. I have also been said to have 'child-bearing' hips, and, shucks, I didn't even put those to good use.

I had to occupy my body before feeling free to not procreate. I had to listen and get to know my body more intimately, and more quietly, from the inside. This was in contrast to a childhood and youth of listening to others tell me their views about my body, good or bad, punishing or loving. Again, sadly this is an experience particularly common to girls growing up and conditioned into family and society's view of rights and wrongs. In occupying my body, I was able, in the words of Peterson and Engwall (2013), to hear for the first time the silence of my childfree body. I resonate with their words:

> ...women can resist gendered discourses through constructing an embodied childfree identity. The naturally childfree position and the 'silent body' have transformative power to contest the meanings attached to womanhood and could increase freedom for women to experience womanhood in a variety of ways. (Peterson and Engwall, 2014: 387)

I love their emphasis upon 'freedom for women to experience womanhood in a variety of ways'. I am fascinated by the embodied aspect of childlessness – the coming together of the experiences of being a body and the experience of being a childless woman. If, in the words of the title of the book by Mardy Ireland (1993), we are 'reconceiving womanhood' then what does being without child mean for our experience of being a body? I am not just interested in this because I work as a Body Psychotherapist, but because in paying attention to our child-lessness on a bodily level we are moving beyond the conventional framing of the childless woman as lacking something, historically being met with pity, or worse still, scorn, rather than being recognized for her potential abundance and, as Peterson and Engwall point out, the myriad possible ways of being a woman. My embodied experience of choosing childlessness resonates closely with that of Mills':

> As a feminist, I assumed that I should determine the purposes my body would serve, and I must have intuited that for me the writer's life would be incompatible with parenthood. My renunciation was, in fact, epicurean, and it has abetted my simplicity. (Mills, 2002: 7)

Saying no to childbearing on an embodied level has enabled me to find a new, clear, 'yes' to other things; new horizons and baby-sized projects. Perhaps that is simply because I have made a clear – if not always easy – decision to not bear children. Occupying my childlessness has been freeing, particularly compared with living with the conflict of indecision, which, energetically, I personally found quite divisive. The thought of occupying one's childfree body in order to feel freer might at first seem counter-intuitive, particularly given the physicality of pregnancy and birth, with mothers who have had that experience being seen as 'proper' women.

This capacity to occupy my body was a political moment, as well as being an embodying, relaxing, releasing moment. It was, on a personal, bodily level, rather like the 'Occupy' movement folk setting up camp in key public places a few years ago: St Paul's in London, Wall Street in New York, and closer to home, College Green, in central Bristol. To me the Occupy movement is, and was, an attempt to reclaim power and decision-making, in the face of capitalist inequalities. I can see a direct parallel with my own, childless situation. I have a sense of occupying, or re-occupying my body, which has given me confidence and a greater capacity to speak out – with kindness, I hope, and maybe fiercer kindness. Soulé's words spring to mind:

> ...Fierceness is not the same as cruelty. Our fierceness is what gives us the energy to want to change things in a positive direction. It's also what mothers feel when somebody attacks their children. And that's a healthy thing. We need to re-embrace that kind of fierceness and indignation, not from an egoistic point of view but from a compassionate perspective. We can't let the world be destroyed, and we need to be fierce – not violent or cruel, but fierce about it. (Soulé, 2005)

As important as occupying our own body, knowing our own

agency and potency, is how we find ourselves occupying the planet; how we treat other life on earth, human and other-than-human. I have explored elsewhere in detail why embodiment matters (see Kamalamani, 2012: 51-62), and the parallel between the disembodiment of humans and mistreatment of the world and her other-than-human species, so I will not repeat that here. Suffice to say that we need to continue to heal the splits we find in our experience between mind and body, self and other, human and 'nature' (that complex word again), and other-than and more-than-human. Because of our recent history of accelerating disembodiment and the emphasis and dependence upon technology, we excel in acting as though we have mastered nature, failing to see the damage we are causing as humans. The more we abuse and exploit the earth's resources and other species in an unskillful way, the harder it is to look at the damage we have caused, hence the importance of the emphasis upon grief and hope in the work of practitioners like myself, facilitating wild therapy, through to the work of the well-known and much-respected ecophilosopher Joanna Macy (see Macy & Johnstone, 2012).

Healing the splits works and brings greater contentment. In my happiest moments these days my body feels like a garden in full bloom, bejeweled and warmed by sunlight. In my quietest moments my body is like that of a soft, curled up animal in a burrow: nowhere to go, nothing to show or hide or prove. I see the physicality of my sister-in-law's embodiment – soon to be a mother again – and marvel at the miracle of conception, pregnancy, birth and her ability to return to her regular size and shape (Emily is awesome. She runs 25 miles a week, is svelte, stylish, funny, and loves, teaches and plays with her growing brood.) And it is such a different experience to that of being in my body.

It is a relief to be past the point where childbearing is a hot issue and I occupy my body without child – that is not to say it will not become hot again, of course, this can be a messy and long-winded process, rather like birth itself. A few female friends feel that their life is complete because they have given birth. On one hand, I can imagine that sense of completeness and that timeless, sacred link with all the mothers and babies who have ever gone before. On the other, I know that it is only true for some women, it is not representative of the whole picture of childbirth. Some friends have felt disengaged after giving birth and have been unable or will not bond with their newborn – often through no fault of their own. Others are overwhelmed by the circumstances of their lives. Some experience a blissful feeling of completion and purpose. I am interested in all the different moments in this life when we realize this blissful sense of completion. Maybe at the full blossoming of adolescence or the arrival of 'krone-hood' in our elder years, or maybe after finishing an important project (I confess I am hoping to feel it when I upload this manuscript for final publication. But it is best not to predict moments of bliss...). Giving birth is a fruitful moment, with the potential for bliss and insight. And it is not the only one.

In the words of Bartlett: 'The space in the child-free woman's life is not empty and barren, but full of potential'. (Bartlett, 1994: 233)

And Morell: 'Vacant emptiness may be reunderstood as a radical openness that allows for various possibilities – for growth, expansion, exploration'. (Morell, 2000: 318)

Reverie

How has your relationship with your body been over the years? Map or draw your body on paper, or map how it has changed over time, or how your relationship with it has changed. This can be a helpful exercise in under-

---

standing not only how 'in touch' or embodied we feel overall, but helps us to notice different bits of our body with which we feel more or less ease. What sense do you personally have of 'occupying' your body? Has it been easier to occupy your body since deciding not to have children, perhaps resonating with Peterson and Engwall's words regarding the potential silence of the childfree body? Or, conversely, do you feel a sense of loss in your body as a result of that decision? What have been your moments of bliss? When were they? Where were you? Who were you with, or were you alone? If you are a parent, how did the birth(s) of your child(ren) change your body and your relationship with it?

Chapter 28

An emerging consciousness

The new story for me is a story of reunion. Reconnection...we are connected with nature, we are part of nature, what Thich Nhat Hanh, the Buddhist master says, we are 'interbeing', we are interdependent, we are interrelated. Nothing is separate...Large numbers of young people are waking up. And they are saying "we are not here just to work for multi-national corporations and make money for them, we are here to live. We have to live, to find a meaning for life". The old story is the story of measurement and the new story is to bring measurement and meaning together. You cannot measure everything, you cannot measure meaning. And in this emerging story people are moving away from the fossil fuel-based economy to a more renewable economy. (Kumar, 2014)

We are living in extraordinary times, and, yet, superficially, it looks like business as normal. Phenomena such as climate change and the sixth extinction crisis are finally entering – uneasily – public consciousness here in the UK. There seems to be a greater awareness of the realities of climate change and less climate skepticism. There is growing awareness of the effect of human life and work on the lives of other-than-human species. These themes are on the news frequently in contrast to a few years ago and I am noticing how the tone, for example, around climate change, is gradually changing. It is no longer about whether or not climate change exists, but how we address it – and new reports about the dire consequences of climate change are emerging all the time.

There has also been a tangible rise in public protest, from the

'Occupy' movement to an everyday surge in folk who might not normally protest but are beginning to do so, whether that is in response to austerity measures, calling for reform of the financial system, opposing fracking, challenging the tax breaks of large corporations, or campaigning to stop the dismantling of the UK's National Health Service.

Spiritually-speaking in the 20 years that I have been practicing meditation and Buddhism there has been a huge surge in interest in mindfulness in living with stress, illness and in pain management. Perhaps this is part of the broader shift in consciousness, with the recognition of the importance of a more inward, reflective aspect to life. Perhaps it is an inevitable process of meditation being secularized and mindfulness being commoditized in a capitalist culture. I do not know, but I know that there has been a change, and access to meditation and ways into spiritual practice have become much more commonplace. In terms of the central theme of this book, I am also noticing an increase in media coverage about childlessness, particularly in looking at the attitudes towards intentionally childless women. I am not sure that the views towards intentionally childless women are changing all that quickly, but at least a debate is happening, with prominent women talking about their choices, for example: Cameron Diaz, Jennifer Aniston, Helen Mirren, and Lucy Worsley, whom I mentioned earlier.

Awareness of the ordinary and extraordinary is an important part of my everyday life. Personally I do not go along with the idea that every time has its challenges and this time is no exception. Of course every time *does* have unique challenges, and at no other time have there been such extreme challenges: climate change, loss of biodiversity, the 6th generation extinction crisis, and capital controlled by a global elite; complex themes I have touched upon throughout this book. It seems obvious to me and a handful of people around me, that we are entering, albeit very slowly, 'great turning times', moving from an Industrial Growth

Society to a Life-Sustaining Society (Macy & Young Brown, 1998: 17). Macy calls for the need for 'shifts in perception of reality, both cognitively and spiritually' as one of three areas which need addressing during the great turning times (Macy and Young Brown, 1998: 21).[9] For me this parallels talk and practice in Buddhist circles about a turning around at the deepest seat of our consciousness in the process of becoming enlightened.

It seems obvious to me and many of my tribe that we need structural change right now in the way we live, work, and how the financial and trade systems work – or do not work, for billions of the world's inhabitants. We can change our individual behaviors, knowing that that makes important ripples, *and* we need urgent change at a policy level. Recognizing and engaging with this 'tipping point' can feel liberating at times, as well as anxiety-provoking. I have not always felt this sense of liberation. I have had, and they can come and go, feelings of despair, grief and despondency in response to the way in which we have treated and continue to treat the planet, our home, each other, and other-than-human species. A vital part of these times of a new, emerging consciousness is to be part of a community of people, for support, action, and reflection. I am reminded in particular of a recent talk by a friend and colleague at an event called 'The Green Earth Awakening' organized by Buddhafield in Somerset:[10]

> Amidst all of that bad news...it can be hard to stay afloat in that kind of tsunami of bad news...So where is the good news? Where is the good news we need to keep us afloat? So although it can be hard to see this, in a certain sense, the bad news is the good news. The mere fact that information about the perils of our times is being made available is a crucial factor in the healing of our times. And listening, hearing those signals, is the necessary starting place for any change. That

the danger's actually being felt and sensed. That we are beginning to identify the problems. That the bad news can be heard – that is the good news. It is like Thich Nhat Hanh says: "What we really need to do to help the world is to hear the sound of the earth crying". So we live in times of great peril, but also times of great promise. (Guhyapati, 2014)

I am heartened by the insights of those doing similar work. As Guhyapati says, at least we are waking up to what is going on in the world, hearing those signals, as we decide how to respond individually and collectively. I feel grateful that I engage at this interface between self and world: with clients, supervisees working in often intense and resource-stretched organizational settings, trainees, and fellow Buddhist practitioners. For those of you who are dipping your toes in exploring these themes for the first time, then the work of ecophilosopher Joanna Macy is helpful in not only understanding why a response of grief is useful and important as we do the 'work that reconnects' but also in cultivating 'active hope', part of the title of her latest book, co-authored with Chris Johnstone (see Macy & Johnstone, 2012).

In engaging with the great turning times I am reminded of my early experiences of practicing Buddhism and being taught to reflect upon impermanence. As I delved deeper, I learned more about recognizing life's impermanence, unsatisfactoriness and insubstantiality (known as the 'three lakshanas' in Buddhism, see Sangharakshita, 1957: 194). I found it a relief to understand how we prolong our suffering as we attach and seek pleasure from things which are by nature impermanent, unsatisfactory, and insubstantial. I was struck by how this was received by non Buddhists. For some, Buddhism seems to become associated with a focus upon suffering or thinking about death in a morbid way. It is a shame that Buddhism is grasped in this back-to-front way. In my mind reflecting on beginnings and endings (not just death, but birth *and* death) and recognizing the impermanent, unsatisfactory, and insubstantial nature of phenomena, has been liberating.

Being an apprentice bodhisattva and ecosattva is vital work in staying as present as possible in these times. It also takes time, effort, and focus. I would love it if more of us decided to forgo having children, instead giving more time to nurturing the earth, limiting our destructive ways in lessening further planetary damage – regardless of whether climate change is irreversible. Bodhisattvas are not only known for their deep longing to save all sentient beings, they are also well known for their great ability to approach what appear to be arduous tasks with lightness and play. They show us the way into the heart of enlightened practice. As Shantideva reminds us in the Bodhicaryavatara, translated as 'a guide to the bodhisattva's way of life':

> Thus in order to complete this task,
> I shall venture into it
> Just as an elephant tormented by the midday sun
> Plunges into a (cool, refreshing) lake.
> (Shantideva, 1979: 98)

We need this combination of facing the reality of the world as well as the ability to play, experiment, and explore, as we enter new territory, individually and collectively. As much as anything, our ability to loosen and play with our existing worldviews and our fixed self views will be as important as analyzing where we have come from and where we are heading.

We also need this faculty to play in sustaining ourselves in our own version of doing the work that reconnects. This arena is challenging and can take us to our edges. Life as we know it, both human and other-than-human, is under threat, yet we need to find ways to keep on living and engaging with life and the wonder of the world. Cultivating curiosity can help with this, as can a keen awareness of doing things which affirm life and acknowledge and honor death. Of course, having children can be a great affirmation of life, so those of us without children perhaps need to be a bit more creative in knowing what it is that affirms life in its newness and beauty as our horizons grow.

A pregnant pause

In this chapter we have moved again into looking at wider themes, in particular, a new, emerging consciousness, and shifts in consciousness. Is that something that you agree with, are aware of, and part of? Is your desire to remain childless part of that wave of shifting consciousness? What matters most to you about life on earth, beyond the lives of your immediate families and friends? What are your thoughts in response to the play of the bodhisattva? And the idea that the 'bad news is the good news'? Take time to note what you contribute, and what you would you like to contribute even more in your work and life.

Chapter 29

Giving the gift of confidence

> So this is my confession. I am a woman who does not want children. I know I am not alone in this. I hope that if more women confess to also harboring this dark secret, that people will begin to accept that this is a legitimate mind-set. I hope that one day women who choose to go without children will no longer be given a pitying stare, a condescending head-tilt. I hope that people will stop questioning their decision, that they will realize it was not made flippantly, that they will respect it and understand that a childless woman can still live a joyful and accomplished life. (Hunter, 2014)

I, too, long to live in a world where it is okay not to have children, and I admire Hunter for stating her hopes so openly in the quote above. I long to live in a world where those who have decided to be childfree are celebrated as much as family life is sometimes haloed and idealized. In my late twenties, training for ordination, one of the most useful things that was said to us was to do everything we could to build our own confidence, particularly as women. The team of women ordaining other women witnessed, time after time, this chronic lack of confidence of women in the ordination process. Not only that, but what women needed in being supported in their lives and Dharma practice was to be given the gift of confidence; the message that you are on track and doing okay. Back then I wasn't familiar with the notion of giving the gift of confidence, now it is something I have grown to love and value.

This lack of confidence sometimes, maybe often, tips easily into self-harm and aggression. I am reminded of the words of the Buddhist teacher Pema Chodron. She points out how:

When we start to meditate or to work with any kind of spiritual discipline, we often think that somehow we are going to improve, which is a subtle aggression against who we really are...But loving-kindness – maitri – towards ourselves does not mean getting rid of anything. Maitri means that we can still be crazy, we can still be angry. We can still be timid or jealous or full of feelings of unworthiness. Meditation practice is not about trying to throw ourselves away and become something better. It is about befriending who we are already. (Chodron, 2004: 11)

Generosity is an important quality to cultivate in building our confidence and befriending who we are, whether or not we meditate. Generosity (or 'dana' in the Sanskrit language) is one of the six perfections of the bodhisattva.[11] Generosity is multi-faceted and includes giving the gift of confidence to ourselves and others, including having the generosity of spirit to befriend who we are already, in Chodron's words. Giving the gift of confidence has been an important aspect of my work leading Buddhist study and supporting women in their ordination process. It is also an important aspect of working with psychotherapy clients and in supervising therapists. We live in a culture with a huge propensity for self-criticism rather than self-confidence. It saddens me. We are busy analyzing, pulling apart and criticizing. Even when that criticism is constructive and growthful, sometimes there is a place to let things just be and to gently reassure.

I am grateful to the women who gave me the gift of confidence in deciding not to have children. The person who particularly comes to mind is Jennifer Matheson, then known as Sarvabhadri, who was supporting a retreat I was on one summer at Taraloka, a women's retreat centre in Shropshire. I was in the phase of talking to as many interested people as possible about having children, and Jennifer was particularly supportive, engaging and interested.

I am reminded of the words of the writer Natalie Goldberg, who, in her book *Wild Mind: Living the Writer's Life*, asks the question: 'Who gave you permission?' (Goldberg, 2009: 123). Goldberg's question is asking who gave you permission to write, but equally, this question could be asked of giving permission to live a life without children. As Goldberg points out, this is not permission in terms of authority, but permission in offering encouragement and friendship in writing, or in this case, living without children and pursuing baby-sized projects. As I look back now I think it was Jennifer who, in some senses, gave me permission to contemplate a life with or without children. She taught me that the most important thing was to engage with the process with kindness and patience.

The giving of the gift of confidence is vitally important during and after the decision to remain childless. May the kindly witness, the attendance of the traditional 'gentlewoman' in our inner experience, give us the gift of confidence as we change and grow. Better still, may we have friends who give us this gift, as we give it to them. Consider becoming part of the emerging childfree movement (Park, 2002: 39) as a way of meeting with like-minded people and as a way of challenging the pronatal notion of childbearing as the central aspect of female identity. May these communities of people also give the gift of confidence to those deciding whether or not to have children.

A pregnant pause

Perhaps the notion of giving the gift of confidence is new to you – it certainly was to me before I started practicing Buddhism. Very often generosity is associated with giving material things, like money or gifts, so learning that giving time and confidence is of equal, if not more, importance,

---

and can be a breath of fresh air. When have you been given the gift of confidence in your life? As an intentionally childless man or woman would you feel able to give the gift of confidence to someone else mulling over the baby question? If you have decided to remain childless, was there a particular person or people who gave you confidence in making this decision? Have you found, or might you find connections with other people without children helpful as you make the transition into new horizons, creating a new community of people?

Chapter 30

Family healing and the 'ancestor syndrome'[12]

> ...how can we escape from the invisible threads of our family history, from the...frequent repetitions of difficult situations? In a way, we are less free than we think we are. Yet we can regain our freedom and put an end to repetitions by understanding what happens, by grasping the threads in their context and in all their complexity. We can thus finally live 'our own' lives, and no longer the lives of our parents or grandparents... (Ancelin Schützenberger, 1998: 3)

My decision not to have children relates, in part, to a need for family healing. This has become increasingly clear to me since I decided not to have children, as if creating and entering a space, or clearing, in which I can acknowledge family ghosts and help lay them to rest. I imagine this healing might have taken place if I had had children, except it would have taken place differently, perhaps at a later stage in my life, maybe after the intensity of parenting younger children. The decision to remain childless has itself been a healing process for me, particularly in the latter stages of the process, although I could never have known that in my late twenties.

The need for healing in various lines of my family became patently clear to me in my genealogical research, which began about eight years ago. In researching your family tree you come across patterns, links, gaps, unknowns, brick walls, and, sometimes, uncannily repetitive events. What most motivated me to take my part in my family's healing work was discovering the dislocations in family history in both my mother's and father's lines. My part in family healing emerged from a deeper awareness in understanding the unfinished business which has passed, as it does, between the generations of families (see Ruppert, 2008 & Mucci, 2013).

Family healing occurs in many ways. My contribution to this work has been to practically find out more about the family members who have gone before: the rifts, the miscommunication, the contact lost through emigration, and simply filling in the gaps of what we did not know. I have had the chance to dwell on these family members in the fullness of their lives: who they were, what they did, what happened in their lives, both for them, and in the wider world around them. I made family pilgrimages, for example, to the final resting place in Scandinavia of my paternal grandfather, as well as making new pilgrimages to find the graves of other relatives, estranged from my family of origin.

We each do our work in this family healing, consciously or not, and I am not for one minute suggesting that not having children is necessarily part of this work. It has been for me, and yet I can see that my brother's part in this work has been to procreate and be a hands-on dad. We each do what we do in living our lives as consciously as we can, rather than in reaction to the habits which were automatically handed down to us, or in automatic pilot mode. Our work and our place in the family jigsaw puzzle becomes clearer to us, the more we do this work. Perhaps not having children has the potential to put those of us choosing childlessness more acutely in touch with our place in things, given our lack of ascribed place, and given the cultural prevalence of the pro-family agenda.

In researching family history an 'x factor' happens, which I think is partly why genealogy has experienced a popular resurgence, beyond facts, figures, tattered, fading photos and the confirmation of family stories passed down through the generations. I find it hard to put into words what this 'x factor' is, but it seems to be something to do with finding out more about where we belong (a sense of our land and place), who we belong with (our immediate people), which wider group we belong to (our wider tribe or community, past or present) and how our people individually and collectively made sense of their lives through their work, faith and how they spent their time (beliefs, identity, etc).

I also found and find myself discovering a strong sense of particular family members who are long gone. This is perhaps not so surprising; we share DNA, I dwell on their life and times, in some senses bringing back to life their experiences when they were here on earth, perhaps they trod the same earth I tread. That can – unintentionally or intentionally – be a strong practice of invocation. It is this invocation aspect which interests me with regards to family healing and the decision whether or not to have children.

As stories come back to life, people are stirred, or enlivened, or sometimes fear the process of looking back – so sensitivity is needed. We cannot know what we'll find, which is half the fun and half the fear. We not only get a deeper, more embodied sense of what it means to be a member of our particular family, we also get a stronger sense of the joy, sorrows, successes, and disappointments which comprise a human life and which get woven together in the fabric of family stories across the generations. All families have stories. They may be secret or shared stories, and celebrated or invisible stories. They may be stories of heroes and heroines or of hardship and survival against all odds. We each have our own stories too, some of which are linked to, or arise from, our relationship with our family, for example, the 'black sheep', 'prodigal son', 'daddy's girl'.

As you listen to these stories perhaps start to notice how you have lived out and continue to follow these family stories. I am reminded of a conversation with Daisy, my niece, when she was five. To my surprise she recollected, without prompting, the story of how her great granddad died in an airplane in the Second World War. That event was an important backdrop in the childhoods of both myself and my brother, and a huge loss in the fabric of my family's life. My grandfather, what he stood for, and what was lost as a result of his death, live on, yet the trauma of his death eases in the re-telling and re-feeling.

We all have our examples of these stories and the effect they have had on our family lives. They might be mundane and ordinary to others, but to us they are what has formed, shaped and made us who we are today, even if we only bring them to mind once in a while, perhaps on an anniversary or birthday or when we are going through a certain life event. We might even not be consciously aware of them, yet they still have an effect on our present day family constellation.

Some stories are traumatic. In fact, working as a psychotherapist, I have noticed how much trauma there is in our lives, leaving lasting marks on individual and collective psyches. I remember being taken by surprise when learning about my own family tree in doing something called 'family constellations' work; a therapeutic approach originated by Bert Hellinger (2003) and developed further by recent generations of practitioners. Doing this work confirmed my gut feeling that it was wise for me personally not to have children, and that that decision is an important aspect of my own family's healing, in particular, my female line. I cannot describe this rationally, but on a gut-level it made, and still makes, absolute sense. Skipping a generation of childbearing and rearing feels helpful and healing.

On a more practical level this is because my time is freer to focus on being an aunt – a role I take seriously – and being in the position of offering support and love because I am not preoccupied with raising my own children. I remember my nephew suddenly asking me a few years ago if I was definitely not going to have kids. "No, still no plans to". A smile played on his lips. "If you had your own children you probably would not love me as much as you do now, would you? Cos, like, you'd always love your own children more wouldn't you?" "Yep, you are probably right, Thomas, even though I would never stop loving you". It was an 'out of the mouth of babes' moment. In a largely urbanized, geographically mobile world in which the extended family and supportive, close community is often sadly lacking, aunties, uncles, cousins and close family friends and neighbors are increasingly important. Knitted up communities are important for the healthy raising of children, whether we are their parents, aunties, uncles, grandparents or friends.

Reverie

Allow this notion of family healing to seep into your reflections and day dreams. Are there events in your ancestor's lives which continue to impact you or your family, covertly or overtly? Are there particular recurring patterns or behaviors, sometimes destructive, which continue to pass down through the generations? Find time to sketch a family tree, recalling as much detail as you can about your family. Notice recurring patterns, cycles, and events when you reflect on your family's tree. If you are an auntie or uncle (whether by birth or through friendship) notice the importance of that role in supporting the growth and learning of the next generation. Perhaps being an auntie or uncle was a factor that meant that you were freer not to have children of your own?

As a result of your own family's healing, or perhaps even through deciding not to have children of your own, do you resonate with Schützenberger's quote that 'we can thus finally live 'our own' lives'?

Chapter 31

Minority Report

One day there will be a word for a woman without a husband or children that is not pejorative; a single word that conjures up the image of a strong, sexual and feminine woman who revels in her voluntary freedom. When that word becomes common currency, then we'll know that the present stereotypes have lost their stranglehold. Until then our sexuality and fertility are not our own: they are the property of a patriarchal society which fears women's freedom and penalizes deviants like spinsters, lesbians, unmarried mothers and the childless. (Muldoon, 1987)

It is not compulsory to have children in order to be an accepted, valid, human being and member of society. I will say that again, because it is so rarely said aloud. It is not compulsory to have children in order to be an accepted, valid, human being and member of society. An important dimension in my post-baby-making decision landscape has been raising awareness about this through research, teaching, writing, and in conversation. Right now, I am particularly interested in raising awareness that it is not compulsory for a woman to have a child in order to be an accepted, valid human being and member of society. Not surprisingly, there are still stronger pressures for women to procreate than men, but I want to include men here, too.

This story made me laugh, and then feel sad, nodding with some recognition:

"Okay, here's the truth: I cannot have children" I told my cabdriver somberly. I attempted to look distraught, my lips quivering. And my ploy worked. Finally, this man, who'd relentlessly argued that I would change my mind about my decision to not have children, clammed up and began focusing intently on the road. Yes, after years of being told by complete strangers that I did not know my own mind, I had finally learned the secret to get people to stop insisting, "You'll eventually want to have kids". I just had to lie about it. (Datt, 2013: 16)

Whilst I really understand Datt's decision, feeling she 'just had to lie about it' (and having employed my own strategies of diverting conversations to avoid actually lying) I would love it if those of us who are intentionally childless share more openly our reasons for our decision, as and when we can. Not with the intention of building our entire identity around our intentional childlessness, well, that is not my personal cup of tea, but to broaden the narratives around childlessness and to normalize the trend of increasing intentional childlessness. The discourses around childlessness can easily become polarized. Let's create better visibility around the subject of choosing childlessness, so that those choosing childlessness are not simply seen as 'career driven', selfish, or subtly pitied (and maybe sometimes secretly envied?) for not having been blessed with children.

I am reminded here of the words of Polly Higgins, the awesome lawyer who loves the earth enough to be campaigning for an international law of ecocide.[13] Her recently published book is entitled *I Dare You To Be Great* (Higgins, 2014). I am inviting the same thing in this chapter, so I will borrow Polly's words. I am daring you, as a voluntarily childless woman, to be great. Great in terms of how you take your place, great in how you live your life, great in how you communicate your decision to remain childfree and how life has been since, giving the gift of dialogue and confidence to others.

We need to remember our greatness and potency, because it can be difficult to be part of a minority, particularly a minority at the forefront of a new cultural shift; namely, an increase in intentional childlessness. In her work interviewing intentionally childless women, Gillespie (2000: 232), points out how resisting traditional, pronatal cultural discourses offers the potential for the transformation of these discourses. There is great potential for new discourses around the role of childless women and their role in society.

I also agree with Gillespie as she points out that there are high personal costs in being in this resistance role. It is a fine art, making one's point without coming across as reactive, polemical or reinforcing one's 'otherness'; particularly if the deviant label lingers. From my research and the research of others it seems that many of us who are childless have experienced being dubbed selfish, deviant or abnormal, given that we have failed to reproduce, which strikes at the heart of our identity. As Bartlett reminds us:

> ...prejudice against child-free women is vehement, because like most social change, it is a slow process that meets resistance all the way. The question 'why did you have children?' is rarely asked; there is an assumption that parenthood is inevitable, 'only natural' and as such is not open to query. (Bartlett, 1994: xi. Original italics)

Perhaps those of us who are childless by choice and those of us who are childless by circumstance can support one another in being part of this minority, given the potential high personal cost of being a minority. We can be, in Gillespie's words (2001: 143) part of the 'new femininity' which is arising from women increasingly engaging in broader social roles and more paid work, leading to new discourses on womanhood (Gillespie, 1999). We can not only raise awareness and create a more healthy dialogue around the diverse reasons why people remain childless, but also share notes on how it is to be part of this minority, rather than silenced by the prevailing pronatal norms, regardless of the reason for our childlessness.

I am aware acutely of this in my own personal experience of being a childless woman. I have absolutely no interest in going round preaching the benefits of intentional childlessness as preferable to childbearing, and I would prefer it if my decision-making process and my decision to remain childless were equally respected. I find it particularly inspiring and refreshing when I have discussions about my life with dear friends who are mums. It feels liberating to understand how they are, what motherhood means and what it does not mean to them and how central it is to their life, as well as their joys, frustrations and resentments.

For me this sharing of experience is important whether or not we are parents. It can also practically be difficult to orchestrate. I know that I have lost contact with friends, particularly when their children are young and our timetables and priorities rarely coincide. I was surprised by the response when my first article about voluntary childlessness was published in a therapy publication (Kamalamani, 2009). Women who were not mothers both by choice and by circumstance wrote and thanked me for the article, encouraging me in my future work. It is time that the voices of this often invisible group of men and women are heard, given that they have an important role to play in voicing how and why they decided not to have children, broadening the expectations, norms, and horizons of today's consensus reality.

In the meantime, let's remember the words of Polly Higgins, as we take our place in the world as women – and men – who happened to decide to not have children:

Greatness brings with it a challenge: stay safe and play safe or be open to a very different kind of adventure. It is not about feeling better – it is about getting better at feeling what it is to be truly alive. I can honestly say that when you dare to be great, your life will never be dull. (Higgins, 2014: Prologue)

A pregnant pause

If you are without child notice whether the idea of being part of a minority is a familiar one. Does it feel uncomfortable, or okay, or even supportive, knowing you are not alone in this minority? Take time to think through how, why, when and whether you have felt at the edges of mainstream life as a result of not having had children. What has, or would, support you in feeling part of a childless minority? To what extent do you see yourself as part of a movement of people developing new ways of living? Reflect on whether that feels attractive or daunting. In what ways have you been aware of creating a new awareness of intentional childlessness, even if only within your own circle of family and friends? What have you learned about your own decision-making process from friends who are parents?

Chapter 32

Ebbs and flows: never saying never?

> I do not have children, and I am not sure if I have wanted them or never wanted them. It is weird not to be able to decide. (Cho, 2013)

For most of us the desire to procreate follows a winding rather than a linear path, with stops and starts, unless, that is, it was clear to you from early life that you did not want to become a parent. Or perhaps you experienced bouts of baby urges, or never even questioned the thought of having children until recently, assuming that this was your destiny.

Part of your post-decision-making landscape might be understanding more fully the ebbs and flows of your own process, becoming more emotionally literate, maybe more at ease in relationship to your own doubt and restlessness. It can be a significant watershed to finally decide that you are never going to try for children, and from what I can ascertain I am not sure that all that many people come to a conscious 'never' decision. I used to find it interesting to occasionally review my own decision-making process with greater water under the bridge between then and now. More latterly the decision seems quite remote and far less important than it once was.

This was not always the case. At one point in my late twenties this question was on my mind every month. And, of course, there may well be other stages yet to come in this process. I imagine that around the time of the menopause it might feel poignant to realize that my potential chance to bear children has passed. The 'baby question' generates its own sense of urgency and immediacy at different times and in as many different ways as there are people on the planet, with the decision-making process having its own ebbs and flows. As I recollect the ebbs and flows in my decision-making process, track your own, perhaps noticing similarities and differences, if that is helpful.

Different life cycles bring a range of insights, struggles and questions. I was at my most 'broody' at 19. I experienced a strong, sudden, physical urge to have a child and was shocked at the strength of my instinct, the dramatic yo-yoing of adolescent hormones.

I experienced a milder set of baby urge pangs after the death of my grandmother in my mid twenties. I knew that I did not want children with the man I was with, so the urge was not strong enough to override the reality of how I felt about my ex and our relationship. I was somewhat surprised when I did not have a huge upsurge of desire to have a child after the death of my father when I was 32. Given the circumstances of his death, which I wrote about in Part II, I can see why this might have been the case.

During the process of preparing to be ordained as a Buddhist I spent a fair amount of time talking to other women – mothers and non-mothers alike – and thinking through my own response. A central part in preparing for ordination is becoming as clear as you can about the conditions which are most conducive to practice a life of meditation, study, spiritual friendship etc. That is not to say that women do not have children after being ordained, it is more that the ordination process itself, usefully, is an invitation to intensify and focus one's conditions for practice.

Having reached the gradual decision to not have children, there have been further ebbs and flows. This has been reflected in my approach to writing this book. When I first started writing this at the age of 31 it was just too hot a topic to write about! I was still too full of the fear of 'what will people think if I write about that?' and 'but what if I change my mind and suddenly wake up and want children?'

Picking up this writing project nearly 11 years later in my

early forties was an altogether different proposition. I have lived through the phases/stages that I talk about in this book, particularly in Part III. Namely: developing baby-sized projects, engaging more consciously with ancestral healing, acknowledging that I am in a minority, and having been given the gift of confidence, often in the form of other childless women wanting to read my book, to help make sense of their own decision-making process.

What cut the difference in the ebbing and flowing of this decision-making process for me was the day I realized that deciding not to have children is not an ending, it is a beginning, and the chance to decide to do something other than procreate. It is not necessarily about loss and doom and gloom – as it is sometimes portrayed or maybe misunderstood through others' projected sympathy – but a potential gain and a different expression of creativity and nurturing.

This may sound obvious, but it was not at all obvious when I was in my twenties or early thirties. It took some time to realize the extent of the impact of my own conditioning upon both my decision to remain childless and my ability and capacity to conceptualize and write about it without focusing on lack rather than choice and abundance. In mainstream culture not only is bearing children seen as the 'norm', but childlessness is still often presented in terms of lack, loss, grief, and loneliness.

Deciding not to try for children, and naming that process, felt like a significant coming out. I was acutely aware of being part of a minority. This might be quite different for you. Until recently I have found it hard to be straight and honest about that decision without feeling a nagging urge to explain, justify, water down, or politely change the subject. Perhaps this is because I fell into the 'I will have children one day' camp or, in the words of Berrington (2004) the 'perpetual postponers'. My intuitive sense is that I have a body which would be happy to go with making babies. I was never one of those (fortunate?) women who said 'oh no, I have never wanted children, it's just never been important to me'.

So it is something of a relief to sit here at 44 and feel equanimity surrounding the question of procreation. As I write, a young mother feeds her baby behind me in the cafe where I am sitting. I am acutely aware of the beauty of newness and possibility associated with this tiny new life. I no longer automatically jump to a fleeting sense of 'I'll never do that', as I see the woman breast feed. The thought of that loss no longer occurs to me. Instead I feel glad to be sitting here writing; creation in another form, all under one roof.

I am reminded again of the Buddhist teaching to which I referred in the introduction and in Part I: the eight worldly winds of pleasure and pain, loss and gain, fame and infamy and praise and blame. I am struck by how much of the arena of childbirth and rearing (or not) are subject to pleasure and pain, loss and gain and praise and blame in particular. In terms of pleasure and pain I see the pleasure in the eyes of my breast-feeding cafe neighbor, contrasted with the immense pain of a friend who has been through two rounds of failed IVF treatment. I am reminded of the praise a woman can receive for being a good mum contrasted with the blaming of women who decide to not have children, sometimes being accused of being selfish and self-centered.

The Dharma, the teachings of the Buddha, point out how hard the worldly winds blow through our lives much of the time. We can resist and react to them or we can gradually learn to see them for what they are; the inevitable ups and downs of life:

...they (the worldly winds) can teach us about the texture of life. They can reveal its heights and depths. They can show us ourselves at our noblest and our most petty. They can draw from us new qualities and dimensions of being. (Vajragupta, 2011: 106)

Reverie

Track your journey in both wanting and not wanting to have a child. There may have been times when the desire to procreate was stronger than others. Pay attention to your thoughts, reflections, dreams, and conversations as you follow this journey. Remember the events and triggers which surrounded those changing urges. Notice whether your reflections around whether or not to have children followed a linear, or somewhat more circuitous path. Did you decide at some point that you would never have children? Can you relate to yourself as a 'perpetual postponer' when it comes to this decision? (Berrington, 2004) Recall when you started to know for sure that you didn't want children. What situation were you in and when did you make that decision? Can you relate to me saying that stating openly that I would not be having children felt like something of a 'coming out'? Has it felt similar or quite different to you? If yes, what was the most important thing you learned about yourself from that experience?

Chapter 33

Landscapes of the body and divine women

The varied lives of women who are not mothers support the idea that motherhood is more of a culturally embedded mandate than a biological or psychological mandate. (Ireland, 1993: 138)

The electric moments of all creation still in your body. Despite everything, be it grief, be it fear, making you glad. The story of how it all began being told inside you. And youf own birth and your own death, every passing and all that is coming to be in your body too. The entire wave, washing through you, in you, even at this instant, taking you now. (Griffin, 1999: 328)

My relationship with my body continues to change as I enter my middle years. Things happen; not just the obvious, visible stuff, like wrinkles, cellulite, and a greater ease in being in my own skin, but a greater attunement to my body's processes and cycles. This is, in part, due to my body awareness, and my relationship with others' bodies, which has deepened through working as a Body Psychotherapist and writing a book concerned with this theme (Kamalamani, 2012).

This relationship has also been influenced by my choice to not become a mother, as I explored in the earlier chapter 'Occupying your body in taking your place on earth'. These days the landscape of my body is my land, my earth, the place to which I am drawn after a long day, a highly-tuned resource in my work as a therapist, the place into which I retreat when lonely and frightened, and the land I share with friends and lovers in joy and pain. Provisionally, at least, my body is the way I conceive of 'my place' on earth, which is kind of handy, given that I take it with me wherever I go.

The more I understand and practice ecopsychology – the study and practice of human relationship with the other-than-human – the more I feel at home in my body, at home on the earth, and at home in terms of being with a wider body of people with whom I feel connected. Robinson defines ecopsychology beautifully:

> In Greek, *oikos* or 'eco' means 'home', *psyche* is 'soul', and *logos* is the 'word' or the 'story'. So a poetic translation might be 'the story of the home of the soul' or 'the story of the soul of home.' (Robinson, 2009: 26. Original italics)

The landscape of my body is my place on earth, in a moving, transient form. It was my beginning place, as I became incarnate, and will take me (or, rather, I will be taken) to my final physical resting place in this skin; returning to the earth as a decaying body or ashes. There is no other place which feels so much like 'mine'. And, of course, this body is not me and is not mine, either. I continually borrow the elements and live in intimate connection with them on a daily basis, whether or not I realize that truth. I drink water then pee water. I constantly borrow air to breathe as I move through this shared space of life on earth. The more I inhabit and dwell in my body, the more I can give attention to the work that I need to do, and the less chance I have of falling into 'spiritual bypassing', the term Welwood coins in noticing how a spiritual seeker can 'avoid dealing with their emotional unfinished business' (Welwood, 2000: 5).

My sense of home has gradually drawn inwards, rather than being an outer place. In parallel, I realize more and more all the webs of life in which I am entangled and woven. Perhaps through experiencing the safety and location of a provisional home, in and through my body, the totality of my life energies have the freedom to extend far beyond the earlier more limited self view of what is me and mine.

It has taken until my early forties to get a sense of my own embodied identity as a woman who is not a mother or, as described earlier, a girl destined to be a mother 'one day'. It has taken me years to figure out what it means, and how it looks and feels, to be a woman without having created a child, particularly in a society in which childless female role models are few and far between – although thankfully gaining more attention in recent years. I mentioned in passing, to a woman who came to one of my meditation days, that I was writing about embodiment from the point of view of childlessness. Her response was fascinating, informed by the fact she is a mum and has recently finished writing about embodiment for her PhD:

> I am very curious about what the embodied meaning is for you regarding not becoming a mother. For me, pregnancy, breast feeding, and all the many other mum bits are so much inscribed on my body and part of body memory...but then so is so much other life experience that in combination is my unique body signature. (Personal communication with Woodspring, 2013)

I, too, imagined until my thirties that pregnancy, giving birth, and breast-feeding would be inscribed upon my body. So this post-decision horizon has been a time of realizing and digesting, on an embodied level, that this isn't what is happening now. This has been a process of updating myself with what is true now, and now, and now, compared to the 'one day' myth of becoming a mother. And, of course, I still have a woman's body! If I choose, I can still honor and learn from the changing cycles of my body each month, rather than ignore them, and I can decide to age and grow older gracefully.

The process of reclaiming my body has paralleled a time of witnessing some friends and family being largely occupied with baby-making and rearing. Conception and birth are miracles, whether in human or the billions of other species of life. It can be curious to not be conceiving and giving birth, whilst seeing it all around you. It has made me realize that birth is not the only creative miracle. Each stage of our life offers endings and new beginnings, and the more we notice and honor these, the more fully we can be who we are and know how to live. For me, it has been a relief to grow into a more comfortable relationship with being flesh, bone, blood, still channeling and expressing creativity and care without being a mother.

The landscapes of our bodies are shaped by the landscapes of our minds and cultural impacts upon this landscape. There is a lot going on here, which I find increasingly fascinating in my work as an ecopsychologist and in supporting the women who visit my therapy room to love and accept their bodies. Accepting their bodies as they find them, from the inside, rather than judging them from the outside and how they 'should' look, often through the critical eyes of others and societal messages. My wish is for all of us to come to a point of reconciliation, or even a suggestion of reconciliation, in which we can accept our bodies, our rich lives embedded in our bodies – mother or other – rather than judge our flesh and blood from an externally-oriented, largely paternalistic, white, wealthy, 'able-bodied', cosmeticized, fashionista agenda which prevails in mainstream views of bodies. And, in parallel, challenge the patriarchal viewpoints which police the rules and norms about how we 'should' look and behave.

The traditional female rites of passage and archetypes tend to include motherhood, for example: maiden, mother, crone. This makes it interesting to know how to make sense of one's embodied identity when it is devoid of procreation. Where do we fit in this schema if we are without child? Do we need a new schema? Or do we put up with being the minority at the margins? How do those of us who are childless women relate to this all-important archetypal level with a major archetype – mother – missing? You might argue that this is irrelevant and abstract, but I would disagree, given the vital role archetypes play in our psychic patterning which shapes everyday life.

Fortunately there are goddesses who are childless, but it takes a bit of researching to uncover them – they are not big in popular culture. This is a shame, because they are important figures in their own right. For me the virgin goddesses of Artemis, Athena and Hestia are important to bear in mind, as are the Buddhist female deities, such as Prajnaparamita, who is seen as the mother of all the Buddhas, rather than earthly mothers. There are plenty of examples of divine childless women....

Perhaps an important next phase for us collectively is to encourage the creation of a culture in which newly envisioned or largely forgotten female archetypes can breathe fresh, new life into the mythical, archetypal realm. In that way we can encourage diversity, bridging the gap between difference and acknowledging the place and role of women who choose to remain childless. Role models which embody the childfree, extending far beyond the over-worked, inaccurate view of the stereotypes of the childless woman either being career-driven, vocationally guided, or religiously-converted women.

Why does it matter to enliven our archetypal landscape? Because if the landscapes of our bodies are determined, or at least shaped, by prevailing symbols of what it means to be female, then we need to look at non-mother symbols, rather than symbols which focus on our status as a mother, wife and home-maker alone. It is also important to guard against a utilitarian view of our female bodies. I have caught myself, during my most intense moments of period pain, wondering what the point is in periods and hormones when I am not even making babies. That view can be crystallized by the mainstream view that we are not proper women if we have not made babies. So we need a live exploration of how it is to be childless at different stages in our lives, as important in our peri and menopausal phases as when we are in the prime of childbearing.

Landscapes consist of many different textures, colors, shapes, formations, histories and interrelationships with human use, and, at times, abuse. Let us respect women and men, whether parents or childless, to explore and be at ease with their own bodily landscapes. As Morell so eloquently says:

Childless women, whether childless by choice, chance or circumstance, need a symbolic world that affirms a child-free life as normal, imaginable and desirable. To think about childlessness in new ways calls for the development of alternative vocabularies and thought models that reinscribe the validity of a child-free life. (Morell, 2000: 321)

Reveries

Dwell on these themes, or, more importantly, invite your body to turn over the themes of this chapter as you go to bed at night, listening to what your body has got to say...

How have the landscapes of your body changed over time? Notice whether the decision to bear children, or not, has influenced your embodiment; your experience of being a body. Did you or do you think that being a mum would be 'inscribed' on your body and body memory? Are there particular archetypes, maybe goddesses or maybe other role models, which you have found powerful in mulling over the baby question? What do you make of Morell's words, calling for a 'symbolic world that affirms a child-free life as normal, imaginable and desirable'.

How might you contribute to the creation of that symbolic world as you choose childlessness? Writers, artists, musicians, therapists, amongst other practitioners

---

in all walks of life have a role to play in not only normalizing, but also creating positive images and narratives around childlessness. I am mindful of quote I have just heard from Ursula Le Guin during an acceptance speech given at the 65th National Book Awards in the USA:

I think hard times are coming when we'll be wanting the voices of writers who can see alternatives to how we live now and can see through our fear-stricken society and its obsessive technologies to other ways of being, and even imagine some real grounds for hope. We will need writers who can remember freedom. Poets, visionaries – the realists of a larger reality. (Le Guin, 2014)

Chapter 34

Inspiring women

> Philosophers, artists, writers, travelers, political activists, nuns, nurses and doctors all rank amongst the child-free women who make up our heritage. But these women have been the exceptions, drawn away from motherhood by their talents. Now ordinary women too have a choice... (Bartlett, 1994: 189)

I have been fortunate in being helped along the way in my decision-making by other women who have happened to, or decided not to have children. The women below; living or dead, personally known or unknown to me, have been an inspiration in the way they have chosen to live their lives.

Elizabeth I (1533-1603). I admire Elizabeth's clarity and steeliness, from such a tragic childhood of loss, betrayal and cruelty. From what I read and understand she was a lot more than just clear-headed and steely. To rule England for 45 years seems admirable in itself, let alone bearing in mind the times in which she was Queen of England.

Georgia O' Keefe (1887-1986) was the first woman of more modern times who came to my attention as someone who was consciously childless. Keefe was a New York actress and artist. I will be honest, I did not know much about her apart from the fact that I love her work.

Joan of Arc (1412-1431), the awesome French freedom fighter. She would certainly be someone I would add to my fantasy dinner party guest list.

Julian of Norwich (1342-1416). The English anchoress – which means one who has retired from, or in Buddhist parlance, 'gone forth' from the world – who lived in the 14th and 15th centuries, is often regarded as one of the most important of the Christian mystics, even though she has never been canonized or beatified. She must also have been a radical optimist, being credited with writing the well-known verse: 'all shall be well, and all shall be well and all manner of things shall be well' (Norwich, 1998: 80). What's more, *Revelations of Divine Love*, her work of 1395, is the first book in the English language known to have been written by a woman (UNESCO, 2012).

Lottie (1878-1967), my maternal great grandmother, to whom this book is dedicated. Lottie apparently made no secret of the fact that she never wanted children and ended up having eight. It mightn't have been so great for her children's sense of self worth that she was an ambivalent mother, but I appreciate knowing that I am not alone in my desire not to reproduce, and feel fortunate living in an age with effective contraception.

Maitreyi, my friend and preceptor; the woman who ordained me as a Buddhist. I respect deeply Maitreyi's life of service to the Buddhist order to which I belong. She certainly lives up to her name: 'the kindly one'.

And lastly, and by no means least, my appreciation to Stephanie Mills, who kindly wrote this book's foreword, and whose work I talked about in the introduction. When I have wavered in this writing project I have thought of Stephanie delivering her college graduation speech 'The Future is a Cruel Hoax' back in 1969, announcing to her class mates that the most humane thing for her to do is to have no children at all.

A pregnant pause

Bring to mind your most important role models. Perhaps some are without child, living lives which may have taught you something valuable about childlessness. Think back to your reflections at the end of the 'By the time I'm 30'

---

chapter. For whom are *you* now a role model? What qualities, experiences and characteristics do you embody and exemplify which are invaluable to the next generation? Take time with this – and remember that no one has to look at your reflections! – as you identify and acknowledge the inspiration you bring to the people and the world around you. Are there similarities between those who inspire you – maybe similar qualities, or lives? What light does this shed on how you wish to live the rest of your life?

Chapter 35

Going forth

Enlightened wisdom sees the interdependence of all beings and forgoes the fiction of private choices that do not impinge on the rest of the matrix of life. Enlightened compassion cherishes all beings, not merely one's family, tribe, nation, or species, as worthy of one's care and concern. (Gross, 1997: 306)

In many Buddhist traditions 'going forth' refers to the act of leaving behind the known, the familiar, and the predictable and taking a leap of faith into the unknown, with the intention of committing more of one's energy to Dharma practice and contemplation. Going forth traditionally refers to the act of monks and nuns leaving their home or monastery for the homeless, or non-home-owning, possession-less life, moving from worldly complexity towards stillness, simplicity and contentment. Bringing stillness, simplicity and contentment into one's life is itself an important 'precept' or training principle in Buddhist practice. As in many traditions, going forth is a process that is encouraged within the order and movement within which I practice.

Going forth can also refer to the giving up of certain views and actions in moving towards new ways of being. So you do not always have to leave home to go forth, although some friends practice 'brahma carya'; going forth from home ownership and sexual relationships in pursuing a simpler, celibate life through which they can go deeper in their practice of meditation and the Dharma. In creating the conditions conducive to spiritual practice, going forth is a spiritual act with potentially far reaching consequences. Perhaps the best known example of going forth is Siddhartha Gautama, the historical Buddha, leaving home on his path towards enlightenment at the age of 29 (see Blomfield, 2012).

Of course, you do not have to be the Buddha to practice going forth. Going forth without following the traditional path of leaving home can consist in gradually letting go of views, assumptions or behaviors, which are limiting or constricting. In going forth from one thing, we are moving towards something else. Perhaps a new, or at least, slightly different reality to the one we might have once imagined, as we engage more deeply in our spiritual practice.

A small example of going forth in my pre-Buddhist life was becoming a vegetarian when I was 15, which I mentioned earlier. For years I had felt growing unease towards eating animals. This was compounded by learning about factory farming, animal cruelty and the tampering with animals being bred for their meat. Becoming a vegetarian was a going forth from being a meat-eater to being an herbivore, deciding to limit the harm whilst meeting my own nutritional needs and wants.

The decision to become a vegetarian was an act of going forth because it was concerned with giving up one set of actions and moving towards a new way of relating to animals, causing less harm. It was also a going forth in as much as it meant I was a bit different to those around me – vegetarianism was not quite so commonplace in the mid 1980s. It was interesting, and painful, seeing how others saw me in the light of my decision to become vegetarian. Whilst I felt more congruent, more in line with how I wanted to live my life, and less conflicted when faced with a chunk of meat, I was surprised to find that others were threatened and skeptical, waiting for this odd phase to come to an end.

Choosing to not have children has been a strong, long-term process of going forth throughout my twenties, thirties, and, to a lesser extent, in my early forties. In many ways, having children would have made sense to me. I like children, they often seem to like me. I hope I would have been a diligent mother, and loving and playful too. My family members, and those of my partner, would have been delighted had we decided to try for children: more cousins for playing, more babies to coo over, more interesting conversations about child-rearing, child-bearing, parenting, education, and the creation of precious new lives.

I have realized that going forth as an act comes about in stages – or more aptly, in scenes! – as has my decision to not have children. My first tentative steps towards provisionally deciding to not have children are now far behind me. A process took place in which I moved from focusing on a provisional decision not to have children, to a more definite decision to remain childless. Between the provisional and the definite there was a phase of great uncertainty; a kind of no man's and no woman's land. This is an apt description from a societal point of view, given that we are in the throes of figuring out – individually and collectively – how to define women who do not have children, aside from the established and long outdated labels 'spinster', 'barren', or 'career woman'.

The shifts between choosing not to have children and identifying as definitely being 'out there' as childless have been subtle ones, with no easily identifiable stages. There have been important landmarks along the way. It has taken a few 'baby-sized projects' to feel a sense of ease – even liberation, to be honest – at being childless.

Like all acts of going forth, there have been long nights of the soul. There have been the poignant existential pangs I have mentioned, recognizing that I will have no direct descendents, and when my life ends it will be business as normal for all bar the grieving of a handful of friends and family. There is also the loss of the societal status of being a mother, living in the archetypal half light somewhere between marrying maiden and crone. The mother is a vital archetype to which, childless or not, we need to pay attention, whether or not we are earthly mothers. It offers the chance to nurture ourselves, others, and the world, and if we have no actual earthlings, our time is freer, with the potential for nurturing beyond what would traditionally be our immediate family.

I am fortunate in feeling a sense of resolution about not being a mother. These days I have more creative outlets than ever, including nurturing roles where my care and attention matters. I have realized many of my work dreams and ambitions. I have a fulfilling and often demanding practice of the Dharma and meditation, which gives me the ethical tools and potential for a transcendental perspective – albeit fleeing. I am, in short, blessed. Not complacent, and it has not all been plain sailing, but blessed with interesting work, mainly good enough health, good friends and a community of fellow Buddhist practitioners refining the art of muddling through with the help of the three jewels: the Buddha, Dharma and Sangha.

I would urge all women who decide not to try for children to think carefully about life as a non-mother and the social and cultural implications of that. I tend to move in circles where I know several women of my age who are without child, as well as knowing lots of friends with children, so I am in a relatively supportive context in the face of the more extreme pronatal societal prejudices. I think it is important to think through how the decision not to have children will pan out in the long run, particularly in terms of social support.

Of course none of us can know how life will be, with its twists and turns, and I am not encouraging too much speculation, but do think through your friendships, networks and family contexts in thinking through being a childless woman at 50, as well as at 32. I am free to write, see clients, see friends, babysit for my nephew and nieces and a whole host of other things. I can meditate and follow a changeable routine. This would be far less the case had I decided to become a Mum. However, I am in the

fortunate situation of being surrounded by people who understand and largely accept the decision of me and my partner to not
have children, which is not the case for everyone.

Going forth and living from a greater awareness of the
practice of stillness, simplicity and contentment can give rise to a
strong sense of freedom: freedom to choose and freedom to act. I
certainly appreciate that freedom in my own life, and I am also
well aware of the tyranny of not choosing and living in a constant
state of not being able to commit to anything: people, events, our
lives, even everyday decisions. What has been most significant in
the act of going forth from having children is letting go of the
idea of myself as first and foremost a mother. I, and thousands of
women like me, have stepped into less known, less culturally
affirmed roles. In this moving away from being 'mum' I move
towards a whole host of other opportunities. What most holds
my attention is finding new forms of creative and nurturing
expression in my life; hopefully a life which is of benefit to
others, not just me, and in supporting others who are childless to
find their own creative, nurturing expression.

A pregnant pause

Going forth may well be an alien notion to you – it was to
me before I started practicing Buddhism, apart from
knowing a few monks who chose to live simply, stepping
away from material concerns. Notice your responses to
going forth – whether it attracts or repels you as you
ponder the following questions:

Does the notion of 'going forth' make sense to you?
Does it appeal to you in terms of increasing the conditions
for stillness, simplicity and contentment? Think of the
times in your own life when you have 'gone forth', even if
you may not have given it that name.

Which habits or life circumstances would you like to go forth from in your life? If you are without child, has letting go of the role of mum or dad felt like a going forth, in terms of your identity and life purpose? Notice the feelings accompanying that sense of letting go.

Chapter 36

Big mind and parental mind

Early in Part I of this book I introduced a traditional Buddhist teaching called the metta sutta. I was reflecting on how the world might be if we paid attention to the part of the sutta which says: 'a mother's mind for her baby, her love, but now unbounded'. I asked how it might be to live in a world in which we each felt that boundless love towards one another – and other-than-human life.

Zen Buddhism takes this one step further in terms of introducing what is known as 'big mind' and 'parental mind'. When we experience big mind every single thing, every single person we encounter becomes our life, so long as we are able to: 'throw out our ordinary way of viewing things' (Kōshō Uchiyama Rōshi, 2005: 51). I love this notion – that whatever we encounter, whoever we encounter, is our life, becomes our life. This flies in the face of our habitual ways of seeking to create, plan, and control circumstances, events and people, in creating our own sense of identity and building our egos. As Shoshanna points out:

> Just stop looking for what is wrong with the other and what is right with us. Stop looking out for number one. In fact, number one includes everyone....In order to develop Parental Mind, we must take ultimate responsibility for everything that appears in our lives. We do not choose one thing and reject another – the homeless man on the street is just as precious as our own child. (Shoshanna, 2004: 89)

If we decide to devote our entire life to each and everything that we encounter, practicing 'big mind', the notion of 'parental mind' starts to make more sense. Parental mind is the notion that whatever we are doing, whoever we are relating to, we do that task, or we act with the same caring attitude of a parent towards his or her child. In the words of Dogen:

> Whether you are the head of a temple, a senior monk or other officer, or simply an ordinary monk, do not forget the attitude behind living out your life with joy, having the deep concern of a parent, and carrying out all your activities with magnanimity. (Dogen, 1237, translated by Kyokun, see web source)

Practicing and cultivating the qualities of deep magnanimity give rise to this sense of being a parent to all that lives, with a loving, caring, wise, all-encompassing orientation to life. Whether or not we physically conceive, give birth, or rear children, according to this teaching and practice we can still have that 'parental mind' for all that lives. It is important to know that this love extends beyond the human realm, to the other and more-than-human life. It is said that when the Buddha attained enlightenment – waking up and becoming completely wise and kind – he said: 'I attained the way simultaneously with the whole world and all sentient beings. Everything – mountains, rivers, trees, grasses – all attained Buddhahood' (quoted in Kōshō Uchiyama Rōshi, 2005: 51).

Reverie

I find these teachings inspiring and mind expanding! We can act as parents without producing more earthlings, if we adopt big mind and parental mind. I also find it reassuring that the Buddha saw the potential for enlightenment in all of life, flying in the face of Buddhism

---

sometimes being portrayed as a rather dry, detached form of philosophy. See what you make of the teachings of 'big mind' and 'parental mind'. Do they seem far-fetched, or can you imagine how they could be helpful in throwing light on how to live creatively and with self and other in mind, giving expression to parental qualities?

Chapter 37

Stillness, simplicity, and contentment

As time passes I increasingly realize there is an interior dimension to silence, a sort of stillness of heart and mind which is not a void but a rich space. What became obvious to me as I thought about this is that for me there is a chasm of difference between qualities like quietness or peace and silence itself. (Maitland, 2009: 26)

At the point of ordination as a Buddhist I took up ten traditional Buddhist precepts, rather akin to training principles. The third one of these was to abstain from sexual misconduct. In its positive form, this precept is expressed as: 'with stillness, simplicity and contentment I purify my body' (FWBO, 1999). Contentment is the opposite of sexual misconduct. It is easy, culturally approved, in fact, to be intoxicated. There are the obvious intoxicants like sex, drugs, food, and alcohol, through to the less obvious, such as watching TV to the point of being Zombie-like and craving all forms of stimulation and distraction. Then there are all the degrees of subtlety in how we live a life infused with stillness, simplicity and contentment in a mainstream culture largely obsessed by distraction and a constant craving for the next best thing or attainment: car, facelift, house, job, and partner. On the surface, the precept sounds idyllic and easy to practice. In reality it is deeply counter-cultural.

I was struck by the resonance between this third precept and the point of view of a seasoned ecologist friend who thinks the main way forward in terms of doing less harm to the planet is to simply do less: drive less, fly less, eat less, look seriously at how we live and slow it all down. Again, this suggestion sounds so obvious, almost too simple. Yet if all of us, especially in so-called more developed countries, practiced doing less there would be profound consequences for our use of carbon, let alone our peace of mind and contentment levels, once we became re-acquainted with our own company and a slower pace of life, which might in itself create something of a social revolution. It feels like we have got a way to go in being prepared to understand our contribution to carbon usage, to have the capacity to look at the distressing prediction about climate chaos, let alone being able to envisage a post-carbon world.

The third precept 'with stillness, simplicity and contentment I purify my body' can take us a long way, personally and collectively. This precept can be misread as being about passivity, as could the notion of doing less. For me this is not about a complacent contentment, quite the opposite. The more spacious my mind, the more capacity I have to engage with what matters, a bit like the reminder from the previous chapter to adopt big mind or parental mind. When I am in a mindful and emotionally robust state, the flotsam and jetsam of everyday life (the car breaking down, bills needing paying, difficult communication around me) is less preoccupying and I can keep a broader horizon beyond me and mine.

Of course, the flotsam and jetsam of everyday life is our lives and how we engage with those things is an important part of practice. Personally, I do not find it all that helpful drawing a distinction between what some call the 'mundane' and the 'spiritual'. To me, how we live our everyday lives is a reflection of the effectiveness of our practice – the meeting place of the so-called 'mundane' and 'spiritual'. My practice is not in some other place, waiting for the time when I am kind and wise enough to engage. It is right here this minute. Do I order my tea respectfully, taking in the other person, or am I rushing and disregarding the woman on the cash till? Those things matter – the minutiae of our lives and relationships.

I am interested in that minutiae yet I do not want to become obsessed with it – becoming too locked in to my own little life, at the cost of having a broader duty of care to other beings and important actions which have an influence well beyond my life. What is conducive to stillness, simplicity and contentment? For me it is regular meditation, writing, and spending time outdoors, remembering my place in things and getting my shoes muddy, rather than having an intense relationship with my laptop.

I am glad that I have the time to reflect on the precepts and time to keep a broader horizon, which gives me the capacity to work as a therapist and the chance to write books like this one. If I were in the midst of motherhood I know it would be much harder to practice the precept of stillness, simplicity, and contentment. This is partly because of the considerable practical, physical, emotional and time demands of being a parent, partly the societal pressure I see being put upon parents, and partly because of the pace of life itself.

I feel like a tightrope walker in a constant balancing act between being and acting 'in the world', as the phrase goes, punctuated by quieter contemplation, roaming outside, and reflection. In the next chapter I will introduce the bodhisattva called Red Tara. A key aspect of both Red Tara's and Green Tara's symbolism is that these female figures are seated in a posture with one leg up, one leg down, reflecting the enlightened balance between the life of the bodhisattva saving all sentient beings, reflected in her leg stepping down to the world, and her other leg tucked up in meditation posture, meditating, reflecting and turning inwards. For me this balance is very much part of the horizon of being voluntarily childless. I am pretty sure I would not be able to do these things and bring up children. That is not to say you cannot have a rich, fulfilling practice bringing up children, of course you can, and people do. And, of course, the natural priority of most parents is the welfare of their children and family, with all their joys and demands. More and more I think that this time in earth's history – and all of our histories – could do with more people doing less and reflecting more. Practicing stillness, simplicity, and contentment for the benefit of ourselves, others and the world.

Reverie

Notice how you have felt whilst reading this chapter. See whether the notion of 'stillness, simplicity and contentment' is attractive or a bit threatening and unfamiliar in your experience. Take time in exploring your own relationship with silence, peace, simplicity, and stillness. Are these aspects of life conducive to contentment for you, or are you more at ease when you are busy and doing things? How has your experience of yourself changed when you have had periods of more stillness and silence? What do you make of the idea that the world could do with people doing less and reflecting more? Does that make sense to you in deciding to be without child?

Chapter 38

Red Tara's fascination and boundless love

> *Mettā* is a beautiful word, just five letters signifying the purity
> of our own heart, the heart essence, often obscured yet always
> available. (Khema, 1991: 26, original italics)

I love the richness of meditation practice and the cosmology of
Tibetan Buddhism. When I first started to practice I most appreciated the commonsense, road map like guidance of the Dharma,
the teachings of the Buddha and the Buddhist path. Nowadays I
wonder at the diversity of teachings, organizing around the
centrifugal practice of going for refuge to the Buddha, Dharma
and Sangha.

By 'going for refuge' I mean continually placing the example
of the Buddha, the teachings of the Dharma, and the connection
of the Sangha, or spiritual community, at the heart of my life.
Back in 1995 I would never have imagined that I would
encounter a bodhisattva carrying a bow and arrow made of tiny,
beautiful lotus flowers. That is until she appeared in my
dreaming consciousness not long after my ordination. At that
point I did not know about the bow and arrow, just this nagging
and alluring sense of the color red in enlightened, female form
whenever I sat to meditate.

In Tibetan Buddhist cosmology this alluring bodhisattva
figure is known as Red Tara. She is a particular aspect of Tara,
who is a well-known and well-loved bodhisattva embodying the
enlightened quality of compassion. Aspects of Red Tara's
symbolism are similar to her spiritual sister, Green Tara. She is
also seated in a posture with one leg up, one leg down. As I said
at the end of the last chapter, this signifies the enlightened
balance between the life of the bodhisattva saving all sentient

beings: one leg stepping down to the world, and the other leg tucked up in meditation posture, contemplating, reflecting and turning inwards. I am also drawn to Tara's compassion and her care for all that lives: '...[Tara] has a mother's compassion and instant response to suffering. She cares for all beings as though each were her only child. Like a mother she is very accepting' (Vessantara, 1993: 177).

In one of Red Tara's hands is a vase of the nectar of immortality. In the other she holds the stem of a lotus flower. Balanced at the calyx of the flower is an exquisite bow and arrow made of tiny, perfectly formed white lotus flowers. Red Tara fires arrows into the hearts of humans, symbolically at least, so that they fall in love with the Buddha, Dharma and Sangha. Red Tara is a transcendental enchantress. In terms of the Tantric 'rites', she represents the rite of fascination and deep compassion for all lives. She shows us how loving-kindness can be extended to all beings in the way she is stepping down into the world, as well as her unending attempts to capture the hearts of men and women everywhere.

I love the fact that there is a bodhisattva originating from the Tibetan Buddhist tradition who uses a bow and arrow to light up our hearts with compassion, who fascinates us with her beautiful red form. She puts me in mind of an enlightened manifestation of the great huntress Artemis, who 'in the myths...acted swiftly and decisively to protect and rescue those who appealed to her for help' (Bolen, 1984: 47). What I appreciate most about the imagery linked to Red Tara and her rite of fascination is her desire to fascinate *all* beings, rather than just one special significant other, be that our lover, our child, our parent, sibling or best friend. She embodies the possibilities of how our hearts can feel and express, our love now unbounded and uncolored by the more narrow constrictions of romance, or parental love, or sibling love, or the love of friendship. Dwelling with Red Tara is not about making pretty pictures in one's mind eye:

The practice of Red Tara is a supreme vehicle for arousing both intellectual understanding and meditative realization of nondual awareness. While the name of Tara is Drolma, the name of this particular emanation as Red Tara is...Goddess Who Brings Forth One's Own Natural Awareness. (Khadro, 1986: 25)

I envisage a world in which we embody the scope of this compassion and care for all sentient beings. A world in which there would be less violence, less poverty, fewer orphans, refugees, and an end to torture, slavery and those left homeless by the ravages of war, soil erosion and climate chaos. A world in which we remember more often love, play, laughter, wisdom and abundance. I find myself wondering whether Red Tara's practice could fascinate us back into remembering and reconnecting with our sense of awe and wonder for the earth? I am not interested in romanticizing other-than-human life, but I would love it if we could find our way back to remembering that we are not the only species and that how we live currently is creating suffering and extinction, and if left unchecked, will lead to the demise of our own species in the not too distant future.

In the realm of Red Tara we are fascinated by and fascinate all beings, not just our one true love of our own son or daughter, but any being who happens to cross our path. We have the discriminating powers of the Buddha Amitabha to see the unique and particular beauty and characteristics of each individual, yet we do not discriminate in terms of who we love. This is refreshing in a world which can so over-emphasize romantic and parental love, at the cost of all of the myriad forms of love which exist.

The Red Door
by Padmavajra

O friends
I ask you
come
come to the red door
red door at the back of the heart

Just for a while
friends
leave the mind
that calculates and measures
and come
come to the red door
red door at the back of the heart

O friends
have courage
open the door
just a crack will do
be generous
be warm
have courage
open the door
red door at the back of the heart
Then, O friends
bliss from another world
will flood you
flood through the red door
red door at the back of the heart

For you must know
friends

that the red door
is a goddess
and she leads to the palace of wisdom

O friends
I ask you come
come to the red door
red door at the back of the heart

Chapter 39

Holding to nothing whatever

There are pleasures that one gives up when one decides not to have children. But as I keep telling myself: you cannot have everything. Choices have to be made, and consequences have to be lived with. The act of choosing inevitably brings loss. It is a difficult lesson to understand and accept. I keep trying to relearn it. (Klepfisz, 2000: 27-28)

Five years ago my friend and work colleague and his family suffered the most heartbreaking of human tragedies; his little daughter died. Suddenly, overnight. She was nearly two years old, a bright star of a little girl who was ready to play, laugh and who oozed life. Her Mum, Dad, and older sister have done amazingly well in living after such an incredible shock and loss.

I remember clearly hearing the news of her death. My brother called me that Sunday morning. Despite the regular chirpiness of his voice, I could tell intuitively that there was something devastatingly wrong. "There is some terrible news, I am afraid." I found myself blurting down the phone "not Thomas or Daisy – are they okay?" My first response, my absolute gut response, was to check on my nephew and niece. He assured me they were fine and went on to break the tragic news about my friend's daughter.

Sometime afterwards I felt humbled as I reflected on my response of "not Thomas or Daisy?" Remembering now, I can recall the tightly bound fear in the pit of my stomach at the thought of any danger coming to those young ones, my own flesh and blood. On an instinctual level there is something inherently wrong about the premature death of a child, which is particularly marked if it occurs in your own family.

Of course, I can intellectualize death and impermanence and

can see that my acceptance of the truth of impermanence is greater since meditating and practicing Buddhism. But when that impermanence comes knocking on the front door of our own homes there can be a glaring difference between what we like to think we know and what our guts tell us we actually know.

I am reminded of a memory of visiting my Dad in the oncology department of the Bristol Royal Infirmary during the last month of his life. I walked into the ward where he was resting. I was shocked to see this aged, shrunken, shadow of a man who bore a striking resemblance to my Dad, head back, asleep in an armchair. There was a screech inside me "NOT my Dad. Death can come and get everyone else but NOT my Dad". It was a sudden, shocking experience. Those of us who live in the West, in the 'more developed' world are cosseted from images of death, many of us living in relative material ease which seems to mean that we cannot take too much of the everyday realities of old age, sickness and death.

We – I – bargain with life in trying to make sense of what can sometimes seem like its absurdities and cruelties. Of course they are not absurdities and cruelties, if we see life as it is, without overlaying our own views, assumptions, expectations. Life's full of itself – and there is no life without death. Accidents happen, children die, relationships end, we get old and sick and die ourselves. The more we can align ourselves with these truths, even though it is a practice calling for huge courage, kindness, and patience, the more we are able to die well and live well.

I can only imagine the unthinkable heartbreak of my friend and his wife and daughter as they lived through their daughter's sudden, shocking death. I witnessed little pockets of their quiet hell. I saw the profound, empty, listlessness in their eyes and felt their deadened life energy. I imagine they got up and got dressed because they had to, with their older daughter to feed, nurture, reassure, love, and live for.

One day follows another and so on and so on and the

remarkable creatures that we are, we form new habits in vastly-altered realities. The trauma of losing her will always be with them, not far below the surface. I remember the horror in the air at her funeral. Grief is contagious, particularly amongst a community of parents and friends, with parents clutching for dear life onto their own children. I also remember the amount of love and appreciation and was struck by the creativity and beauty of her funeral arrangements. I remember the aftermath of the funeral. I visited my friend and his wife most weeks for a while; showed up, listened and tried to provide a link to their life as it had been, and would be again, in tremendously altered form. I am glad to have been able to show up and listen – it was the least I could do.

Perhaps I was a little more able to show up precisely because I did not have my own little beings back at home. Perhaps knowing of their daughter's death was too horrifying for those tucking their own small children up in bed. It was not so close to home for me to witness my friend's loss, because I have not, this lifetime at least, had a child to lose. Perhaps more of me could be there because I knew I did not have a child I could or can lose? I know the loss of not having a child, but not the loss or fear of losing a cherished son or daughter.

Having children changes our lives radically. I was struck when a friend gave birth for the first time, and, a few days later, declared that she now knew why she was on the planet. And I know many other friends who were not struck by the same sense of euphoria, in fact, they struggled to bond at first, even though they love their children. I remember another friend and a client voicing their fears that they simply would not be able to carry on if something happened to their children, given the strength of their bond.

In bringing to mind the worldly winds of loss and gain, pleasure and pain, which blow through the realm of child-bearing, I am reminded of the story of Kisa Gotami. Kisa is a young woman who is wracked with grief following the death of her baby. She goes to the Buddha desperately seeking a way of bringing her child back to life. The Buddha sets her one simple task: to bring back a single mustard seed from someone's home. The mustard seed, the Buddha said, must come from a home in which no one has ever died. Kisa Gotami sets about determinedly to find a seed. She goes to house after house, but simply cannot get a mustard seed, because she's unable to find a home where there has been no death. She returns to the Buddha, as it gradually dawns on her why he set her this task and she ends up following his teachings and slowly overcoming her grief.

I love this story; like all good stories it points to the truth that we can only know things through our own experience and awareness. I might know intellectually that all beings die, and I will die, but a substantial part of me does not want to accept it. It must be harder still, so much harder, to come to terms with the death of your child. For me, these stories are so precious in that they transmit the universal truths of suffering and loss, also pointing out that compassion is a way of going beyond these limitations.

What I also love about this story is that it highlights the Buddha's skill and care in the way he communicated with this despairing, grieving woman. He did not preach at her, or squash her grief with religious superiority. No, he set her a task, often beneficial for those consumed with grief, encouraging her to talk to others and discuss their losses in the doorway of each house she visited.

Impermanence is a continuous and constant feature of our everyday lives, taking shape all around us, all the time. We are born and we die as sure as spring follows winter. We cannot know the length of our own lives, or the lives of those we love. One aspect of the loss and freedom of being childless feels akin to a line from a renowned Buddhist teaching I practice: 'holding to nothing whatever, but dwelling in prajna wisdom' (FWBO,

1999). This is a line from the 'Heart Sutra', one of the most well known Buddhist teachings. Reflecting on this verse in parallel with letting go of being a mother is one way in which I can begin to have a sense of the profound letting go that this verse implies. Of course, the verse refers to going beyond *all* attachments, for example, to child, partner, identity, car, job, house, body, views, etcetera. In my life so far not becoming a mother has been one of my most significant acts of letting go. There has been a loss in not having children, even though it has been my choice, and for me the right choice. At times I have been aware of the physicality of that lack. I would also imagine that, for very different reasons, those who have outlived their child might ultimately feel a sense of 'holding to nothing whatever' as they face the new reality of life without that being and the deep loss of relationship and holding.

In not having a child I have grown to realize that I feel parallel loss and freedom. Loss that I will not ever experience that bond with our child, and freedom from that deep bond to another human life – a bond which is a healthy and important part in the somatic and psychic development of any infant. This deep bond, like all deep bonds, brings intense joy, fear, and sadness. Of course, there is loss and gain in being in an unbonded state, being without child. There have been times in the past when I have winced at hearing a child call "Mummy!" knowing that person will not be me. Yet there has also more latterly been a sense of growing freedom in roaming new horizons.

> In my opinion, any woman who does not have a child – and I include myself – is missing something, whether she knows it or not. I will never have the unique relationship with a child that a mother has, and she will never have the degree of personal freedom that I have – we're both giving up something, and we're both getting something too. (Safer, 1996: 4)

A pregnant pause

Take plenty of time and space to reflect on these themes, given their sensitivity. Take particular care if you have lost a child yourself. Notice for yourself whether or how deciding not to have children has been a loss, as well as a positive choice. Acknowledge the effect that decision has had on all the different parts of you. Of course, some people do not experience loss and regret in choosing childlessness. Others have been through much grief, particularly if their childlessness is more ambiguous – part choice and partly circumstance deciding for them. Have you shed anything in deciding not to have children? What's been lost and gained? How do you relate to 'holding to nothing whatever'?

Chapter 40

The personal is political

> How can we celebrate women's 'difference' without allowing the ideology of difference to subordinate us and negate our rights (as has happened in the past)? How can we affirm the significance of motherhood while still trying to free women from the obligation to mother? (Schwartz, 1993: 63)

I am very appreciative of the waves of the women's liberation and feminist movements in the 20th and 21st centuries. Without them, and my practice of Buddhism, I would not be sitting here with the time to write, being financially independent, and free to make the choice to not have children. Whilst there are still stigmas around being childless, these are minimal compared to the inequality women faced a century ago. And yet we have still got work to do.

A movement called 'Women Against Feminism' has been growing online in the past year, with the trend of young women posting a 'selfie' photo, holding a written statement as to why they personally do not feel they need feminism. Feminism, predictably, is portrayed as being about man hating, being a victim, blaming patriarchy for your woes, not being a feminist because you love your husband, etcetera. Most of the selfie statements are not about feminism, but a misunderstanding of it, so far as I can tell.

Some commentators are laughing this movement off, but I find it harder to do so. I wonder whether my generation were, in large part, a rather lost generation in terms of social and political awareness and this trend, and widespread complacency, is largely carrying on down the generations. We were growing up as 'Thatcher's children' – well, I wasn't, but it is the name sometimes given to my generation – sold the dream of individualism at the cost of community cohesion and the message of greed being good. By the time we graduated there were few jobs and plenty of disillusionment. The focus on the individual striving has been at considerable cost to a community orientation, important social and political causes and a global awareness.

Feminism has been invaluable in highlighting the realities of motherhood, rather than its often over-romanticized illusions, and has sought to separate womanhood from motherhood. Yet, Morell (2000) points out how 'Feminists, perhaps unwittingly, have contributed to this new pronatalism. Attention to motherhood in academic feminism is so prevalent that there is now a brand of feminism known as 'maternal feminism' (Bulbeck, 1998: 11). The relationship between feminism and childbearing is an interesting and complex one which has changed over the decades, in and through the different 'waves' of feminist thought and action. Some men and women have felt empowered by remaining childless, recognizing:

> …the notion of motherhood as essentialist, determinist, fixed, inevitably fulfilling and central to feminine identity for all women is firmly entrenched in industrial, urban and rural societies. (Gillespie, 2001: 141)

Others have recognized that motherhood has the potential to honor women's potency, embracing it as an important aspect of their lives. As Morell says:

> Unless nonreproduction and reproduction are both envisioned and supported as viable options, women are not liberated. Mothers and non-mothers in Western countries may struggle with different circumstances, yet we are united by our social experiences as women in patriarchal societies. (Morell, 2000: 321)

Feminism, too, has its limitations. I was struck hearing the reflections of my teacher, Maitreyi, who ordained me as a Buddhist. Having been a squat-living, dedicated feminist in the early 1970s before encountering Buddhism, she is an interesting person to talk to on this theme:

> From a Buddhist perspective feminism is clearly not enough. It is only a possible starting point in our efforts to develop true individuality. For while feminism asks us to look at our gender conditioning, Buddhism asks us to look at our conditioning as human beings, asks us to look at how the poisons of greed, hatred and delusion bind us to the wheel of samsara (the suffering of conditioned existence). While feminism investigates the dichotomy between men and women, male and female, Buddhism urges us to strive to overcome the dichotomy of self and other in the process of which we eventually transcend identification with being either male or female. (Maitreyi, 1994: 9)

However, there is still much I can learn and act upon encompassed by the slogan 'the personal is political'. This was used as a political argument in the rallying of both the student movements and second-wave feminism of the late 1960s and was popularized by the feminist Carol Hanisch in her 1969 essay of the same name (Hanisch, 1970). Hanisch's essay highlights the connections between her personal experience and wider social and political structures, and was a challenge to the nuclear family and conventional family values as the accepted norm.

Nowadays 'the personal is political' is used more widely and is as relevant in conversations about carbon usage and childbearing as it is anything else. 'The personal being political' is still a useful way of remembering to remember how each and every one of our lives has an effect on the wider world, perhaps opening up dialogues about how we live and seeing the impact we have in the world. In terms of the teachings of the Buddha, 'the personal is political' slogan also reminds me of the traditional teaching of things arising in dependence upon conditions and ceasing in the absence of those conditions, which is known as 'pratitya samutpada' or 'conditioned co-production' (Sangharakshita, 1957: 109) or which Joanna Macy, the ecophilosopher, refers to as 'mutual causality' (Macy, 1991).

Now is the time for each of us to deepen our capacity to respect the differences in how we each decide to live our lives. I am mindful of Bartlett's words here: 'Women are very sensitive to the differences between them, but learning how to celebrate and honor the variation is a challenge that we cannot ignore' (Bartlett, 1994: 116).

This bridging of difference is vital for how and whether we can care for our world and the children of the next generation – whether or not we have given birth to them – as well as ceasing the harm we cause to other-than-human life. It is this bridging of difference that will, in part at least, create the resilience we will need to face the challenges ahead. Bridges between mothers and non-mothers, those who choose to have children and those who are unable to have children, the married and unmarried, to name but a few. I will end with a quote from Zoe Williams in *The Guardian* earlier this year, which so well summed up the zeitgeist:

The endpoint of liberation will be when we rejoice in the fact that any two women can live their lives as differently as any two men can, and can say so without the necessity of an existential threat to anybody. When the second-wave feminists said the personal was political, they did not mean this. They did not mean the personal instead of the political. (Williams, 2014)

A pregnant pause

Notice whether your decision-making around child-lessness has felt like a political decision. How do you relate to the phrase 'the personal is the political'? Is it familiar to you, interesting, or do you feel it has nothing to do with you? How has feminism impacted upon your life and, in particular, deciding to remain without child? What is or could become your personal contribution in celebrating and honoring the differences between women: mother and other?

Chapter 41

Doing womankind a massive favour?

Every woman who chooses – joyfully, thoughtfully, calmly, of their own free will and desire – not to have children, does womankind a massive favour in the long term. We need more women who are allowed to prove their worth as people; rather than being assessed merely for their potential to create new people. (Moran, 2011: 45)

...the choice to have children calls for more careful justification and reasoning than the choice not to have children simply because in the former case a new and vulnerable being is brought into existence whose future may be at risk. (Overall, 2012: 3)

When I first started to research the area of voluntary childlessness in the late 1990s there was little literature available, apart from the work of a few female academics, to whom I am most grateful. This has changed and is fast-changing. Intentional childlessness is becoming a much more recognized and acknowledged set of circumstances. Not only in academic circles, but in popular circles, as reflected in the quotations above from women from two very different work backgrounds: Caitlin Moran, the British broadcaster, TV critic and columnist, and Christine Overall, Professor of Philosophy at Queen's University, Kingston, Ontario in Canada.

I find it interesting that both Moran and Overall are mothers. In our topsy-turvy world it is still the case that it is far less of a taboo for women who are mothers to comment on the situation of intentional childlessness, than those who are childless themselves. Nevertheless, I am glad they do, raising awareness of childlessness and how it is woven together with a woman's identity in social commentary. It seems that celebrities are starting to be more vocal about childlessness, with the childless actress Cameron Diaz saying a few years ago, "I think women are afraid to say that they do not want children because they're going to get shunned. But I think that is changing too now" (Singh, 2009).

In this post-horizon landscape let's keep that change happening. Of course I can see the safety in talking about intentional childlessness from a position of already having had one's children. In my thirties there were times when I nearly shelved this writing project, just in case I changed my mind and ended up having babies, and through fear of being further stigmatized as a childless woman for discussing themes evoking strong and difficult emotions. These days I am inclined to agree more openly with Caitlin Moran that each of us who chooses not to have children is doing womankind a massive favor in the long term. Let's further the tradition of openly and creatively discussing intentional childlessness...

In a world where alternative life styles are growing in number and acceptance, voluntary childlessness should be considered as the ultimate liberation...Far from being a sign of immaturity or maladjustment, the child-free state indicates self-understanding and self-discipline. (Movius, 1976: 62)

Chapter 42

Coming of age: pregnant with possibilities

> Childless women today are on the precipice of redefining womanhood in the most fundamental way ever...What is most remarkable is that those spearheading that groundbreaking change are unmindful of their position...the women I spoke with are not only unaware, but they feel they are alone; they do not know they are surrounded by a silent multitude. (Cain, 2002: xii-xiii)

> Women's thinking is revolutionary: redesigning their personal lives and the nature of relationships, women are deciding what they do and do not want life to be, clarifying their own philosophy. (Hite, 1993: 378)

It is 17 years since I first started reflecting on and researching the area of voluntary childlessness. Now's the time for this baby-sized project, or, in fact, almost grown-up project, to take off, spread its wings and to have a life of its own. *Other Than Mother* is coming of age and so am I, in relationship to this area of research. What began life as a research project has now taken shape as a book. Issues that used to feel so very pressing (Will I be a mother? Will we have a child?) are now part of the tapestry of my recent past. The decision-making process I went through was an important part of who I am, but not something that defines me.

Early on I was keen to talk to anyone I could about child-bearing and motherhood. Nowadays, it feels like I 'happen not to have children', similar to the colleague to whom I referred in Part II of this book. However, in terms of research around voluntary childlessness, it is early days in understanding how my generation without children will experience later middle and old age. If you are as yet undecided as to whether or not to have children, I urge you to keep engaging with the process, remembering that ultimately, there is no 'right' or 'wrong' answer.

It's alright not to have children. We cannot have everything in this world. Sometimes it's smart to see our limits. On this subject, in fact, I often say that it is wonderful not to have children. And wonderful to have them. Each is its own kind of wonderful. (Aron, 1999: 164)

A pregnant pause

These are the final reflections of *Other Than Mother*. Flick back through this book, noticing which themes need more of your attention. Also make sure that you take time to digest, remembering the importance of kairos time. You may still feel undecided as to whether or not to have children, in which case, in the words of Stephanie Mills: 'search your conscience and follow your heart' (Mills, 2010). Take stock as to where you are now, perhaps reflecting on the similarities and differences between your imaginings for your life and what actually happened. My mind turns to a quote from the writer J.M. Barrie: 'The life of every man is a diary in which he means to write one story, and writes another; and his humblest hour is when he compares the volume as it is with what he vowed to make it' (Barrie, 1891).

Conclusion

'A child of all life'

> I am a child of all life, and all living beings are my brothers and sisters, my children and grandchildren. And there is a child within me waiting to be born, the baby of a new and wiser self. (Snyder, 1995)

As I write, it is a few weeks until the winter solstice, Christmas and the turning of the year. Light sparkles in the damp darkness, illuminating beads of rain and wavering cobwebs. The light and shade of the sky in the past week have been a delight; soft pinkish blue shades against the few remaining green bewildered leaves hanging on for dear life to the tree branches. Most of the branches are stark, bare, and naked. Winter is having her own quiet drama. Not the blousy drama of early spring flowers being too full of themselves, like the coral-colored Camellia in our spring garden. Instead the exposed, uncovered nature of life gathering its underground strength ready to start the cycle all over again. Bare, naked, chilly loveliness.

Into this phase of entering the darkness – with its faint promise of renewal and newness – enter the rituals and celebrations of the solstice and Christmas. I sense the spirit of renewal deep in my bones and am reminded of the need to go into the dark as fully as I can, so that I emerge at the other side, in a new season, with a new year and new beginnings. Christmas and the solstice bring irresistible stories of new life, new light, and all the sights, smells, sensations, sounds and tastes of newness. However commercialized, consumer-driven and over-the-top Christmas celebrations have become, the truth is that the promise of new life, more light and the new shoots of renewal are a *sine qua non* of living. Our expression of that might have become a bit twisted and turned, but the underlying celebration is vital to the rhythm of the year.

That promise is present in every child born, every being that is hatched, and birthed, and every forming new bud – no wonder we want to reproduce! At best we have the potential of creating a cherished life, taking our place in the cosmic drama – sometimes Greek tragedy – of life and death. Whatever the circumstances, new life in all its myriad forms, human and other-than-human, are a vital reminder of creation, potency and renewal.

May we become intimate with a sense of ease and grace at each life stage: birth, the fragility of new beginnings, growth, blossoming, maturity, death, renewal. There is no sense in welcoming one and fighting another. Of course, we do, because we are human and fallible and we have, *en masse*, strayed from the path of living with a simple, ordinary awareness of being more attuned to one another and the planet we share. May we equally be more at home in our own skins, living our unique lives.

The reminder of new life, in the form of the turning of the year, or the arrival of a child, fuels my wonder for life. I am reminded of the bodhisattva named Vajrasattva. He is envisaged as being as white as snow – so, seasonally timely – and associated with primordial, un-blemished purity. His enlightened wisdom reminds us to embrace every moment of our lives with fresh eyes and hearts. Each moment is a new moment, bringing a new breath. Each new moment brings the choice of following the well-worn track of our habits or treading a new path and going beyond the well-worn stories of ours and others' lives.

Each breath reminds us that there is the start of a new moment. Continuity and change. In the spirit of 'Life is King', the poem I quoted at the end of Part I, the challenge ahead for us in our world, whether with or without child, is to find a way to dialogue about where we are as a species, acknowledge our impact on the planet and find new ways of living sustainably.

Living our private lives, which are lit by a greater awareness of global concerns. This will call for immense compassion, patience, and the wisdom to listen and understand ourselves, one another, and the world; our home.

May we learn to dance with the worldly winds, rather than allowing them to knock us to the ground. May we each soften our views, stereotypes, judgments and assumptions about one another, taking time to seek understanding, rather than leaping to defending ourselves, our identities, and lifestyles. May we explore new dialogues in how we talk about parenthood and non-parenthood, opening up new possibilities, developing a new language, new networks and communities of people who can dwell amongst one another, living lightly on the earth.

Endnotes

1   For example, an article from the American weekly news magazine *Time* explored voluntary childlessness: 'The Childfree Life: When having it all means not having children' (see Sandler, 2013) and was criticized by the nonprofit organization *Grist* (see Hymas, 2013) for failing to consider, in Hymas's words, the 'green angle' in deciding not to have children.

2   For those of you who are involuntarily childless I would highly recommend looking up the work of Jody Day, founder of Gateway Women who is doing outstanding work in developing networks, giving a voice to women who are childless by circumstance, and being a powerful advocate: http://gateway-women.com/ Also see Day (2013).

3   Roszak (1995: 3) defines the field of ecopsychology in the following way: 'A new generation of psychotherapists is seeking ways in which professional psychology can play a role in the environmental crisis of our time'.

4   The well-known British analyst Wilfred Bion's concept of maternal 'reverie' is the capacity to sense, and make sense of, what is going on for the infant (Jacobus, 2005: 169). He also noted the importance of the therapist's use of 'reverie' in the therapy process, as an important tool in his or her response to the patient's material: 'it is this capacity for playing with a patient's images that Bion encouraged' (Casement, 1990: 37).

5   Research emerging from the London School of Economics examines the links between intelligence and maternal urges in women, claiming that more of the former means less of the latter (reported by Walshe, 2013). Satoshi Kanazawa, the psychologist behind the research, discusses the findings that maternal urges drop by 25% with every extra 15 IQ points in his book *The Intelligence Paradox* (Kanazawa, 2012).

Kanazawa also sees voluntary childlessness as 'truly unnatural' (2012: 177).

6 This is a phrase borrowed from Gray (1992: 15).

7 'SWOT' analysis involved listing Strengths, Weaknesses, Opportunities, and Threats.

8 These three category names are borrowed from Ireland (1993).

9 The two other areas are: "Holding actions' in defense of life on Earth' (political, legislative and legal work required to slow down the Earth's destruction) and 'Analysis of structural causes and creation of alternative institutions'. (See Macy and Young Brown, 1998: 21)

10 Buddhafield is a community of men and women dedicated to following the Buddha's spiritual path and is part of the Triratna Buddhist community. Buddhafield's people are drawn to nature as the primary context for life and Dharma practice, recognizing:

> our urgent need for a more harmonious relationship with nature, we wish to welcome others into our community and to actively go out to them, teaching the Dharma and sharing our inspiration, experience, and value. Source: http://www.buddhafield.com/?page=vision

11 The other perfections, traditionally known as 'paramitas', are: ethics, patience, energy, meditative concentration, and wisdom (Sangharakshita, 1994: 59). For a more detailed explanation of 'dana', translated as generosity, see Sangharakshita 1999: 95.

12 The 'ancestor syndrome' is borrowed from Anne Ancelin Schutzenberger's book of the same name. See Ancelin Schutzenberger, 1998.

13 On her website Polly speaks of 'the power of a law of Ecocide to enable individuals, communities, governments and NGOs to bring to court prosecutions to examine the

evidence of a given Ecocide and have the support of the law to prevent, prohibit and in some instances pre-empt the mass damage and destruction that is causing or is likely to cause significant harm'. See: www.pollyhiggins.com

References

Abbott, M. (2003) *Family Affairs: A History of the Family in 20th Century England*. Routledge.

About Time (2013). Directed by Richard Curtis. Universal Pictures International (UPI).

Alexander, R. (2012) 'Dollar benchmark: The rise of the $1-a-day statistic'. *BBC News Magazine*. Source: http://www.bbc.co.uk/news/magazine-17312819.

Anderson, L. (1998) 'The Right Not to Bear: Nonmother Stephanie Mills', *Women's International Net Magazine*, Issue 16, December 1998.

Aron, E. (1999) *The Highly Sensitive Person: How to Thrive When the World Overwhelms You*. Thorsons, an imprint of Harper Collins.

Ashurst, P. & Hall, Z. (1989) *Understanding Women in Distress*. London: Routledge.

Bartlett, J. (1994) *Will You Be Mother? Women Who Choose to Say No*. Virago Press Ltd.

Barrie, J.M. (1891) *The Little Minister*. Lovell Coryell & Company.

Basten, S. (2009) 'Voluntary childlessness and being childfree'. The Future of Human Reproduction: Working Paper No. 5, St. John's College, Oxford & Vienna Institute of Demography.

Bates, G. (1972) *Steps to an Ecology of Mind*. The University of Chicago Press.

Bauer, F. 'No kidding', *The Guardian Weekend*, 14th August 2004.

Baum, F.E. (1983) 'Orientation towards voluntarily childlessness', *Journal of Biosocial Science*, Vol 15, No 2, p.153 quoted in Lisle, L. (1999) *Without Child: Challenging the Stigma of Childlessness*. Routledge, p.5.

Beck, K. (2011) ' Everyone should care about children – even those of us who are not mothers', Mommyish website. Source: http://www.mommyish.com/2011/08/12/everyone-should-

care-about-children-even-those-of-us-who-arent-mothers/#
ixzz3PSkE3OwS

Bensching, D. quoted by Larson, V. (2011) 'How not to save a marriage', *Huffington Post*, 13 August 2011. Source: http://www.huffingtonpost.com/vicki-larson/how-not-to-save-a-marriag_b_920464.html

Berrington A. (2004) 'Perpetual postponers? Women's, men's and couple's fertility intentions and subsequent fertility behavior', *Population Trends* 117, UK Statistics Authority. Pp.9-19.

Blackstone, A. & Dyer Stewart, M. (2012) 'Choosing to be childfree: research on the decision not to parent'. Sociology School Faculty Scholarship. Paper 5. Source: http://digital-commons.library.umaine.edu/soc_facpub/5

Blackstone, A. (2014) 'International childfree day, 2014 edition!' Blogpost 14th May 2014. Source: http://werenothaving ababy.com/childfree/nominate-childfree-man-woman-year/

Blomfield, V. (2012) *Gautama Buddha: The Life and Teachings of the Awakened One*. Quercus.

Bolen, J. (1984) *Goddesses in Everywoman: A New Psychology of Women*. Harper Perennial.

Breathnach, S. B. (1997) *Simple Abundance: A Daybook of Comfort and Joy*. Bantam Books.

Bulbeck, C. (1998) *Re-orienting Western Feminisms: Women's Diversity in a Postcolonial World*. Cambridge University Press cited in Morell (2000) 'Saying No: Women's Experiences with Reproductive Refusal', *Feminism and Psychology*, Vol 10, No 3, pp.313-322.

Cain, M. (2002) *The Childless Revolution: What it Means to be Childless Today*. Perseus Books.

Campbell, A. (1999) *Childfree and Sterilized: Women's Decisions and Medical Responses*. London: Cassell.

Cannold, L. (2004) 'Declining Marriage Rates and Gender Inequity in Social Institutions: Towards an Adequately Complex Explanation for Childlessness'. *People and Place*, Vol

12, No 4, pp.1-11.

Carroll, C. (2000) *Families of Two: Interviews with Happily Married Couples Without Children by Choice*. Xlibris Corporation.

Carroll, L. (2015) *Alice's Adventures in Wonderland*. Macmillan's Children's Books.

Casement, P. (1990) *Further Learning from the Patient: The Analytical Space and Process*. Routledge.

Casey, T. (1998) *Pride and Joy: The Lives and Passions of Women Without Children*. Beyond Words Publishing.

CDC: National Health Statistics Reports, Number 51, April 12, 2012. 'Fertility of men and women aged 15–44 years in the United States: national survey of family growth, 2006–2010' by Martinez, G., Daniels, K., and Chandra, A., from the Division of Vital Statistics. Source: http://www.cdc.gov/nchs /data/nhsr/nhsr051.pdf

Chamie, J. & Mirkin, B. (2012) 'Childless by Choice: More people decide against having children, presenting quandaries for governments and the elderly'. *YaleGlobal Online*, 2nd March 2012. Source: http://yaleglobal.yale.edu/content/childless-choice

Cho, M. 'I would not know where to begin' in Mantel, M. (2013) (ed) *No Kidding: Women Writers on Bypassing Parenthood*. Seal Press.

Chodron, P. (2001) *The Wisdom of No Escape: How to Love Yourself and Your World*. Element, an imprint of HarperCollins Publishers.

Chodron, P. (2004) *Comfortable with Uncertainty: 108 Teachings on Cultivating Fearlessness and Compassion*. Shambhala Publications.

Cohen, P. (2010) 'Long Road to Adulthood Is Growing Even Longer', *The New York Times*, 13th June 2010.

Connidis, I. A., & McMullin, J. A. (1996). 'Reasons for and perceptions of childlessness among older persons: Exploring the impact of marital status and gender', *Journal of Aging*

Studies, Vol 10, pp.205 - 222.

Coorey, P. (2012) 'PM v Obama: who has it harder?' *The Sydney Morning Herald,* 2nd April 2012. Source: http://www.smh.com.au/federal-politics/political-news/pm-v-obama-who-has-it-harder-20120401-1w6qa.html

Copur, Z. & Koropeckyj-Cox, T. (2010) 'University students' perceptions of childless couples and parents in Ankara, Turkey', *Journal of Family Issues,* Number 31, pp.481–506.

Crawford, E. (2000) *The Women's Suffrage Movement: A Reference Guide 1866-1928* (Women's & Gender History). Routledge.

Dally, A. (1982) *Inventing Motherhood: Consequences of an Ideal.* Schocken Books.

Daniluk, J.C. & Herman, A. (1984) 'Parenthood Decision-Making', *Family Relations,* Vol 33, Issue 4 (October 1984), pp.607-612.

Datt, B. (2013) 'What to Expect When You're Never Expecting' in Coolidge, J. & Mantel. H. (eds) *No Kidding: Women Writers on Bypassing Parenthood.* Avalon Publishing Group.

Davis, A. (2012) 'TV historian Dr Lucy Worsley: I was educated out of having children', *The London Evening Standard.* 24th April 2012. Source: http://www.standard.co.uk/news/uk/tv-historian-dr-lucy-worsley-i-was-educated-out-of-having-children-7675602.html

Day, J. (2012) 'Julia Gillard and the fear of the childless woman'. *The Guardian,* 25th October. Source: http://www.theguardian.com/commentisfree/2012/oct/25/julia-gillard-childless-woman

Day (2013) *Rocking the Life Unexpected: 12 Weeks to Your Plan B for a Meaningful and Fulfilling Life Without Children.* CreateSpace Independent Publishing Platform.

Defago, N. (2005) *Childfree and Loving It!* London: Fusion Press.

Dowrick, S. (2010) *Forgiveness and Other Acts of Love: Finding True Value in Your Life.* Allen & Unwin.

Dubofsky, C. (2014) ''Childless' or 'childfree': the difference

matters'. R H Reality Check. Source: http://rhrealitycheck.
org/article/2014/05/08/childless-childfree-difference-matters/

Ehrlich, P. R. (1968) *The Population Bomb*. Ballantine Books.

Eisenberg, E. (2000) *The Ecology of Eden*. Picador.

Ellen, B. (2014) 'Haven't had a baby? That's you written off, then'.
The Guardian, 31st August. Source: http://www.theguard
ian.com/commentisfree/2014/aug/31/jennifer-aniston-
childess-women-judged-unfairly

Emin, T. (2011) 'Who do you think you are?' Series 8, Episode 10,
first screened on BBC1 on 12th October 2011.

Engel, B. (1998) *The Parenthood Decision: Discovering Whether you
are Ready and Willing to Become a Parent*. Mainstreet Books.

Esquivel, L. (1993) *Like Water for Chocolate*. Black Swan.

FAO (Food and Agriculture Organization of the United Nations)
(2012) 'The State of Food Insecurity in the World'.

Farming First (2009) ''Silent hunger crisis': FAO estimates over 1
billion hungry in the world'. Posted 24 June 2009. Source:
http://www.farmingfirst.org/2009/06/silent-hunger-crisis-fao-
estimates-over-1-billion-hungry-in-the-world/

Fielding, H. (1997) *Bridget Jones's Diary*. Picador.

FWBO (1999) *Puja: the FWBO book of Buddhist devotional texts*.
Windhorse Publications. 6th edition.

Gibran, K. (1991) *The Prophet*. Pan: New Ed Edition.

Gies, E. (2012) 'Even conscientious people have an eco-footprint'.
Earth Island Journal: News of the World Environment, Spring
2012. Source: http://www.earthisland.org/journal/index.php/
eij/article/even_conscientious_people_have_an_eco-
footprint/

Gillespie, R. (1999) 'Voluntary childlessness in the United
Kingdom', *Reproductive Health Matters*, Volume 7, No 13,
pp.43-53.

Gillespie, R. (2000) 'When no means no: Disbelief, disregard and
deviance as discourses of voluntary childlessness', *Women's
Studies International Forum*, Vol 23, No 2, pp.223-234.

Gillespie, R. (2001) 'Contextualising voluntary childlessness within a post-modern model of reproduction: implications for health and social needs', *Critical Social Policy*, Volume 21, No 2, pp.139-159.

Goldberg, N. (2009) *Wild Mind: Living the Writer's Life.* Rider Books.

Gordon. L. 'Voluntary motherhood: the beginnings of feminist birth control ideas in the United States' in Walzer Leavitt, J. (1999) (ed) *Women and Health in America: Historical Readings.* The University of Wisconsin Press. 2nd Edition

Gray, J. (1992) *Men Are from Mars, Women Are from Venus: A Practical Guide for Improving Communication and Getting What You Want in Your Relationships.* Thorsons: an imprint of HarperCollins.

Griffin, S. (1999) *What Her Body Thought.* HarperSanFrancisco (a division of Harper Collins Publishers).

Gross, R.M. (1997) 'Buddhist resources for issues of population, consumption, and the environment' in Tucker, M.E. & Ryuken Williams, D. *Buddhism and Ecology: The Interconnection of Dharma and Deeds.* Harvard University Press, pp.291-311.

Guhyapati (2014) 'Connect-empower-liberate'. The first of three talks given by Dharmachari Guhyapati at Buddhafield's Green Earth Awakening Event in Somerset, UK, July 2014. Source: http://www.ecodharma.com/articles-influences-audio/ecodharma-audio

Hanisch, C. 'The Personal is Political' in Firestone, S. & Koedt, A. (1970) *Notes from the Second Year: Women's Liberation: Major Writings of the Radical Feminists.* New York: Pamphlet, 1970.

Hellinger, B. (2003) *The Art and Practice of Family Constellations: Leading Family Constellations as Developed by Bert Hellinger.* Carl-Auer-Systeme-Verlag und Verlangsbuchhandlung GmbH.

Henley Centre (1999) 'The paradox of prosperity: a report for the Salvation Army'. London: Henley Centre/Salvation Army.

Hewlett S.A. (2002) 'Executive women and the myth of having it all', *Harvard Business Review*, Issue 80 (April), pp.66-73.

Higgins, P. (2014) *I Dare You To Be Great*. Clink Street Publishing.

Hite, S. (1993) *Women as Revolutionary Agents of Change: The Hite Reports and Beyond*. Bloomsbury Publishing.

Hoffman, P. (2012) 'Should environmentalists breed?' Piper Hoffman's blog: 'Rock the boat: law, society, and social justice'. Source: http://piperhoffman.com/2012/03/04/should-environmentalists-breed/

Hoffman, P. (2013) 'Are childfree people destroying America?' Source: 'Choosing childfree: you do not have to be a parent' blog, 12th September 2013: http://www.choosingchildfree .com/are-childfree-people-destroying-america/

Hunter, S. (2014) 'Coming out as a woman who does not want children', *HuffPost Lifestyle*, 19th March 2014. Source: http://www.huffingtonpost.co.uk/sian-hunter/women-who-dont-want-children_b_4981515.html

Hymas, L. (2010) 'Say it loud – I am childfree and I am proud: the GINK manifesto', Source: http://gristo.org/article/2010-03-30-gink-manifesto-say-it-loud-im-childfree-and-im-proud/

Hymas, L. (2011a) 'I decided not to have children for environmental reasons', 27th September 2011. *The Guardian Environmental Network*. Source: http://www.theguardian.com /environment/2011/sep/27/not-have-children-environmental-reasons

Hymas, L. (2011b) 'How green are the childless by choice?' 17th May 2010. Source: http://grist.org/article/2010-05-17-how-green-are-the-childless-by-choice/

Hymas, L. (2013) 'Time magazine catches on to the childfree movement, misses the green angle', 3rd August 2013. Source: http://grist.org/living/time-magazine-catches-on-to-the-childfree-movement-misses-the-green-angle/

Ibsen, H. & Watts, P. (Translator) (2003) *A Doll's House and Other Plays*. Penguin Classic.

Jacobus, M. (2005) *The Poetics of Psychoanalysis: In the Wake of Klein*. Oxford University Press.

Jeffries, S. & Konnert, C. (2002) 'Regret and psychological well-being among voluntarily and involuntarily childless women and mothers', *International Journal of Aging and Human Development*, Vol 54, No 2, pp.89-106.

Johnson, G., Roberts, D. & Brown, R. et al. (1987) 'Infertile or childless by choice? A multipractice survey of women aged 35 and 50', *British Medical Journal*, Volume 294, 28th March 1987.

Jung, C. (1988) *Zarathustra seminar*. Edited by James Jarrett. Princeton, NJ: Princeton University Press. P.151. Quoted in Sabini, M. (2002) (ed) *The Earth Has a Soul: C.G. Jung on Nature, Technology & Modern Life*. North Atlantic Books. P.73

Kamalamani (2009) 'Choosing to be childfree', *Therapy Today*, Vol 20, Issue 6.

Kamalamani (2012) *Meditating with Character*. O Books.

Kanazawa, S. (2012) *The Intelligence Paradox: Why the Intelligent Choice Isn't Always the Smart One*. John Wiley & Sons.

Kelly, M. (2009) 'Women's voluntary childlessness: a radical rejection of motherhood?' *Women's Studies Quarterly*, Vol 37, Nos 3 & 4, Fall/Winter, pp.157-172.

Khadro, C. (1986) *Red Tara Commentary: Instructions for the Concise Practice Known as Red Tara: An Open Door to Bliss and Ultimate Awareness*. Pilgrims Publishing.

Khema, A. (1991) *When the Iron Eagle Flies: Buddhism for the West*. Penguin Group.

Kirchgaessner, S. (2015) 'Pope Francis: not having children is selfish'. *The Guardian*, 11th February. Source: http://www.theguardian.com/world/2015/feb/11/pope-francis-the-choice-to-not-have-children-is-selfish?CMP=fb_gu

Kitzinger, S. (1978) *Women as Mothers*. Fontana Original.

Klepfisz, I. (2000) 'Women without children; women without families; women alone' in Ratner, R. (editor) *Bearing Life: Women's Writing on Childlessness*. The Feminist Press at the

City University of New York, pp.19-28.

Kōshō Uchiyama Rōshi (2005) *How to Cook Your Life: From the Zen Kitchen to Enlightenment*. Shambhala Publications Inc.

Kyokun, T. Translator of 'Parental mind' by Zen Master Dogen. Source: http://www.mro.org/mr/archive/24-4/articles/parenta lmind.html

Ireland, M. (1993) *Reconceiving Women: Separating Motherhood from Female Identity*. The Guilford Press, New York.

Kumar, S. (2014) 'The new story'. A talk delivered at the new story summit at Findhorn, Scotland. Source: https://www.youtube.com/watch?v=GjgdwI6p9Ks

Le Guin, U. (2014) Acceptance speech for the National Book Foundation's medal for distinguished contribution to American letters at the 65th Annual National Book Awards held in New York City on 19th November 2014. Source: http://www.filmsforaction.org/watch/ursula-le-guin-speech-challenges-the-inevitability-of-capitalism/

Letherby, G. (1999) 'Other than mother and mothers as others: the experience of motherhood and non-motherhood in relation to 'infertility' and 'involuntary childlessness'', *Women's Studies International Forum*, Vol 22, No 3, pp.359-372.

Lisle L. (1996) *Without Child: Challenging the Stigma of Childlessness*. Routledge.

Lorber, J. and Moore, L.J. (2007) *Gendered Bodies: Feminist Perspectives*. Los Angeles: Roxbury.

Maitland, S. (2009) *A Book of Silence*. Granta Books.

McAllister, F. with Clark, L. (1998) Family Policy Studies Centre, summary of 'Findings: a study of childlessness in Britain', published by the Joseph Rowntree Foundation.

Maitreyi (1994) 'Why feminism?' in *Dakini Magazine*, Summer 1994, Issue 13. Published by Friends of the Western Buddhist Order.

Mackey, M. (2000) 'This is a question I do not answer' in Ratner, R. (editor) *Bearing Life: Women's Writing on Childlessness*. The

Feminist Press at the City University of New York, pp.29-30.

Macy, J. (1991) *Mutual Causality in Buddhism and General Systems Theory: The Dharma of Natural Systems*. The Suny Series, Buddhist Studies. State University of New York Press.

Macy, J. & Young Brown, M. (1998) *Coming Back to Life: Practices to Reconnect Our Lives, Our World*. New Society Publishers.

Macy, J. (2009) 'The greening of the self' in, L. & Chalquist, C. (ed) *Ecotherapy: Healing with Nature in Mind*. Sierra Club Books, pp.238-245.

Macy, J. & Johnstone, C. (2012) *Active Hope: How to Face the Mess We're in Without Going Crazy*. New World Library.

Mantel, H. (2013) *No Kidding: Women Writers on Bypassing Childhood*. Seal Press.

Marshall, G. (2014) *Don't Even Think About It: Why Our Brains Are Wired to Ignore Climate Change*. Bloomsbury USA, New York.

May, E.T. (1995) *Barren in the Promised Land: Childless Americans and the Pursuit of Happiness*. Cambridge, MA: Harvard University Press.

Merlo, R. & Rowland, D. (2000) 'The prevalence of childlessness in Australia'. *People and Place*, Vol 8, No 2, pp.21-32.

Mills, S. (1989) *Whatever Happened to Ecology?* Sierra Club Nature & Nature Philosophy Library.

Mills, S. (2002) *Epicurean Simplicity*. A Shearwater Book, Island Press.

Mills, S. (2010) The closing excerpt from 'Stephanie Mills: On (not) having children & living sustainably'. A YouTube video from the Post Carbon Institute: https://www.youtube.com/watch?v=9_DA_tWrTHw

Mindell, A. (2002) *Dreammakers Apprentice: Using Heightened Awareness to Interpret the Waking Dream*. Hampton Roads Publishing Company, US.

Moran, C. (2011) *How To Be a Woman*. Ebury Press.

Morell. C. (1994) *Unwomanly Conduct: The Challenges of Intentional Childlessness*. New York: Routledge.

Morell C. (2000) 'Saying no: women's experiences with reproductive refusal', *Feminism and Psychology*, Vol 10, No 3,
pp.313-322.

Movius, M. (1976) 'Voluntary Childlessness. The Ultimate
Liberation', *The Family Co-ordinator*, Vol 25, Issue 1 (Jan 1976),
pp.57-63.

Muldoon, K. (1987) 'Childless by choice', *New Internationalist*, No
176, October 1987.

Mucci, C. (2013) *Beyond Individual and Collective Trauma:
Intergenerational Transmission, Psychoanalytic Treatment, and the
Dynamics of Forgiveness*. Karnac Books.

NICE (National Institute for Health and Care Excellence) (2014)
'Intrapartum care: care of healthy women and their babies
during childbirth'. Source: http://www.nice.org.uk/guid
ance/CG190

Norwich, J of., Spearing, A.C., & Spearing, E. (1998) *Revelations of
Divine Love*. Penguin Classics.

Office for National Statistics (ONS). '1 in 5 women are childless
at 45' Report released 7th March 2013. Source:
http://www.ons.gov.uk/ons/rel/fertility-analysis/cohort-
fertility—england-and-wales/2011/sty-1-in-5-women-are-
childless-at-45.html

Overall, C. (2012) *Why Have Children? The Ethical Debate*. The MIT
Press.

Rich, A. 'Motherhood: the contemporary emergence and the
quantum Leap', pp.259-273 in Rich, A. (1984) *On Lies, Secrets
and Silences: Selected Prose 1966-1978*. London: Virago.

Packham, C. (2011) 'Stop having children instead of bleating
about conservation, says wildlife expert'. EcoEarth.Info
Environmental Portal & Search Engine. Source:
http://www.ecoearth.info/shared/reader/welcome.aspx?linki
d=216414

Park, Kristin (2002) 'Stigma management among the voluntarily
childless'. *Sociological Perspectives*, Number 45, pp.21–45.

Peterson, H. & Engwall, K. (2013) 'Silent bodies: childfree women's gendered and embodied experiences', *European Journal of Women's Studies*, Vol 20, No 4, pp.376–389.

Pohlman, E. (1969) *The Psychology of Birth Planning*. Cambridge: Schenkman.

Preece, R. (2006) *The Wisdom of Imperfection: The Challenge of Individuation in Buddhist Life*. Snow Lion Publications.

Ratner, R. (2000) (editor) *Bearing Life: Women's Writing on Childlessness*. The Feminist Press at the City University of New York.

Rich, S., Taket, A., Graham, M. & Shelley, J. (2011) ''Unnatural', 'unwomanly', 'uncreditable' and 'undervalued': The Significance of Being a Childless Woman in Australian Society', *Gender Issues*, Vol 28, No 4, pp.226–247.

Robinson, L. 'Psychotherapy as if the world mattered' in Buzzell, L. & Chalquist, C. (2009) *Ecotherapy: Healing with Nature in Mind*. Sierra Club Books, pp.24-29.

Rogers, C. (1994) *On Becoming a Person*. Constable.

Roszak, T. 'Where psyche meets Gaia' in Roszak, T., Gomes, M.E., & Kanner, A. D. (1995) *Ecopsychology: Restoring the Earth, Healing the Mind*. Sierra Club Books, San Francisco.

Ruppert, F. (2008) *Trauma, Bonding & Family Constellations: Healing Injuries of the Soul*. Green Balloon Publishing.

Safer, J. (1996) *Beyond Motherhood: Choosing Life Without Children*, Pocket Books.

Salzberg, S. (2002) *Lovingkindness: The Revolutionary Art of Happiness*. Shambhala classics.

Samuels, A (2002) 'A new anatomy of spirituality: clinical and political demands the psychotherapist cannot ignore'. An edited version of a lecture given in the series 'Psychotherapy and Spirituality' at the London Centre for Psychotherapy on 26 October 2002. Source: http://www.andrewsamuels.com

Sandler, L. 'The childfree life: when having it all means not having children', *Time Magazine*, 12 August, 2013. Source:

http://time.com/241/having-it-all-without-having-children/

Sangharakshita (1957) *A Survey of Buddhism: Its Doctrines and Methods Through the Ages.* Windhorse Publications, seventh edition.

Sangharakshita (1994) *Who is the Buddha?* Windhorse Publications.

Sangharakshita (1995) *Transforming Self and World: Themes from the Sutra of Golden Light.* Windhorse Publications.

Sangharakshita (1995) *Complete Poems 1941/1994.* Windhorse Publications.

Sangharakshita (1998) *What is the Dharma? The Essential Teachings of the Buddha.* Windhorse Publications.

Sangharakshita (1999) *The Bodhisattva Ideal: Wisdom and Compassion in Buddhism.* Windhorse Publications.

Sangharakshita (2002) *Creative Symbols of Tantric Buddhism.* Windhorse Publications.

Saunders, A. (1957) *Reader's Digest.* January 1957. I found this source from: http://quoteinvestigator.com/2012/05/06/other-plans/

Schützenberger, A.A. (1998*) The Ancestor Syndrome: Transgenerational Psychotherapy and the Hidden Links in the Family Tree.* Routledge.

Schwartz, J.D. (1993) *The Mother Puzzle.* Simon and Schuster, New York.

Shantideva & Batchelor, S. (translator) (1979) *A Guide to the Bodhisattva's Way of Life.* Library of Tibetan Works and Archives, Dharamasala.

Shantideva & Williams, P., Crosby, K., & Skilton, A. (translators) (2008) *The Bodhicaryavatara.* Oxford World's Classics: Oxford Paperbacks.

Shaw, R.L. (2011) 'Women's experiential journey towards voluntary childlessness: an interpretative phenomenological analysis', *Journal of Community & Applied Social Psychology*, Vol 21, pp.151–163.

Shoshanna, B. (2004) *Zen Miracles: Finding Peace in an Insane World*. John Wiley & Sons.

Shriver, L. (2005) 'No kids please, we are selfish'. *The Guardian*, 1st September 2005.

Singh, A. (2009) 'Cameron Diaz: women afraid to admit they do not want children', *The Telegraph*, 10th June 2009.

Snyder, G. (1995) *A Place in Space: Ethics, Aesthetics, and Watersheds*. Counterpoint Press.

Solnit, R. (2006) *A Field Guide to Getting Lost*. Canongate Books.

Somers, M. (1993) 'A comparison of voluntarily childfree adults and parents', *Journal of Marriage and the Family*, Vol 55, Issue 3 (August 1993), pp.643-650.

Somé, S. (2013) Quoted in the editorial of the summer 2013 international newsletter of the Global Ecovillage Network (GEN). Source: http://gen.ecovillage.org/en/content/gen-internatio nal-newsletter-summer-2013-editorial

Soper, K. (1995) *What is Nature? Culture, Politics and the Non-Human*. Wiley Blackwell.

Soulé, M. (2005) 'The whole package', *Tricycle: The Buddhist Review*, Summer 2005. Source: http://www.tricycle.com /special-section/whole-package

Stanley, J. & Loy, D. (2011) 'Why the Buddha touched the earth'. Source: http://www.huffingtonpost.com/john-stanley/budd hism-and-climate-change_b_925651.html

Stobert, S. & Kemeny, A. (2003) 'Childfree by choice', Canadian Social Trends, *Statistics Canada* – Catalogue No. 11-008, Summer 2003.

Thanissaro Bhikkhu (1997) *Samaññaphala sutta: The fruits of the contemplative life*. DN 2 PTS: D i 47. Source: http://www.access toinsight.org/tipitaka/dn/dn.02.0.than.html

The Shawshank Redemption (1995). Directed by Frank Darabont. UK: Rank Film Distributors.

Tran, M. (2014) 'Kirstie Allsopp tells young women: ditch university and have a baby by 27'. *The Guardian*, Monday 2nd

June 2014.

UNESCO (2012) '10 things to know about Norwich': Source: http://www.unesco.org.uk/uploads/Norwich%20UNESCO%20City%20of%20Literature%2010%20things.pdf

United Nations (1999) 'The world at six billion'. By the Population Division Department of Economic and Social Affairs United Nations Secretariat. 12 October 1999.

Vajragupta (2011) *Sailing the Worldly Winds: A Buddhist Way Through the Ups and Downs of Life.* Windhorse Publications.

Van Luven, L. (ed) (2006) *Nobody's Mother: Life Without Kids.* Heritage House Publishing

Veevers, J.E. (1975) 'The moral careers of voluntarily childless wives: notes on the defense of a variant world view', *The Family Coordinator*, Vol 24, Issue 4, pp.473-487.

Veevers, J. E. (1980) *Childless by Choice.* Butterworth (Canada), Ontario.

Vessantara (1993) *Meeting the Buddhas: A Guide to Buddhas, Bodhisattvas, and Tantric Deities.* Windhorse Publications.

Vipassi (translator, date unknown) *The Karaniya Metta Sutta.* The original karaniya metta sutta can be found in the Suttanipta (Sn 1.8) of the Pali Canon.

Walker, E. (2010) *Complete without Kids: An Insider's Guide to Childfree Living by Choice or by Chance.* Greenleaf Book Group LLC.

Walker, E. (2011) 'Childfree for the environment's sake', *Psychology Today.* Source: http://www.psychologytoday.com/blog/complete-without-kids/201109/childfree-the-environments-sake

Walshe, S. (2013) 'Should we care that smart women are not having kids?' *The Guardian*, 7th August 2013.

Watt, N. (2007) 'Carry on flying, says Blair – science will save the planet', *The Guardian*, 9th January 2007. Source: http://www.theguardian.com/business/2007/jan/09/theairlineindustry.greenpolitics

Webb, A. (2009) 'The division over multiplication', *Earth Island Journal: News of the World Environment*, Summer reports. Source: http://www.earthisland.org/journal/index.php/eij/arti cle/the_division_over_multiplication

Welldon, E. (1988) *Mother, Madonna, Whore: The Idealization and Denigration of Motherhood.* Free Association Books, London.

Welwood, J. (2000) *Towards a Psychology of Awakening: Buddhism, Psychotherapy and the Path of Personal and Spiritual Transformation.* Shambhala Publications Inc, USA

Williams, Z. (2014) 'Let's not savage Kirstie Allsopp for having a view on motherhood: Until we allow women the freedom that we give to men, they will continue to receive vitriol simply for speaking out', *The Guardian*. 3rd June 2014.

Wintle, A. (2013) 'Lucy Worsley: My family values', *The Guardian*. 12th April 2013.

Woodspring, Dr. N. (2012) Personal communication via email, 27/3/13.

Bibliography

Alaimo, S. (2000) *Undomesticated Ground: Recasting Nature as Feminist Space*. Cornell University Press.

Batchelor, M. (1996) *Walking on Lotus Flowers: Buddhist Women Living, Loving and Meditating*. Thorsons, an imprint of HarperCollins publishers.

Brin, E. (1998) 'Women happy about their choice to be childless', *Milwaukee Journal Sentinel*, 28th October 1998.

Burgess, C. (1996) 'Childless by choice'. Web article. Source: http://www.raleighnokidding.com/articles/burgess.html

Callan, V.J., (1983) 'Childlessness and partner selection', *Journal of Marriage and the Family*, Vol 45, No 1, February 1983.

Cannold, L. (2000) 'Who's crying now? Chosen childlessness, circumstantial childlessness and the irrationality of motherhood: a study of the fertility decisions of Australian and North American women'. PhD thesis. Source: https://minerva-access.unimelb.edu.au/bitstream/handle/11343/39435/72411_00000675_01_01_front.pdf?sequence=1

Chancey, L. & Dumais, S. (2009) 'Voluntary Childlessness In Marriage and Family Textbooks, 1950–2000', *Journal of Family History*, Vol 34, No 2, April 2009, pp.206-223.

Claremont de Castillejo, I. (1973) *Knowing Woman: A Feminine Psychology*. Shambhala.

Cline, S. (1993) *Women, Celibacy and Passion*. Optima. A division of Little, Brown and Company (UK) Ltd.

Doyle, J., Pooley, J.A., & Breen, L. (2012) 'A phenomenological exploration of the childfree choice in a sample of Australian women', *Journal of Health Psychology*, Vol 18, No 3, pp.397-407.

Dykstra, P.A., & Hagestad, G.O. (2007) 'Roads less taken: developing a nuanced view of older adults without children', *Journal of Family Issues*, Vol 28, No 10, pp.1275-1310.

Gaard, G. (ed) (1993) *Ecofeminism: Women, Animals, Nature*.

Temple University Press, Philadelphia.

Gibbs, N. (2002) 'Making time for a baby', *Time Magazine*, 15th April 2002. Source: http://content.time.com/time/magazine/article/0,9171,1002217,00.html

Gieve, K. (ed) (1989) *Balancing Acts: On Becoming a Mother*. Virago Press.

Giles, D., Shaw, R.L., & Morgan, W. (2009) Representations of voluntary childlessness in the UK press, 1990–2008, *Journal of Health Psychology*, Vol 14, No 8, pp.1218-1228.

Gillespie, R. (2003) 'Childfree and feminine: understanding the gender identity of voluntarily childless women', *Gender & Society*, Vol 17, No 1, February, pp.122-136.

Griffin, S. (1978) *Woman and Nature: The Roaring Inside Her*. Perennial Library. Harper & Row, Publishers, New York.

Hagestad, G.O. & Call, V.R.A. (2007) 'Pathways to childlessness: a life course perspective', *Journal of Family Issues*, Vol 28, No 10, pp.1338-1361.

Harcourt, W. (2009) *Body Politics in Development: Critical Debates in Gender and Development*. Zed Books.

Hendrixson, A. & Gies, E. (2015) 'Argument: if you care about climate change, should you have children?' *New Internationalist*, March 2015.

Hoch Smith, J. & Spring, A. (1978) *Women in Ritual and Symbolic Roles*. New York: Plenum Press.

Kalyanavaca (ed.) (1997) *The Moon and Flowers: A Woman's Path to Enlightenment*. Windhorse Publications.

Kent, T.L. (2011) *Wild Feminine: Finding Power, Spirit & Joy in the Female Body*. Atria Books & Beyond Words.

Khema, A. (1997) *I Give You My Life: The Autobiography of a Western Buddhist Nun*. Shambhala.

Lewin, E. (1985) 'By design: reproductive strategies and the meaning of motherhood' in

Letherby, G. (1994) 'Mother or not, mother or what?' *Women's Studies International Forum*, Vol 17, No 5, pp.525-532.

Homans, H. (ed) *The Sexual Politics of Reproduction*. Gower Pub. Co., Aldershot, Hants, United Kingdom.

MacNamee, J. (ed) (2008) *In Her Element: Women and the Landscape – An Anthology*. Honno Autobiography.

Magrid, B. (2002) *Ordinary Mind: Exploring the Common Ground of Zen and Psychoanalysis*. Wisdom Books.

Malson, H. & Swann, C. (2003) 'Re-producing 'woman's' body: reflections on the (dis)place(ments) of 'reproduction' for (post)modern women', Journal of Gender Studies, Vol 12, No 3, pp.191-201.

Moran, C. (2011) *How To Be A Woman*. Ebury Press.

Northrup, C. (2006) *Women's Bodies, Women's Wisdom*. Piatkus.

Ory, M.G. (1978) 'The decision to parent or not: normative and structural components', *Journal of Marriage and the Family*, Vol 40, Iss 3, pp.531-539.

Pearce, L.D. (2002) 'The influence of early life course religious exposure on young adults' dispositions towards childbearing', *Journal for the Scientific Study of Religion*, Vol 41, No 2, pp.325-340.

Peterson, H. (2014) 'Fifty shades of freedom: voluntary childlessness as women's ultimate liberation', *Women's Studies International Forum*, Vol 0, No 0, pp.1-10. Published online ahead of print.

Ratner, R. (2000) 'Electing to remain childless', *Chicago Tribune Internet Edition*. Source: http://articles.chicagotribune.com/ 2000-01-09/news/0001090140_1_childless-fertility-stories

Richman, S. (2014) *Mended by the Muse: Creative Transformations of Trauma*. Routledge.

Shepherd, R. (2003) 'Happily unblessed', *The Observer*, 19th October 2003.

Singer, J. (1998) *Modern Woman in Search of Soul*. Nicolas Hays.

Srimala (1996) *Breaking Free: Glimpses of a Buddhist Life*. Windhorse Publications.

Wager, M. (2000) 'Childless by choice? Ambivalence and the

female identity', *Feminism & Psychology*, Vol 10, No 3, pp.389-395.

Williams, Z. (2003) 'The Parent Trap', *The Guardian Weekend*, 18th October 2003.

info@kamalamani.co.uk
www.kamalamani.co.uk

EARTH

BOOKS

Earth Books are practical, scientific and philosophical
publications about our relationship with the environment.
Earth Books explore sustainable ways of living; including green
parenting, gardening, cooking and natural building. They also
look at ecology, conservation and aspects of environmental
science, including green energy. An understanding of the
interdependence of all living things is central to Earth Books,
and therefore consideration of our relationship with other
animals is important. Animal welfare is explored. The purpose
of Earth Books is to deepen our understanding of the
environment and our role within it. The books featured under
this imprint will both present thought-provoking questions and
offer practical solutions.